The Victorians in the Rearview Mirror

THE VICTORIANS IN THE REARVIEW MIRROR

Simon Joyce

Ohio University Press
Athens

Ohio University Press, Athens, Ohio 45701
www.ohio.edu/oupress
© 2007 by Ohio University Press

Printed in the United States of America

Ohio University Press books are printed on acid-free paper ⊗ ™

14 13 12 11 10 09 08 07   5 4 3 2 1

Library of Congress Cataloging-in-Publication Data

Joyce, Simon, 1963–
   The Victorians in the rearview mirror / Simon Joyce.
      p. cm.
   Includes bibliographical references.
   ISBN-13: 978-0-8214-1761-4 (hc : alk. paper)
   ISBN-10: 0-8214-1761-4 (hc : alk. paper)
   ISBN-13: 978-0-8214-1762-1 (pb : alk. paper)
   ISBN-10: 0-8214-1762-2 (pb : alk. paper)
   1. English literature—20th century—History and criticism. 2. Literature and history—Great Britain—History—20th century. 3. Great Britain—History—Victoria, 1837–1901—Historiography. 4. Great Britain—Civilization—19th century—Historiography. 5. Authors, English—20th century—Political and social views. 6. Authors, English—20th century—Aesthetics. 7. Modernism (Literature)—Great Britain. 8. Social values in literature. 9. Nostalgia in literature. I. Title.
   PR478.H57J69 2007
   820.9'358—dc22
                                                                            2007019541

Contents

Illustrations

Acknowledgments

A book like this one is, inevitably, less a survey than a sampling of related topics, each of which hopefully contributes to a coherent argument. Those topics necessarily reflect my own interests—and they are an eclectic bunch. Thanks, then, to all of those people over the years (and it has been a lot of years) who have shared or simply humored those interests. Some people listed here might swear that this book came out a long time ago.

I think of myself a reluctant Victorianist, and of this book as an attempt to work through my reservations about the nineteenth century, and more particularly the professional study of it. Too often, it feels like a period freighted with too much baggage, most of it negative—which means that people in my position can sometimes make a pretty good living essentially denouncing the thing they study. In working through my argument, I seek to draw out what I see as some unmitigated positives from the Victorians, things they can still teach us, in addition to pointing to some of the ways in which we have learned to misrepresent the period.

It helps that I have rarely worked as a strict Victorianist. In many ways, this book is an unintended consequence of the dreadful academic job market of the 1990s (and beyond). While I feel lucky to have found any work at all, I am even more lucky to have found institutions that have not wanted to hire in narrow boxes. The early chapters of this book took shape when I taught at Texas Christian University, where I was supposed to display some expertise in nineteenth- and twentieth-century fiction. In trying to prove my credentials in the later period, I somehow worked up an idea about modernism, so I am very grateful to colleagues and students who indulged me while I did so—most especially Melissa Blackman, Chu-Chueh Cheng, Linda Hughes, and Elizabeth Macleod-Walls.

The bulk of this book was written after I was hired at the College of William and Mary, which rashly thought I could direct a program in literary and cultural studies. Faculty colleagues in the English department and in the LCST program have kindly indulged my teaching forays into

x   film studies, heritage culture, and contemporary fiction, only occasionally asking me to say something about the Victorians. The last three chapters of this book are the results of those forays, and of a generous release program offered by the College of Arts and Sciences, which gave me a year off to write. Among the many friends that have made me very welcome in Williamsburg, I most want to thank Elizabeth Barnes, Varun Begley, Colleen Kennedy, Arthur Knight, Jack Martin, and Deborah Morse (with whom I first thought through the material of chapter 3, in a conference paper and team-taught course on "The Victorians and Film"). Rob Nelson provided invaluable assistance in preparing the illustrations.

Elsewhere, I have benefited from the advice, friendship, and expertise of Tammy Clewell, Barry Faulk, Stephanie Foote, Jim Holstun, Christine Krueger, Andrew Miller, Janet Sorensen, and Joe Valente. David Sanders at Ohio University Press has been supportive from the beginning, as were two very helpful and sympathetic readers of an early draft. I'd like to thank them for some very useful suggestions that helped me rethink the final chapter and epilogue.

The prize for best reader, however, goes to Jenny Putzi, my colleague, partner, and true love. Her careful reading, insightful commentary, and unfailing support have made this book a whole lot stronger; my life, too, has been made immeasurably better by her presence in it. Our son Sam generously put off being born until I finished the manuscript, but he has also made every day delightful since then. I hope that as an Anglo-American child of the twenty-first century, he can learn some things from the Victorians, while rejecting the kind of "neo-Victorian" moralizing that has often passed for political and cultural thought in recent times.

May the road rise with you all.

An early version of the introduction was published as "The Victorians in the Rearview Mirror," in *Functions of Victorian Culture at the Present Time*, ed. Christine Krueger (Ohio University Press, 2002). Chapter 1 first appeared in *Victorian Studies* and is reprinted with the permission of Indiana University Press. Portions of chapter 4 were published as "Victorian Continuities: Early British Sociology and the Welfare of the State," in *Disciplinarity at the Fin de Siècle*, ed. Amanda Anderson and Joseph Valente. © 2002 by Princeton University Press. Reprinted by permission of Princeton University Press.

Introduction

It was probably inevitable that the years 2000–2001 would bring with them another series of reevaluations of the nineteenth century. Just as surely, while the United States and many other industrialized nations dabbled in a momentary technophobia incited by the anticlimactic "millennium bug," Britain obsessed about its relationship with its own past. The *Observer* of 2 January 2000 reprinted articles from 1800 and 1900, noting hopefully that "[t]his time round, our first editorial of the century—and of the millennium—does not have to fear Britain suffering invasion, war and conquest," even though the date technically opened neither the century nor the millennium (and meanwhile, Afghanistan, Iraq, and the so-called War on Terror were all waiting in the wings to mock the paper's false hope).[1] Three days earlier, the *Guardian* had similarly led off with a look back, wondering "What would they make of us now, those cheerful, confident subjects of the old queen, secure in the certainty that Britain was great and progress would make it still greater, who launched us 99 years ago into the 20th century?"[2]

It is an impossible question to answer and a strange one to ask. It assumes that "those cheerful, confident subjects" might all speak with one voice and then agree in their assessments of their own era and of what a new century promised. Predictably, the *Guardian* could only answer

2   with ambivalence, noting that "[i]n some ways, they would find our world
reassuringly familiar," but "elsewhere, our lives would astonish them": the
continuity of the monarchy, cricket matches, and debates about electoral
reform and hunting reflected the former possibility, while space exploration, a greater tolerance for homosexuality, genetic engineering, and the
millennium bug exemplified the latter. The exercise itself is a peculiarly
British one, and self-defeatingly incoherent in ways that recall the official
centerpiece of London's celebrations in 2000, the Millennium Dome in
Greenwich. That structure also claimed to look ahead via a backwards
glance that simultaneously referenced the nation's imperial past, its staging
of spectacles like the Great Exhibition of 1851, and the symbolic significance of Greenwich Mean Time: as one Londoner commented, "We may
no longer own an empire, but we still own time."[3] Ronald Thomas notes that
the dome itself was surprisingly empty of commodities and big ideas, thus
forming the reverse of 1851's Crystal Palace; indeed, as a kind of "entertainment experience" or "pure monument," it almost seemed designed to draw
a negative comparison with the past. "Rather than 'Time for a Change,'"
Thomas observes, "it took as its motto 'Essentially British,' in an effort to
bolster attendance from the 'domestic market' and, it would seem, shore up
the ruins of the lost Victorian fantasy of a distinctly British nationality."[4]

The disease of looking backwards at century's end also infected the
Economist, which under the heading "Still Victorian" pointed out some striking commercial continuities and better-than-expected comparisons: for instance, the British economy had slipped just a little from third to fourth
place worldwide, and investment was still high, surpassed only by levels in
the United States. As if not wanting to sound too complacent, however, it
also noted that "[t]he British citizen, of course, has changed out of all
recognition, and the social structure has been overturned," before shifting
back to a discussion of similarities that seem far less important: "Funny,
though, that crowds still go to Ascot; Eton College remains the country's
foremost school," and so on.[5] There is something both shocking and symptomatic about this focus on the trivia of aristocratic life, as if it might can-
cel out what the *Economist* admits is a fundamental remaking of the British
social structure and citizenry, just as the *Guardian* editorial appears to place
debates concerning the ethics of hunting and genetic engineering as equal
weights on a balance scale. *Inventing the Victorians* (2001), by *Guardian* jour-
nalist Matthew Sweet, also offers an inventory of the ways in which we resemble our predecessors. "Most of the pleasures we imagine to be our own,"
he argues, "the Victorians enjoyed first" in a culture "as rich and difficult

and complex and pleasurable as our own." Indeed, "they are still with us," Sweet concludes, "walking our pavements, drinking in our bars, living in our houses, reading our newspapers, inhabiting our bodies."[6]

It is tempting to infer from such accounts a kind of Victorian vampire that has suddenly reawakened to haunt Britain after a century's rest—except that such positings of an essential and unbroken connection with the past appeared throughout the twentieth century as well. The Victorians, we might say, have attracted as much as they repulsed those that have come afterwards, and each attempt at drawing a definitive line in the sand has subsequently been shown to disguise a more telling continuity, as the following sequence demonstrates. In the year of Queen Victoria's death, 1901, the New Liberal theorist and politician C. F. G. Masterman opened his book *The Heart of the Empire* with the bold assertion that "[t]he Victorian Era has definitely closed."[7] Yet Virginia Woolf, for one, did not agree with his assessment, famously noting in *Mr Bennett and Mrs Brown* (1924) that "on or about December 1910 human character changed."[8] In that essay, as we shall see in chapter 1, she accuses the Edwardians of failing—especially in the cultural sphere—to enact the definitive break with the past that was being predicted on Victoria's death, and which Woolf now associated with the first postimpressionist exhibition in London ten years later. Among others, Robert Graves pushed back her date for the decisive change a few years, so that the experience of military service during World War I became the key transitional moment, just as Leonard Woolf's memoirs later concurred that "the war of 1914 destroyed a new, and civilized or semi-civilized, way of life which had established itself or was establishing itself all over Europe."[9] Yet in 1935 George Dangerfield surveyed the recent history of Britain and wrote critically of the idea that it was the war that finally broke the hold of the past: "It is easier," he notes, "to think of Imperial England, beribboned and bestarred and splendid, living in majestic profusion up till the very moment of war. Such indeed was its appearance, the appearance of a somewhat decadent Empire and a careless democracy. But I do not think its social history will be written on these terms." Dangerfield concludes that an uneven but decisive shift in the national character had in fact already begun, almost subconsciously, in the early years of George V's reign.[10]

Clearly, these commentators found no consensus about what constituted the Victorian "character" or about what might constitute a final break with it. Indeed, if we wanted to bring the sequence up to date, we could add Stefan Collini's tongue-in-cheek suggestion that "in or about May 1979, human character changed," a reference to the election of the Thatcher

4   government with its stated intention of a return to "Victorian values"—presumably the same ones that, if we take his statement at face value, Collini believes had actually been retained up to that point.[11] The entire sequence is strikingly reminiscent of what Raymond Williams once described as a moving escalator of nostalgic remembrance in his work on the literary pastoral.[12] If that genre consistently finds the present wanting when set against an idealized version of the past, usually located in the writer's own childhood, then assertions of modernity seem conversely to privilege the here and now as an escape from the pressing weight of history. On Williams's account, however, we never actually arrive at the golden age of pastoral perfection, since one person's youthful paradise is always also another's debased present: thus, the escalator moves backward from Leavis's disappearing "organic community" to Hardy and George Eliot recalling the 1830s, and back through Cobbett and Clare and Goldsmith and so on, until the search ends at Arcadia or Eden, or some other space that seems to exist outside of history itself. Modernist accounts throw the escalator into reverse, pushing the decisive point of transformation forward instead of back in time, but the effect seems almost identical; indeed, it is tempting to conclude that a pure moment of *modernism*, free from the hangovers of the Victorian past, is just as mythical as the Arcadian paradises of pastoral.

The starting point for this study, then, is the observation that we never really encounter "the Victorians" themselves but instead a mediated image like the one we get when we glance into our rearview mirrors while driving. The image usefully condenses the paradoxical sense of looking forward to see what is behind us, which is the opposite of what we do when we read history in order to figure out the future. It also suggests something of the inevitable distortion that accompanies any mirror image, whether we see it as resulting from the effects of political ideology, deliberate misreading, exaggeration, or the understandable simplification of a complex past. Margaret Thatcher's call for a return to "Victorian values," encoded in a 1983 speech that enumerated hard work, self-reliance, thrift, national pride, and cleanliness among the so-called perennial values inherited from her Victorian grandmother, is perhaps the most famous of these, and incidentally provides us with one example of the surprising closeness of the past.[13]

I argue that such elaborations of the essence of the Victorians provide a particular challenge for people who call themselves "Victorianists." This may equally be the case with other periods, of course, each of which have suffered from the processes of simplification that are the necessary starting point for descriptions of anything like "the Elizabethan World Picture" (in E. M. Tillyard's famous phrase) or other versions of the periodic zeitgeist or weltanschauung. With few exceptions, though, those other periods have not had the kind of purchase on the present that Thatcher's appeal exemplifies, in part because they are simply more distant in time; it is hard, for instance, to imagine anyone taking seriously a similar call to return to Jacobean or Regency values. This is not to suggest that Thatcher found unanimous consent for her particular version of the Victorian past, of course; in a strikingly ineffective example of what I will be describing as a strategy of simple inversion, future Labour Party leader Neil Kinnock responded that "[t]he 'Victorian Values' that ruled were cruelty, misery, drudgery, squalor and ignorance," but his party nonetheless went on to lose the next election by a wide margin.[14]

My argument in this book is that such efforts, however well intentioned, do nothing to unsettle commonsense assumptions about what the Victorians represented and may even paradoxically help consolidate them. Writing about the project of feminist art history, Janet Wolff has identified this strategy as "the politics of correction," arguing that "filling in the gaps" in a male-centered canon of art will only "modify the discourse in minor ways, leaving it essentially unchallenged."[15] I will be arguing something similar about the interplay between a revivalist position like Thatcher's and its critical mirror image, that what emerges from their encounter is a prevailing popular consensus about the defining features of the Victorian age—among which we could list a confidently triumphalist imperialism, a rigid separation of public and private spheres, a repressive sexual morality, and an ascendant hegemony of bourgeois values—that can easily accommodate elements of either argument. Thus, Thatcher's personal morality can appear as the by-product of sexual repression and the Protestant work ethic, while Kinnock's painful social conditions might be glossed as the regrettable flipside of industrialization. (Two press cuttings from 1998 illustrate this particular dichotomy: in one, referencing Thatcher's emphasis on the personal, Britain is praised for "becoming less Victorian" in the wake of Princess Diana's death, having finally abandoned "the phlegmatic belief in coping, the buttoned-up stoicism [that] were once not the outdated fashion of the ruling class, or only male virtues, but a visible part of the national character"; in the other, a striking manufacturing worker holds up a placard that insists on industrial relations as the hallmark of the past century, proclaiming that "BERISFORD/MAGNET ARE VICTORIAN EMPLOYERS.")[16]

6   Faced with the persistence of what Roland Barthes termed the commonsensical "doxa" of public opinion about the Victorians, what should a
Victorianist do? There is the sometimes laborious work of opposition, as
illustrated by Kinnock's counterargument or the assorted reviewers who
painstakingly redressed the blind spots and distortions in Gertrude Himmelfarb's tendentiously Thatcherite diatribe, *The De-moralization of Society*
(1994), which I discuss in chapter 4. Such corrective efforts clearly shade
into ideology critique, asking what John McGowan has termed "the
Bakhtinian question of whom this discourse addresses (answers, contests,
affirms) and to what ends."[17] I want to mention briefly two other strategies
here, each of which has had some success while nonetheless leaving the
basic shape of the doxological Victorian largely intact. The first is exemplified by Steven Marcus's study of nineteenth-century pornography, *The
Other Victorians* (1966), which—as its title makes clear—is interested in
those who do not belong in our received notions of the Victorians. This
approach readily extends to other "others" (feminists, colonial subjects, socialists, sexual minorities, and so on): indeed, historical scholarship in the
twentieth century is full of such efforts to elevate those excluded from the
dominant records, from A. L. Morton's class-conscious *A People's History of
England* (1938) through Sheila Rowbotham's landmark work of feminist recovery, *Hidden from History* (1974), to a text of the same name, edited by
Martin Duberman and others (1989), aimed at "reclaiming the gay and lesbian past."[18] Implicit in this rhetorical framework, though, and made explicit by Marcus, is the way in which it presumes a normative definition
against which "otherness" can be measured: indeed, he notes that "this
otherness was of a specific Victorian kind," and after exhaustive evidence
of this he concludes that "[t]he view of human sexuality as it was represented in the subculture of pornography and the view of sexuality held
by the official culture were reversals, mirror images, negative analogues of
each other."[19] The problem, of course, is that such an approach tends to
leave uninterrogated that "official" view as the normative pole of definition,
although it should be said that the work of Michel Foucault, Eve Kosof-
sky Sedgwick, and others has done much to complicate this kind of binary
thinking.
       A second strategy, which resonates in part with Marcus's "others" and
with Matthew Sweet's archaeology of surprisingly modern Victorian pleasures, is to stress those elements of nineteenth-century society or culture
that most closely resemble our own. In their introduction to a collection
of essays called *Victorian Afterlife* (2000), John Kucich and Dianne Sadoff sug-

gest that "[r]ewritings of Victorian culture have flourished, we believe, because the postmodern fetishizes notions of cultural emergence, and because the nineteenth century provides multiple eligible sites for theorizing such emergence. . . . [T]he cultural matrix of nineteenth-century England," they continue, "joined various and possible stories about cultural rupture that, taken together, overdetermine the period's availability for the postmodern exploration of cultural emergence."[20] Such an approach, which Jay Clayton terms "identitarian" in his *Charles Dickens in Cyberspace* (2003), yields some immediate benefits, enabling a full-fledged narrative—or multiple narratives—of Victorian otherness to be glimpsed beneath the surface, as it were, of our understanding of the period itself.[21]

In suggesting that such an attention to emergent formations allows for a reconsideration of the temporality of historical rupture, by positing instead multiple and overlapping processes of transition, the approach laid out by Kucich and Sadoff would presumably problematize the conventional modernist historiography, which sees "the Victorian" as superseded by something else—variously termed "the modern," "the Edwardian," or "the Georgian." We might, however, see emergence itself as a problematic concept, which only defers the troubled question of definition: after all, if what draws us to the nineteenth century are those ways in which it anticipates the postmodern present, then how do we characterize *that?* As was the case with Marcus's "other Victorians," it is hard to shake the suspicion that our understanding of the norm has remained, even if (as famously for Marx's version of capitalism) it can be shown to contain its own grave diggers; regardless of whether it is seen as being transcended by its own emergent possibilities or challenged by its debased and dissenting voices, a baseline conception of "the Victorian" has essentially stayed the same. In a way, we are back to Thatcher versus Kinnock and a logic of split perception that only reaffirms the ways in which such binaries get set up in the first place. (Who, after all, would question that periods produce their own others and/or anticipate their successors and/or contain unprocessed elements that might turn out to be potentially useful in the future?) One possibility I consider in this book is that our idea of "the Victorian" in fact serves as a condensation of contrary tendencies and oppositions, which we can see hardening over the subsequent century into doxological assumptions and attitudes that are henceforth available for a range of political and cultural forces; these in turn advance by positioning themselves as for or against a partial image of the whole, in the process helping to constitute each other in a form of dialectical spiral. In a sense, "the Victorian" has become a kind

8   of style and is thereby subject to the vicissitudes of twentieth-century fashion, with its rapid cycles of obsolescence and revivalism.

❧

Each of the assessments I have noted up to now has begun by posing what would seem to me to be false questions: was the Victorian age a good or bad thing, and are we for or against it? In each case, what goes unremarked is precisely the extent to which these questions are always already inflected by those doxological assumptions about what the age represents in the popular consciousness. Matthew Sweet's *Inventing the Victorians* is the most obvious example here, with its telling opening inviting his readers to "[s]uppose that everything we think we know about the Victorians is wrong."[22] Setting aside his imagining of a contemporary consensus here— would "we" all agree?—what seems most remarkable about his book is that it focuses so heavily on the everyday lives and mass culture of the nineteenth century: sensation, advertising, drug use, table manners, furnishings, and so on. As each chapter ends with the repeated revelation that the Victorians in fact anticipated contemporary attitudes and amusements, it is hard not to conclude that this could be true in each case and still not fundamentally revise our understanding of the period. Such a conclusion is even more explicit in journalistic accounts like the *Economist's*, which can recognize a continuity in the daily lives of the privileged and also a fundamental reorganization of the national social structure, or the *Guardian's* counterbalancing of space exploration and cricket matches. I am not pointing to a category mistake here, as if economics were necessarily more crucial than entertainment in our retrospective assessments. Instead, it is the central premise of critical judgment that seems to be at fault, with the associated inference that any such listing or balance sheet might point us to "the spirit of the age," to use an appropriately Victorian phrasing.[23] Even Margaret Thatcher and Neil Kinnock could have been equally right about the inheritances of the past and yet hopelessly mistaken to the extent that they each sought to identify the *definitive* values of the time.

Interestingly, there was little consensus about the central meaning of the period on the near-simultaneous ending of the nineteenth century and (a month later) Victoria's reign. Some retrospective summaries in the press might strike us now as just plain odd, as when the normally conservative *Saturday Review* listed as the three abiding features of nineteenth-century life "Darwinism, tractarianism, and socialism," before suggesting that the period dispelled forever "the false sentimentality and ideality which used to ignore the body, or despise it as an impediment to the soul."[24] Looking in the opposite direction, the *St. James Gazette* wrote that the "material progress" of the Victorian age had unfortunately brought with it the debilitating assumption "that mankind was going to settle everything by logic and common sense" or "supply and demand." Darwinism, it noted, has been shown "to account for a little less than was hoped of it," which explained a continuing and even virulent strain of religious enthusiasm and superstition.[25] On the Left, *Reynolds Weekly Newspaper* mocked claims to national progress, commenting that while "the world has seen some changes in the Victorian Era," the labeling of these shifts as "improvements" or "progress" requires us to ask in what *direction* the nation was progressing: "To loftier ideals, a happier common life, a lessening of the strain after sordid things? No; the progress has not been in that direction; on the contrary it has been the reverse."[26]

If these excerpts give us some sense of the public discourse at the moment of Victoria's death, others illustrate the difficulty of looking ahead to a new century or a new reign. On the Right, the *Saturday Review* expressed a palpable hesitation: "Whatever the twentieth century and the reign of King Edward VII may have in store," it editorialized, "we may be sure that it will not be quite like the Victorian age, will probably differ much from it."[27] Toward the political center, we find a similarly cautionary tone in the *Pall Mall Gazette*, which predicted possible disaster in the Boer War: "It is for us to make sure that New Year's Day, 1901, shall not find the Empire of England on the way to the same fate as those out of which it has been built up."[28] On the Left, the certainties of *Reynolds* again: "In our judgment, the first year of the new century will prove to have been the last year of good trade and we must look forward to a period of lean years and to decline in trade as compared with our two great rivals, America and Germany. Unhappily, instead of preparing for this, we have squandered an enormous sum in South Africa and, if we do not make peace, we shall squander much more."[29] Clearly, these statements are articulating real political differences, but what links them is a rhetoric of incipient panic, which predominates whether or not the journal is for the queen, the empire, or "progress."

Each of these statements contains what I take to be a decisive feature of twentieth-century anti-Victorianism: the idea that something termed (on the basis of variable determining factors) "the Victorian" has, for better or worse, now come to an end. One of the most telling responses to the end of Victoria's reign came from the *St. James Gazette*, which wrote on her death of how "[t]he period before her accession, when a King and not a

10   Queen reigned in the land, was a period of long past history, so remote as to seem to belong to a different epoch, a different civilization. . . . She figured in our imagination less as a Person than as an Institution—an Institution immovably fixed in the political and social Order of our age, related to the passing men and passing events of history, but not like them."[30] Here, the age of Victoria stretches back into the recesses of remembered time, while its ending provoked a kind of existential crisis for the nation, which now had to reimagine those institutions and social structures that had seemed so inextricably associated with the monarch herself.[31] In reality, of course, those same structures were readily transformable, in part through a redefinition of the function of the state, which benefited from now being recognized as possessing a relative autonomy from the sovereign. At the same time, Edwardian and Georgian modernists set about the demystification of the figure of the queen, as illustrated by Virginia Woolf's use of the name "Mrs. Brown" for her emblem of stolid subjectivity: as John Madden's 1997 film of the same name reminds us, the epithet was used by *Punch* in particular to mock the widowed queen's relationship with her Scottish servant, John Brown.[32]

     While the Woolfs, Lytton Strachey, and the rest of the Bloomsbury Group are usually thought to have sparked a modernist anti-Victorianism, peaking in 1918 with the publication of Strachey's *Eminent Victorians*, I am suggesting that the groundwork had been prepared immediately on the queen's death—and indeed, in the "decadent" nineties. It is less my project here, though, to trace the roots of this discourse than it is to track its internal contradictions and limits, which led to its continual reassertion and restatement throughout the twentieth century. The Bloomsbury critique of the ruling ideology they inherited from the recent past can seem as vaguely incoherent as the "Group" itself, which renounced any collective identity beyond a loose agglomeration of friends; rejecting this fashioned self-image, Raymond Williams has usefully identified it as a recognizable "*fraction* of the existing English upper class . . . at once against its dominant ideas and values and still willingly, in all immediate ways, part of it." While it came to be connected, in sometimes quite tangential ways, with forces of liberalization and modernism, the Bloomsbury hallmark was, he concludes, its expression of "a new *style*," the keynote of which was an outward projection of the personal register of conscience. Crucially, the various positions they advocated did not need to cohere in any programmatic way, because (as Williams argues) their "individual integration has already taken place, at the level of the 'civilized individual,' the singular definition of all the best people, secure in their autonomy but turning their free attention this way and that, as occasion requires."[33]

Extending this analysis, we might say that for Bloomsbury "the Victorian" also denoted a style, ironically one with its roots in the very areas of culture and domestic life that Matthew Sweet and the *Economist* saw as continuing far into the twentieth century. Such assessments are almost by definition subjective and inconclusive, which helps explain the evident note of disappointment that recurs throughout the early decades of the twentieth century each time commentators such as Woolf, Strachey, Robert Graves, and George Dangerfield recognized that society as a whole had not been fundamentally transformed by a new monarch on the throne, or by postimpressionism, or even by World War I. In this sense, the realization that others did not feel especially "modern" was what could sustain the fractional status of the Bloomsbury vanguard, while also undermining its efforts at a social analysis that always took the Group's own immediate experience as its starting point.

Chapter 1 of *The Victorians in the Rearview Mirror* uses a close reading of the writings of the Woolfs, Clive Bell, and Strachey to suggest that there is little concrete agreement even among the Bloomsbury friends about what actually constituted the sins of the Victorian period; indeed, I argue that *Eminent Victorians* expresses instead the radical unknowability of the previous century, which for Strachey represented an age defined by contradiction. As a result of that instability, as I argue in chapter 2, Bloomsbury anti-Victorianism rapidly gave way to a more positive view of the past that was articulated at the fringes of modernism (and of Bloomsbury itself) by figures such as E. M. Forster and Evelyn Waugh. And yet, the force of earlier critiques conditioned the form and extent of their nostalgia, which never quite manages to articulate a full-fledged endorsement of the Victorians. Instead, texts such as *Howards End* (1910) and *Brideshead Revisited* (1945) situate themselves at an important fault line of modernism, managing at once to argue a necessarily backward vision in the face of an increasingly abhorrent modernity—one that, incidentally, bore many of the characteristics previously attributed to the nineteenth century—as well as the impossibility of an unproblematic nostalgia. In that sense, I see these texts as inheriting from Strachey a view of the past that is internally divided and thus open to a deconstructive close reading that looks to accentuate the conflicted nature of modernist attitudes toward the nineteenth century.

One symptom of that conflict, as I have suggested, is the effort to reduce the Victorian to a style—and one whose primary appeal lay as much

12   in terms of dress and design as in a set of ideological or ethical beliefs. As I highlight at the end of chapter 2, such a move worries a commentator like Roger Fry, whose 1919 essay on "The Ottoman and the Whatnot" mocks the revivalist fashion from within the terms set by Bloomsbury. What it manages to achieve, for him, is the reduction of the nineteenth century to a set of aesthetic objects and, at the same time, the denial of aesthetic value itself, since he can only view a fondness for Victoriana as produced out of an associated set of "historical images they conjure up" that are just as inevitably false. What matters, he concludes with an air of resignation, is that such images "exist for us, and for most people, far more vividly and poignantly than any possible aesthetic feeling."[34] But this reading seems conditioned by the prior assumption that an ottoman can furnish no pleasures other than through its association with a (sufficiently distanced) way of living. What it crucially misses is the spirit of irony that underpins the revival of Victoriana among the social and artistic elites, including a circle of undergraduates at Oxford centered around Waugh. In part, then, this development reflects an outflanking maneuver by a new generation of avant-gardists who sought to displace Bloomsbury by reversing its hatred of the past. As Robert Graves and Alan Hodge describe it in their 1940 memoir *The Long Week-End*, the "neo-Victorianism" of the twenties sought to revive forms of nineteenth-century dress in particular (including bowler hats, stockings, printed chiffon, and cameo jewelry) and yet married it with "the *neo*" of modern materials, such as chrome and Bakelite.[35]

From this point on, I would argue, "the Victorian" serves as a continuous reference point of twentieth-century discourse, whether it is seen primarily in terms of politics or fashion.[36] Chapter 3 examines a later stage in this history from the 1980s, with the phenomenon of "heritage cinema" in Britain at the time of Thatcherism's political ascendancy. Whereas this cycle of visual adaptations (most famously, the films of Ismail Merchant and James Ivory, and the literary productions broadcast on public television's *Masterpiece Theatre*) has typically been seen by critics as a cultural by-product of Thatcher's promotion of "Victorian values," I argue that we need to look elsewhere to understand the connection to the nineteenth century. Their source material is only selectively drawn from the period, with major clusters in the Regency (most notably, the novels of Jane Austen) and at the *fin de siècle*. That latter group of texts, including works by Thomas Hardy, Joseph Conrad, Henry James, and Merchant-Ivory's beloved E. M. Forster, exemplifies a literary impressionism that paradoxically seems particularly ill-suited to visual translation, given their stress on narrative unreliability and perspective.

This insight leads me to consider that what makes heritage cinema seem "Victorian" is its visual style, which emphasizes a concrete material reality through its overriding concern for the authenticity of period details (such as costume, props, and settings). In this sense, I argue along with Jennifer Green-Lewis that we habitually think of the Victorians in retrospect as championing an unequivocally mimetic visual aesthetic, "humorless realists about to be shattered by modernism and the cubist war."[37] In challenging such an assumption, I trace out an alternative trajectory, beginning with Victorian art-photographers like Oscar Gustave Rejlander, who conducted early experiments with combination printing and montage, and extending through antirealist tendencies in early cinema associated especially with Georges Méliès and Sergei Eisenstein. Those influences, I suggest, can be seen in a group of metacinematic heritage films, including *The French Lieutenant's Woman* (Karel Reisz, 1981), *Bram Stoker's Dracula* (Francis Ford Coppola, 1992), and *The Governess* (Sandra Goldbacher, 1997), that seek to place past and present in dialogue through a sustained investigation of the suppressed ideological history of visual techniques. Each film argues that there is no necessary connection between cinematic realism and either the process of literary adaptation or the Victorian period, and instead stages a far-reaching debate about the integrity of cultural texts as they are translated across artistic genres and forms.[38]

Beginning with chapter 3, I shift from the more neutral tone of the deconstructionist, who is content to highlight the internal tensions within modernism's relationship to the past, to a more assertive one that also seeks to restore and revalue aspects of that past that have been consciously occluded in late-twentieth-century public discourse about the Victorians: an experimental visual culture, a commitment to a welfare safety net provided by the state, and a "Dickensian" novel form that stresses the structural interdependence of diverse social groups and classes. In doing so, I hope to resist succumbing to the approach I discussed earlier that holds up repressed or anticipatory elements as the true essence of the period. What marks these elements, as I discuss them in the final three chapters of this book, is the conflicted and contradictory nature of each: art photography, for instance, is initially undertaken and justified as a superior form of mimetic realism; state welfare provision accepts many of the assumptions behind private and philanthropic approaches, especially concerning the moral responsibilities of the individual; and what I term a "neo-Dickensian" literary realism in postwar fiction emerges alongside a simultaneous experimentation with modernist stream-of-consciousness narration.

14   In chapter 4, I address what is perhaps the least acknowledged (or most suppressed) inheritance of the Victorian period, its progressive conception of the responsibilities of the state. Assessing the ideal balance between the central state and the liberal subject is, I argue in the early chapters of *The Victorians in the Rearview Mirror,* one of the key fault lines within the Bloomsbury Group, for whom the Victorians come to represent both a systematic organization of public life (one that presses upon the private individual) and—often at the same time—the principle of laissez-faire. Thus, when E. M. Forster called for a combination of the "new economy" and the "old morality,"[39] he saw the recent past as representing a valuable repository of the latter, needing only to be supplemented by a planned economic system that could centralize the provision and distribution of goods and services; yet this is precisely the kind of thinking to which the Woolfs objected, as a residue of a discredited Victorianism that privileged collective social obligations at the expense of the needs of the individual.

Thatcherism's proposed welfare reforms, by contrast, were rooted in a version of the Victorian period that stressed a minimalist state and maximum freedom for the individual and private enterprise. And yet, by the end of the nineteenth century, there seems to have been a growing consensus that only a centralized state could redress the large-scale problems that were the inevitable consequences of an unstable business cycle, most notably mass unemployment. This is the implication of the descriptive studies undertaken by Charles Booth and other late-nineteenth-century sociologists, and it finds its expression in the policy recommendations of the Minority Report of the Royal Commission on the Poor Laws and the actions of the New Liberal government that came to power in the first decade of the twentieth century. At a more theoretical level, Matthew Arnold's *Culture and Anarchy* (1869) made a parallel case for state education by arguing that only a standardized curriculum would avert the problems that follow from leaving schooling in the hands of particular professions, classes, or churches—a system that stresses sectional identities at the expense of any sense of a greater national good and as such merely reproduces existing political interests and antagonisms. On such evidence, I argue that the Victorians provide a better basis for defending than attacking the foundation of the modern welfare state, which has come under considerable pressure from neoconservatives in Britain and the United States.

Thatcherism's debate about the relative responsibilities of the individual and the state finds a fascinating corollary in a simultaneous division inside contemporary fiction, which moves in one direction to develop high modernism's experiments with first-person narration and in the other back to an earlier model of Dickensian realism. At a time when Thatcher herself proclaimed that there was "no such thing as society,"[40] I argue through a reading of novels by John Irving, Peter Carey, and Sarah Waters that the latter tendency works instead to assert networks of intersubjective connection and dependence, whereas the first-person narratives of novelists such as Irving Welsh and James Kelman suggest a homologous retreat into the (typically damaged) subjectivity of a private consciousness. Irving's *The Cider House Rules* (1985), Carey's *Jack Maggs* (1997), and Waters's *Fingersmith* (2002) all significantly revise and extend the fictional template they inherit from novels like *Oliver Twist* and *Great Expectations*, however: all three, for instance, improvise upon Dickens's orphan stories to comment upon contemporary political debates about public welfare and abortion rights while incorporating a more explicit discussion of sexual identities and practices than the Victorian novelist could. *Jack Maggs* goes furthest, perhaps, in pursuing a revisionary agenda, seeking to rewrite *Great Expectations* from the perspective of the convict Maggs (a modified version of Magwitch), who comes finally to affirm an Australian identity at the expense of a cherished fantasy of Englishness that cannot be sustained once he returns to the imperial metropolis. In this way, as well as in Waters's depiction of the "other Victorian" world of pornography, the prototype of the Dickensian novel is lauded for its effort at representing an expansive and interdependent social world, yet also criticized for placing explicit limits on that world by enforcing the boundaries of national identity and cultural respectability.

In a closing epilogue, "Postcolonial Victorians," I use *Jack Maggs* as a starting point for considering more fully the spatial dimensions of the Victorians' legacy, mindful that their influence was felt throughout the vast expanse of the British empire. Just as it would be absurd to assume that such influence disappeared overnight in Britain itself, whether in 1901 or 1914 or any other date we might select, so we need to understand the precise forms and areas of life in which it has lingered in places like India, Africa, Australia, and the Caribbean. In exploring a number of site-specific examples of a colonial inheritance, I finally consider the possibility that has been implicit at least in much of this book: that "the Victorian" need not be set in opposition to "the modern" and may even be a signifier of modernity in some instances. It is only the persistence of a particular version of modernism, in its earliest revolt against its forebears, that prevents us from recognizing this.

Ultimately, the Victorian inheritance is always a conflicted one that it makes little sense to wholeheartedly endorse or reject. To the extent that

16   people across the globe are still struggling to sort through its influence, marking and celebrating continuities as well as diversions from a supposed "Victorian" blueprint of domestic order and political power, this suggests how little separation we actually have from the nineteenth century. The iconic warning we see when driving, that "objects in the mirror are closer than they appear," thus nicely expresses a feeling we may have about a period that no longer seems as distant as we might like to think, but instead forms the horizon for many of our most pressing debates. In this book I will discuss a series of such moments, when a recognition of a surprising (and perhaps frightening) proximity to the past occurred—at very different times and in different places—to a variety of twentieth-century people.

On or About 1901

The Bloomsbury Group Looks Back

CHAPTER ONE

While the Bloomsbury Group is commonly held to have spearheaded an early-twentieth-century revolt against the Victorians, the relationship of its key figures to the previous century is a complex and often contradictory one. Attempting to summarize their collective attitudes, S. P. Rosenbaum makes two assertions that point in opposite directions: on the one hand, Bloomsbury "reacted strongly against the Victorian family as a means of social organisation," and on the other, "Bloomsbury was born and bred Victorian. The rational and visionary significance of the Group's writing has its origins in Victorian family, school and university experience." Against the impression that is often suggested by their writings (as we shall see), the revolt did not emanate from some Archimedean position of external opposition and critique but from within the conventional social and familial structures that helped to form the Bloomsbury writers. Rosenbaum concludes that "there was in Bloomsbury a basic ambivalence towards nineteenth-century middle-class family life," with one locus of tension being *money*: as we shall see from the memoirs of Leonard Woolf, if it represents a debased standard for judging character or personal worth, what Rosenbaum terms "[t]he puritan foundations of sound saving and careful expenditure on which the essential economic security of Bloomsbury's Victorian households rested . . . appears in most of the family memoirs," forming the basis in particular for a cherished economic independence.[1] Thus,

18   wealth becomes one of a series of objects that are actively disavowed, acknowledged as belonging to an antagonistic set of structures yet at the
same time deemed necessary as the components of an evolving alternative.
It is possible, in this sense, to be wholeheartedly opposed to "Victorianism" as a system while still tied to many of its core elements. Indeed, at
times, the Victorian seems to refer simply to any kind of systematic organization or structural analysis that would constrict the freedoms of the
sovereign individual—including the right to hold such ambivalent and
contradictory attitudes toward the past.

Virginia Woolf's "A Sketch of the Past," from 1939–40, ends on this
point, illustrating a characteristic need to make firm distinctions between
past and present as well as the inevitability that terms begin to bleed into
each other. "No more perfect fossil of Victorian society could exist," she
writes, than the family she recollects from childhood, with her father "a
typical Victorian" and her older half-brother, George Duckworth, as his
natural heir, having "accepted Victorian society so implicitly that an archae-
ologist would find him of the greatest interest."[2] The geological metaphor
suggests the kind of absolute distinction between historical strata that the
memoir makes explicit by counterposing "[t]wo different ages confront[ing]
each other in the drawing room at Hyde Park Gate: the Victorian age; and
the Edwardian age. We were not," Woolf continues, their father's "children,
but his grandchildren," already living in 1910 while throwbacks such as
George Duckworth and Leslie Stephen remained stuck in 1860 (126–27).
It is easy to fill out the terms of this opposition, just as we can for Woolf's
more famous version of it in her 1924 essay *Mr Bennett and Mrs Brown*: living
in 1860, for example, includes her father's sense that "the woman was his
slave," his inability to understand "what other people felt," the "pressure of
society," and a set of public family rituals (125–28). In the last instance, the
distinction is predicated upon a larger split between public and private
space that is itself the hallmark, for Woolf, of a Victorian mode of organization. Since she and her father both retreat for large parts of the day into
their private rooms and thoughts, it is not the public, externalized per-
formances of meals or society functions that define the past so much as the
ways in which they puncture and impinge upon the intervening times
"when we escaped the pressures of Victorian society" (127). In such a context, the past is linked to one column in a set of oppositions—to the public,
social, and ritualized as opposed to the private, reflexive, and spontaneous—
and also to the larger process of binary thinking itself. In specifying the
defining qualities of the Victorians, in opposition to those of the Edwardians, Woolf is paradoxically thinking like a Victorian.

This is only one way in which it proves difficult to maintain the initial sense of an absolute separation between us (living in 1910) and them (stuck in 1860). Woolf acknowledges that she and her sister Vanessa "both learned the rules of the Victorian game of manners so thoroughly that we have never forgotten them. We still play the game." And while that may be "a disadvantage in writing," for reasons that we shall see in a moment, the game itself is said to be "founded upon restraint, sympathy, unselfishness—all civilized qualities" and ones that Bloomsbury would seek to value against a contrasting list (including action, impersonality, and politics) that it also associated with the Victorians. Again, the distinction seems to be unraveling. In one sense, of course, a figure like Virginia Woolf is herself the product of her own late-Victorian upbringing and can play the part of the hostess as well as her mother—"handing plates of buns to shy young men and asking them, not directly and simply about their poems and their novels, but whether they like cream as well as sugar" (129). In another sense, however, such a performance instantiates a kind of "civilized" behavior that is the goal of a post-Victorian ethics, suggesting that the nineteenth century already contained some elements of its own supersession.

What starts out looking like a simple revolt turns out, then, to be a far more complex relationship, shot through with ambiguity and contradiction. In what follows, I first look at some of the more celebrated texts of Bloomsbury anti-Victorianism, including *Mr Bennett and Mrs Brown* and the memoirs of Leonard Woolf and Clive Bell. In each case we see repeated, with minor variations, the same rhetorical gymnastics that shadow any effort to establish a firm line of departure from a past system and set of beliefs that in reality continue to inform the present. In the process, exactly what constitutes "the Victorian" remains permanently unstable, despite—or even because of—Bloomsbury's repeated attempts to dispose of it. This underlying irony is (ironically enough) acknowledged only in the text that has been commonly considered the decisive thrust in Bloomsbury's war with the Victorians, Lytton Strachey's *Eminent Victorians* (1918). There, as we shall see, Strachey comes closest to recognizing the real stakes and motives of modernist revolt and provides the tools by which it can be deconstructed nearly a century later.

Queen Victoria and Mrs. Woolf

Virginia Woolf's famous assertion, in *Mr Bennett and Mrs Brown*, that "on or about December 1910 human character changed" is an intentional overstatement, designed to force readers to question its claim by sheer rhetorical excess. Indeed, the precision of the month and year is offset by the

20   counterbalancing imprecision of "on or about," a tempering that is extended in the following paragraph as Woolf insists that it is not a "sudden and definite" transformation: by now, even the year is in question, as she backtracks further from her initial certainty, saying only that "since one must be arbitrary, let us date it about the year 1910" (4). There is a sense, however, in which the precision of "December 1910" *does* matter, in terms of the priorities it sets for Woolf's essay: it denotes in particular the opening of the first Postimpressionist exhibition in London, organized by Woolf's close friend Roger Fry, and—perhaps more importantly—*not* the death of Edward VII, which had occurred in May of that year. Given the responses to the death of Victoria nine years earlier, and the wide-ranging predictions of a transformed nation and society that accompanied it, Woolf's deemphasizing of monarchical succession is itself significant, and consistent with the larger argument of *Mr Bennett and Mrs Brown* that nominally "Victorian" traits of writing and perception were continued by the Edwardian novelists under discussion: in this, as in many other ways, the Edwardians had failed to engineer a decisive break with the past. Already, we can see the priority afforded to the cultural sphere here, as postimpressionist painting (along with selective "Georgian" literary counterparts) is contrasted with novelistic realism.

It is also significant that the Edwardians she singles out for criticism, H. G. Wells, John Galsworthy, and Arnold Bennett, asserted an activist role for fiction in fomenting social change—and indeed, it is partly on this point that she bases her critique. Just as the change of 1910 is not precipitated by monarchical succession, neither is it the product of explicit political measures: predictably enough, it was first glimpsed for Woolf in literature, in Samuel Butler's *The Way of All Flesh* and the plays of George Bernard Shaw, and then in domestic living arrangements and protocols: reflecting the priority given to the realm of everyday (bourgeois) experience, she compares "the Victorian cook . . . like a leviathan in the lower depths, formidable, silent, obscure, inscrutable," with her Georgian successor, who is by contrast "a creature of sunshine and fresh air . . . in and out of the drawing-room, now to borrow *The Daily Herald*, now to ask advice about a hat." This renegotiated relationship between masters and servants is also named first in a list describing how "[a]ll human relations have shifted," coming before those among "husbands and wives, parents and children." Even more tellingly, as an illustration of Raymond Williams's contention that Bloomsbury writers used their personal and collective experiences as the basis for imagining or projecting larger social changes, Woolf asserts that "when

human relations change there is at the same time a change in religion, conduct, politics, and literature" (5). In such a model, religion and politics are
reduced to second-order phenomena, while literature is afforded first and
last mention as the area of life that both signals a larger transformation and
is at the same time its final manifestation.

Literature can appear as the cause and symptom of such a transformation because—in the same way that "the Victorian" can come to signify binary thinking in general and also one side of a particular opposition—it,
too, is an internally divided sign running in parallel with human character
and relations. In this sense, Woolf's "arbitrary" transition of December 1910
is shadowed by the division of writers into "Edwardians" and "Georgians,"
a distinction that literally would have emerged with the royal succession
seven months earlier. The former are represented, as we have seen, by the
high realist triumvirate of Wells, Bennett, and Galsworthy, while the latter
grouping is more heterogeneous and less obviously contemporary in a strict
sense: while the five named authors (Forster, Lawrence, Strachey, Joyce, and
Eliot) were all born within a nine-year period, between 1879 and 1888,
Forster in particular spans the divide, having already published three novels before the watershed of 1910. The collective identity of the group rests,
for Woolf, on matters of form and style, and each can be identified with "the
Georgian writer [who] had to begin by throwing away the method that
was in use at the moment," a method that she identifies in turn with "the
Edwardian tools" of descriptive detail, external characterization, and social
engagement (18–19). In this way, literature is itself bifurcated around the
same central point of 1910, between those writers who look forward with
a new set of stylistic tools and others who continue on with the old ways.
Summarizing Woolf's position in this essay, Carola Kaplan and Anne Simpson note that it is a distinctively Oedipal one, expressing "the desire and
need to free themselves of the looming figures of their Victorian parents
and, by extension, the Edwardian artists [who] . . . had serious quarrels
with the Victorians" and yet seemed "willing to engage in those quarrels in
the terms their predecessors had taught them."[3] As one revealing characteristic of the new literary movement, for instance, Woolf notes how writers "do not pour out three immortal masterpieces with Victorian regularity
every autumn" (24), an assessment that identifies Bennett and others with
their own nineteenth-century predecessors by denigrating their acceptance of professional protocols and standards for novelists.[4]

As we shall see later in this chapter and in the one that follows, the
polemic involves a necessary form of oversimplification, a kind of willed

22   division into two contesting teams that inevitably slide into each other the more closely we examine the work of the so-called Georgians. The nature of any such division depends, of course, upon the prior statement of distinguishing criteria, yet these paradoxically seem to emerge from the examples themselves in Woolf's essay. With what we might take to be a classically "Georgian" distrust of "analyzing and abstracting," she proposes a story that will illustrate the differences she has presumed, conjuring up a scenario of a woman in a railway carriage which she simultaneously tells us "has the merits of being true" and also embellishes for effect. The most significant use of artistic license is her giving the woman the name "Mrs. Brown," which—in light of *Punch's* jokes about Victoria's relationship with her servant, John Brown—would have made her readily identifiable as the queen herself. Many of the physical details would seem to corroborate this, suggesting an image of the sovereign monarch and defining symbol of her age brought down to earth: there is, for instance, "something pinched about her—a look of suffering, or apprehension, and, in addition, she was extremely small. Her feet, in their clean little boots, scarcely touched the floor." In what seem to be further references to Victoria's later life and her concerns about the wayward Prince of Wales, the narrative imagines that "having been deserted, or left a widow, years ago, she had led an anxious, harried life, bringing up an only son, perhaps, who, as likely as not, was by this time beginning to go to the bad" (6). This self-conscious downscaling of the monarchy seems complete when Woolf imagines the public demanding to know "whether her villa was called Albert or Balmoral" (19).

If we are supposed to read the character as a version of Victoria, the essay works through a form of guilt by association, since we really only get to see how the Edwardian novelists under discussion might tell her story: thus, for instance, "Mr. Wells would instantly project upon the windowpane a vision of a better, breezier, jollier, happier, more adventurous and gallant world, where these musty railway carriages and fusty old women do not exist," while Bennett's eye for detail "would notice the advertisements; the pictures of Swanage and Portsmouth; the way in which the cushion bulged between the buttons" and so on (13). But if these illustrate Woolf's assessment of a literary style that keeps missing the human element itself, we are disappointed in our anticipation of a contrasting "Georgian" approach: as a representative of the new, Woolf concedes, "[a]ll I could do was to report as accurately as I could what was said, to describe in detail what was worn, to say, despairingly, that all sorts of scenes rushed into my mind, to proceed to tumble them out pell-mell, and to describe this vivid, this overmastering impression by likening it to a draught or a smell of burning." By this point, with the joking admission that "I was also strongly tempted to manufacture a three-volume novel about the old lady's son," the Edwardian/Georgian distinction seems to have evaporated, and Woolf admits that she has "pull[ed] my own anecdote to pieces" (17–18). Her stated point is that contemporary novelists have only the Edwardians available to them as role models, but we might equally conclude that the story has less to do with style than with content: the "Georgians" simply would not be writing about Mrs. Brown/Victoria in the first place, while the failed efforts of Wells and Bennett only serve to underscore their status as diminished Victorians, who cling to the old techniques but are no longer capable of contributing to an evolving canon of fiction that Woolf describes in the essay, including works by such nineteenth-century novelists as Charlotte Brontë, Thackeray, and Hardy.[5]

That canon is also distinguished from the work of the Edwardian novelists on account of its attitude toward the external world. Where, for the likes of Jane Austen or Laurence Sterne, "everything was inside the book, nothing outside," writers such as Wells "were interested in something outside," and this produced "incomplete" works for which "it seemed necessary to do something—to join a society, or, more desperately, to write a cheque" (12). A passage like this would seem to cement Virginia Woolf's reputation as lacking any interest in social causes, as (in the words of her husband Leonard) "the least political animal that has lived since Aristotle invented the term."[6] It is not my purpose here to recycle the standard reading of an apolitical Bloomsbury: as Patrick Brantlinger has argued in response to this cliché, the Group's collective record on sexual politics, World War I, and imperialism is a worthy one, even when checked by their own "confessions of naivete and failure, of ineffectiveness and distaste for politics."[7] What seems key in *Mr Bennett and Mrs Brown* is not the simple preference for art over politics so much as the denigration of the latter as a subject *for* art; in a manner that is reminiscent of the writers of the *fin de siècle*, a "pure" form of literature where "everything [is] inside" is held up as superior to the necessarily incomplete style that requires external validation or makes activist demands upon its readers.[8] Such a style is implicitly "Victorian" to the extent that the nineteenth century was itself viewed as a mechanical age, where what often dominated public discussions were precisely the kinds of obligations and responsibilities that tied person to person or a government to its citizens. In that sense, Raymond Williams is surely right that the Bloomsbury Group's ethos and aesthetic were

24 grounded in the individual, even when its members gave support to collective movements and bodies from the Independent Labour Party to the League of Nations.

"The Last Days of Victorian Civilization"?

If, as this suggests, Bloomsbury attitudes were shaped by an Oedipal opposition to a holistic projection of "the Victorians," the best account of the process can be found in Leonard Woolf's autobiography, published in the 1960s, and similar recollections such as Clive Bell's *Old Friends* (1956). Without wishing to force anything so solid as a shared "line" on these memoirs, enough common features exist to indicate areas of agreement that might form the basis for a Bloomsbury orthodoxy: that "Victorianism" is best approached as a set of conventions governing behavior rather than an overt political outlook; that politics is, nonetheless, a category that might be subsumed within the framework of the Victorian, especially as opposed to the more "subjective" mode of feeling; that class is no longer a privileged term for thinking about the opposed forces of progress and reaction—nor for pinpointing what (if anything) united those who came to define the core membership of the Bloomsbury Group itself. In the second volume of his autobiography, *Growing* (1961), Leonard Woolf recalls a youthful letter to Lytton Strachey during his time spent as a colonial administrator in Ceylon, bemoaning that "there is nothing to say to you, nothing to tell you of except 'events.' I neither read nor think nor—in the old way—feel."[9] Events, as they are disparaged here, are closely related to the need "to do something" that Virginia Woolf found so troubling in the novels of the same period; reading, thinking, and feeling are, by contrast, states of being where "everything is inside."

Working in opposition to "feeling" is "Victorianism," a force that often seems to be merely a set of conventions and attitudes that are propagated and recycled through key public institutions, in particular the schools, and that operate to construct and restrict the sovereign individual from the outside. Here, for example, is Leonard Woolf's description of the terms of the struggle, from the first volume of his memoirs:

> Our youth, the years of my generation at Cambridge, coincided with the end and the beginning of a century which was also the end of one era and the beginning of another. When in the grim, grey, rainy January days of 1901 Queen Victoria lay dying, we already felt that we were living in an era of incipient revolt and that

we ourselves were mortally involved in this revolt against a social   25
system and code of conduct and morality which, for convenience
sake, may be referred to as bourgeois Victorianism. . . . People of
a younger generation who from birth have enjoyed the results of
this struggle for social and intellectual emancipation cannot real-
ize the stuffy intellectual and moral suffocation which a young
man felt weighing down upon him in Church and State, in the
"rules and conventions" of the last days of Victorian civilization.[10]

If "Victorianism" is a system, then, it is not one founded in economics or
politics so much as the conventional "code of conduct and morality," the
unspoken and supposedly commonsensical rules of behavior that Louis
Althusser would later identify with the work of Ideological State Apparatuses, among which he gave pride of place to the educational system.[11]

To offer a minor yet instructive example, Woolf remarks that he would
invariably use surnames even when referring to close friends, and that
"[t]he shade of relationship between Woolf and Strachey is not exactly the
same as that between Leonard and Lytton." Blame here again attaches to
"that curious formality and reticence which the nineteenth-century public
school system insisted upon in certain matters," and it is seen as a clear bar-
rier to the expression of intimacy and feeling (*Sowing*, 119–20). Along the
same lines, Clive Bell marks as a significant "date in the history of Bloomsbury" his own engagement to Vanessa Stephen in 1906, when Strachey insisted on congratulating them using first names: "The practice became
general," Bell recalls with a hint of self-mockery, "and though perhaps it
marked a change less significant than that symbolised by the introduction
of the Greek dual, it has had its effect. Henceforth between friends manners were to depend on feelings rather than conventions."[12] The negative
impact of an outdated system of rules of conduct on those who came to be
referred to as the Bloomsbury Group can be glimpsed in other elements of
everyday life, including sexual knowledge and dress styles: of the former,
for instance, Leonard Woolf observes that "[h]ow dense the barbaric dark-
ness in which the Victorian middle-class boy and youth was left to drift
sexually is shown by the fact that no relation or teacher, indeed no adult,
ever mentioned the subject of sex to me" (*Sowing*, 82), while the fashion revolt of "bright green flannel collars" is viewed as "a kind of symptom of the
moral breakdown of the Edwardian era, the revolt against Victorianism,
particularly in so far as it affected the formal male respectability in dress
with its boiled shirt and starched white collar" (*Growing*, 37).

26   What seems deliberately elided here is the question of politics. While speaking of Cambridge, for instance, Woolf notes that "[e]xcept for the Dreyfus case and one or two other questions, we were not deeply concerned with politics" (*Growing*, 25). Bell concurs, saying of the same period that "politics we despised."[13] At times, as with Virginia Woolf's critique of Edwardian fiction, it appears as if politics itself needs to be placed in the column of the Victorians, as something to be transcended by a new civilization predicated on personal freedom and feeling. Both Clive Bell and Leonard Woolf seem to consider World War I in this way, as an unwelcome resurrection of politics to check a collective process of personal growth and experimentation. The former, for instance, speaks of a "new renaissance" in the air but notes acidly that "the statesmen came to the rescue, and Mr. Asquith, Sir Edward Grey and M. Viviandi declared war on Germany. By 1910," he recalls, "only statesmen dreamed of war, and quite a number of wide-awake people imagined the good times were just round the corner."[14] Leonard Woolf's account is similar in its implicit opposition of the politicians and (some) people: "It was, I still believe, touch and go whether the movement towards liberty and equality—political and social—and toward civilization, which was strong in the first decade of the 20th century, would become so strong as to carry everything before it. Its enemies saw the risk and the result was the war of 1914."[15] The key term here, as elsewhere in Bloomsbury writing, is "civilization," which is counterposed to the barbarism of war and politics as well as to the constricting conventions of "Victorianism." Implicitly, at least, the warmongering statesmen of 1914 represent a throwback to the past just as surely as novelists like Bennett and Wells, and each is working against the interests of "wide-awake people."

With such a phrase, we approach another ambiguity in Bloomsbury self-presentation, concerning the question of class. In their protestations to be no more than just "a circle of friends" (a claim I shall examine momentarily), memoirists such as Bell and Woolf assert that the "Group" represented little more, and maybe even less, than the sum of its parts; in other places, however, they seem to spearhead a larger movement for social change, as in the above passage from Woolf or his assertion elsewhere that "we were in the van of the builders of a new society which should be free" (*Sowing*, 161). While this statement echoes the conceptual language of Leninism, with its notion of the vanguard party, it is assuredly not designed to invoke the register of class analysis, which would represent another nineteenth-century holdover. Whenever that language is used, as was the

case earlier with the illustration of the inadequacies of "the Victorian   27
middle-class boy," it is usually yoked to a negative characterization of the
past: indeed, the phrase "bourgeois Victorianism" reinforces the connection, while also suggesting that the significant legacies of the past were
themselves the result of the triumphant hegemony of the middle class. At
times, it seems as if class inequalities have all but vanished, along with *Sowing's* sentimental vignettes of "a vast reservoir of uncivilized squalor and
brutality" in the 1880s and '90s that "no longer exists": from his vantage
point in the twentieth century, Woolf claims to look back and be "struck
by the immense change from social barbarism to social civilization which
has taken place in London (indeed in Great Britain) during my lifetime. The
woman, the policeman, the nurses, the small boy, the respectable passers-
by averting their eyes—all these are inhabitants of a London and a society
which has passed away" (57–58).

   While seeming to wish away the continued existence of the poor here,
Woolf is less certain about the middle class to which he himself belonged.
Sowing begins with a rare—and highly qualified—endorsement of the Victorian bourgeois lifestyle into which he was born. True, he condemns it as
a socialist for "its economic basis and its economic effect upon other
classes," "its snugness and smugness, snobbery, its complacent exploitation
of economic, sexual, and racial classes," and "its innate tendency to . . .
spiritual suburbanism"—and yet it finds praise for its "high psychological
and aesthetic values," the extraordinarily human and humane "relations
that might pertain between peoples if only the world was viewed as either
black or white, good or bad" (36–37). While this is at best a lukewarm affirmation, it does contrast sharply with Woolf's experiences in families like
the Stephens and the Stracheys, who possessed a more secure status among
the traditional British ruling class and among whom "I was an outsider . . .
because, although I and my father before me belonged to the professional
middle class, we had only recently struggled up into it from the stratum of
Jewish shopkeepers." His future in-laws, for instance, had "an intricate tan-
gle of ancient roots and tendrils stretching far and wide through the upper
middle classes, the county families, and the aristocracy" (*Beginning Again,*
74–75), while the Stracheys' dining room contained an atmosphere "of
British history and of that comparatively small ruling middle class which for
the last 100 years had been the principal makers of British history" (*Sowing,* 190).

   It is significant that Woolf seems to want to naturalize his relations with
such families as essentially interclass alliances among the bourgeoisie, at

28   the same time that he records his initial discomforts and distance from them. In such a conflicted response, we can glimpse what Raymond Williams has in mind in terming Bloomsbury "a forerunner in a more general mutation within the professional and highly educated sector, and to some extent in the English ruling class more generally," and thus a "fraction" that is in opposition to traditional and hegemonic values but at the same time the product of them.[16] This "mutation" anticipates the later-twentieth-century development of the "professional-managerial class" (as first defined by Barbara and John Ehrenreich),[17] and its history can be traced back, as Williams notes, to the late-nineteenth-century reforms of the universities and colonial administration that enabled a social connection to be established between Leonard Woolf and his Cambridge friends and future in-laws. But whereas he travels a considerable distance from his "Victorian bourgeois" upbringing, the same is not necessarily so for his wife: while she and her siblings had "broken away from" their own social milieu, "and from Kensington and Mayfair to live in Bloomsbury what seemed to their relations and old family friends a Bohemian life, there was no complete rupture" (*Beginning Again*, 74). In this sense, Bloomsbury speaks to and from within a hegemonic ruling class that contains both the upwardly mobile bourgeoisie and remnants of the old aristocracy, with what Williams terms "a persistent sense of a quite clear line between an upper and a lower class."[18] Left behind, in particular, are those "Victorian" habits of highlighting and multiplying the internal divisions that might have excluded an earlier version of Leonard Woolf from such ranks; by now, as we shall see in chapter 2, the appropriate figure for the outsider might be the aspiring petit-bourgeois bank clerk Leonard Bast, from E. M. Forster's *Howards End*.

A composite picture emerges from these memoirs of an abstracted Victorianism, often particularized as the "Victorian bourgeois" and codified in externalized social prohibitions and rules of conduct, against which is arrayed an equally abstracted force of rebellion. Assessing their shared worldview in this way helps clarify the striking pattern of disavowal that runs through the memoirs of Woolf and Clive Bell concerning the status of a coherent Bloomsbury "Group." Typically marshaled in response to negative attacks, the use of "Bloomsbury" as a term of abuse (Woolf) or "something nasty" (Bell), the immediate defense is to deny the very existence of such a collectivity by branding it "a largely imaginary group of persons with largely imaginary objects and characteristics" (*Beginning Again*, 21), or—as Bell repeatedly does—challenging its critics to define its membership and views.[19] Both, however, acknowledge that the term does have meaning, either as "Old Bloomsbury" for the first generation of friends that came together in 1912–14 or as Molly MacCarthy's affectionately named "Bloomsberries," and they are happy to provide their own senses of who would have belonged: of the fifteen names offered for inclusion by Bell (including four on the periphery), thirteen appear on a similar list drawn up by Leonard Woolf, suggesting a remarkably high correlation between what each offers up as provisional listings of what the latter terms merely "a group of friends" (*Beginning Again*, 23).[20]

The mechanism of disavowal at work here parallels the issue of class, which is simultaneously affirmed and denied as being critical to the opposition between Bloomsbury and "Victorianism." Thus, while Leonard Woolf asserts that the basis of "our group . . . was friendship, which in some cases developed into love and marriage" (*Beginning Again*, 25), he also specifies where and how that circle came together, noting that of the ten men on the list "nine had been at Cambridge, and all of us, except Roger, had been more or less contemporaries at Trinity and King's" (23). As Williams notes,[21] the same sense of incestuous intermixing appears when Woolf recalls the student body at Cambridge, who "intermarried to a considerable extent, and family influence and the high level of their individual intelligence carried a surprising number of them to the top of their professions" (*Sowing*, 186): his own initial exclusion on the basis of family upbringing is deftly deflected by the inclusion of intelligence as an equal factor, once again naturalizing the basis on which a new ruling formation was in the process of emerging.

What remains is the broad generality of a collective rebellion against the enemy of the past, shared among these "friends" but extending far beyond them, in which an undefined "we"—not exactly generalizable as either a class or a generation, but presumably something more than just a small and loose grouping—"found ourselves living in the springtime of a conscious revolt against the social, political, religious, moral, intellectual, and artistic institutions, beliefs, and standards of our fathers and grandfathers" (*Sowing*, 160). As we have seen from Virginia Woolf's *Mr Bennett and Mrs Brown*, the preferred ground for this battle was culture, with artistic style as one of its central weapons. In moving now to a consideration of Lytton Strachey's *Eminent Victorians* (1918), I propose to focus on one of its key sites, a text that fixed the terms of the modernist attitude toward the previous century through an immanent critique of the Victorians' own core beliefs and values. At the same time, Strachey's affinities with Oscar Wilde, a celebrated—if also largely proscribed—figure of the immediate Victorian

30   past, suggest a different line of influence, rooted in a self-reflexive criticism of the period that is often erased by the sweeping generalities that Blooms-bury writing helped to popularize.[22]

Eminent Victorians

As we have already seen with *Mr Bennett and Mrs Brown*, Virginia Woolf was quite content to draw a line between the Georgian/modernist and Victorian-Edwardian/traditionalist on the grounds of literary stylistics. Leonard's rec-ollections describe the same tendency during his days at Cambridge, yet they also suggest a reconsideration of this viewpoint with the benefits of hindsight. Initially, as *Sowing* makes clear, the literary tastes of the group that would form the core of "Old Bloomsbury" had their basis in a simple taxonomy similar to that offered by his wife: thus, Ibsen and Shaw were lauded for "saying 'Bosh!' to the vast system of cant and hypocrisy" inher-ited from the nineteenth century, while Thackeray and Dickens "meant nothing to us or rather they stood for an era, a way of life, a system of morals against which we were in revolt" (165). Arguable cases, predictably enough, could be drawn from the ranks of late-nineteenth-century novel-ists, and Woolf insists on correcting his earlier enthusiasms for Meredith—who "appealed to us as breaking away" from the model set by those two mid-century giants, even though "I am not sure now that he did"—and for James, whom he now acknowledges "was never really upon our side in that revolt" (166).

After admitting to a youthful weakness also for Swinburne, Woolf is led to a reconsideration of the pitfalls of periodization: after all, he now reasons, "Every out-of-date writer of any importance was once modern, and the most modern of writers will some day, and pretty rapidly, become out-of-date. For us in 1902 Tennyson was out-of-date and we therefore un-derestimated his poetry; today another fifty years has evaporated much of his datedness, and his stature as a poet has become more visible. I daresay that we overestimated Swinburne's poetry, but I have no doubt that it is generally underestimated today" (169).

Just as Meredith and James can come to seem less "modern," and in that sense still "Victorian" in some of the same ways that Bennett and Wells would appear to his wife, so too might canonical figures such as Tennyson, Thackeray, and Dickens need to be reevaluated with the benefit of hind-sight. As the above passage suggests, a writer paradoxically might appear less dated as time continues to pass and be relegated to the recesses of his-tory—at which point, Woolf implies, they can be judged more fully on

issues of form and style. The simple binaries of *Mr Bennett and Mrs Brown* 31
make clear, however, that such a reevaluation was difficult to make in the
mid-1920s, when the modernists still struggled with the legacies of the
past and "Victorian" was still a potent term of abuse.[23] Within Bloomsbury
circles, the author who most clearly articulated these problems of historical proximity and distance was actually one of Virginia Woolf's charter
Georgians, yet also one for whom Leonard felt "the eighteenth century
was more congenial and, in a sense, more real than the nineteenth or the
twentieth" (190).

Lytton Strachey's *Eminent Victorians* opens on this issue of distance by
famously asserting that "[t]he history of the Victorian Age will never be
written: we know too much about it." Faced with what Strachey characterizes as "so vast a quantity of information that the industry of a Ranke
would be submerged by it, and the perspicacity of a Gibbon would quail
before it," he recommends instead a more oblique and selective strategy:
dropping "here and there, a little bucket" into such an enormous ocean of
material and attacking it "in unexpected places."[24] Whether entirely sincere
or not, these considerations should at least make us question, as few of its
original or subsequent readers appear to have done, whether Strachey intended a systematic assault on the previous century in his case studies of
Cardinal Manning, Florence Nightingale, Thomas Arnold, and General
Gordon, and whether they are even supposed to be taken as representatives of their age. Echoing Virginia Woolf's mistrust of "analyzing and abstracting" in *Mr Bennett and Mrs Brown*, his preface proceeds to rationalize his
choice of subjects as "haphazard" and "determined by no desire to construct a system or to prove a theory, but by simple motives of convenience
and art." The age is—or at least *was*, at such a short remove—incapable of
being reduced to a simple "précis," just as Strachey himself refuses to follow the example of the period itself by modeling biography as the production of "[t]hose two fat volumes, with which it is our custom to commemo-
rate the dead," and so all he promises at the outset are "certain fragments
of the truth which took my fancy and lay to hand" (viii).

It is worth quoting the preface at some length, because the text has
been consistently read as attempting exactly what it disavows here. As
Strachey's biographer, Michael Holroyd, comments, "The general reader
was taught to think of *Eminent Victorians* as a 'debunking' biography"[25] by its
admirers as much as its critics: thus, for Cyril Connolly it was "the first
book of the 'twenties' . . . a revolutionary text-book on bourgeois society,"
and for Edmund Wilson an effort "to take down once and for all the pre-

32   tensions of the Victorian Age to moral superiority."[26] The more skeptical Edmund Gosse saw its purpose as "to damage and discredit the Victorian Age," motivated by "an intense desire to throw off the shackles of a dying age."[27] In part, such assessments depend upon a consideration of whether Strachey's four subjects are in fact representative of the period and to what extent the designation of their "eminence" is intended literally. The reviewer for the *Times Literary Supplement*, for example, assumes both to be the case, noting that "Mr Lytton Strachey has made a very sincere and scholarly attempt to understand the generation which preceded his own . . . to find out what this time really was" by studying "its eminent figures, the things they really stood for, what motives moved them, and what they contributed of permanent value to the improvement of society and the enlightenment of the human mind." To read *Eminent Victorians* in such a context is, then, already to impute ambitions beyond its own stated purpose and to presuppose what are surely called into question by its title: the issues of who should come to represent the Victorians and on what basis the characterization "eminent" might be conferred on such figures, especially with the benefits of hindsight. On this last question, the reviewer seems to feel that eminence is a negative quality for Strachey, as implied by the consideration of what he might have produced "if he would write not only about 'eminent' but also about those he considers admirable Victorians."[28]

Ironically, something like this had been Strachey's original ambition when he set out to begin a larger project titled "Victorian Silhouettes," with a greater number of biographical subjects and split between positive and negative portraits.[29] The eventual condensation may have come as a result of the outbreak of World War I or the slow pace of composition, caused in part by wartime anxieties, but I would suggest that one effect is to compress that original balance sheet so that a sense of the admirable and detestable features of the period emerge within individual essays—and also within the individuals themselves. It may be that the text now reads as a more positive assessment of the past than it first seemed; U. C. Knoepflmacher has commented that the biographies are "for all their irony, sketched with considerable empathy, even affection," for instance, and notes Strachey's "intense identification with his subjects" in the cases of Florence Nightingale, General Gordon, and Cardinal Newman (as the foil for Manning) in particular.[30] The first of these even momentarily joins the ranks of privileged Bloomsbury authors when Strachey compares her private writing—"a virulent invective upon the position of women in the upper ranks of society"—with the published work of Ibsen and Samuel

Butler, although it is his central point that such criticisms needed to remain 33
private, even for a celebrated figure like Nightingale, possessed as she was
with every advantage except "the public power and authority which belonged to the successful politician" (193, 172).

Among Nightingale's supporters was the monarch herself, a figure who
similarly confused the boundaries between public and private selves, combining a feminine deference that was appropriate for the time with tremendous power and authority.[31] The gendering of such split personalities is
made clear in the case of Nightingale, as Strachey explodes the cliché of
"the Lady with the Lamp" to show in its place a more complex personality
beneath the surface of public mythology: thus, he notes, "[w]hile superficially she was carrying on the life of a brilliant girl in high society," at the
same time "internally she was a prey to the tortures of regret and of remorse,"
and could resolve the conflict only in a massive and unceasing expenditure
of energy to acquire "the experience which alone could enable her to do
what she had determined she would do in the end" (139). Such a split is not
exclusive to Victorian women, though, as something similar emerges in the
study of General Gordon, a man possessed of "intricate recesses where
egotism and renunciation melted into one another, where the flesh lost itself in the spirit, and the spirit in the flesh" (260). If anything, it is this
collapsing of the boundaries between the material and spiritual that is
common to each of Strachey's portraits, uniting those figures he admires
with those he criticizes.[32]

Cardinal Manning, for instance, emerges from *Eminent Victorians* as a
figure who combines Nightingale's struggles with public and private per-
sonae with Gordon's problematic conflation of ego with its renunciation.
The former characteristic appears most fully in Manning's rivalry with
Newman, whose death he privately marked by noting, "Poor Newman! He
was a great hater!" even as he publicly mourned that "[w]e have lost our
greatest witness for the Faith, and we are all poorer and lower for the loss"
(123). Here, as with Nightingale, it is tempting to read the private utter-
ance as emanating from a more truthful self beneath the public façade, or
even—in terms that Strachey would have encountered in Freud—as an underlying id (like Nightingale's "demons") being held in check by the super-
ego.[33] In the matter of ambition, Manning more successfully negotiates the
pitfalls encountered by Gordon by allowing surrogate figures to satisfy his
repressed wants. Commenting on his refusal, even in his private writings,
to acknowledge an appetite for personal recognition and status, Strachey
notes that Manning "vowed to heaven that he would *seek* nothing—no, not

34   by the lifting of a finger or the speaking of a word. But if something came to him—? He had vowed not to seek; he had not vowed not to take" (73; emphasis in original). Reading passages like this, it is hard to distinguish decisively the evils of a Manning, working behind the scenes in the Vatican to undermine Newman yet refusing even privately to admit his culpability, from the heroism of a Nightingale, who similarly employed surrogate figures such as Sidney Herbert to advance her political aims.

The protagonists of *Eminent Victorians* persistently struggle against entrenched authorities, whether in the clergy, army, or government, and sometimes (as with the case of Cardinal Manning) succeed only in joining their ranks. In the process, they experience—or perhaps exacerbate—an internal split in personality that is either beneficial or detrimental to their efforts, depending in part on whether their self-division is seen as inherent, as might be the orthodox Freudian explanation, or instead as symptomatic of a wider social contradiction. The latter point centrally distinguishes Strachey's view of the Victorians from that of the Bloomsbury Group as a whole, which tended to see the ruling culture of the period as essentially mechanical and instrumentalist in its exercising of power. In such a framework, it is relatively easy to see the rigid orthodoxies of the War Office, the Vatican, Thomas Arnold, or the government as institutions against which other individuals—Nightingale, Gordon, Newman, or Rugby schoolboys—engage in a heroic and often fatal struggle. But Strachey's approach is a more complex one, which insists on seeing the Victorian period itself as internally fractured and the popular image of it as coherently one-dimensional as part of the mythology that surrounds it. We can glimpse something of Strachey's revisionism in his portrait of one of Gordon's government adversaries, Lord Hartington, a man who was widely viewed as possessing "an honesty which naturally belonged to one whom, *so it seemed to them*, was the living image of what an Englishman should be" and "the qualities by which they themselves longed to be distinguished, and by which, in their happier moments, *they believed they were*" (322–23; emphasis added). This suggests a closed feedback loop of ideological mystification, within which the Victorian public was brought to consent to supposedly natural qualities—including "solidity" and common sense, in addition to honesty—as the defining characteristics of the national identity, even though neither they themselves nor their official representatives could adequately embody them. We might conclude that Bloomsbury's critiques, with the exception of *Eminent Victorians*, did more to perpetuate this mystification than they did to challenge it, with the result that such character traits and associations still persist in the public imagination a century later.

The figure of William Gladstone most fully illustrates Strachey's reassessment of the period's own complexities. Early on in the essay on Gordon, the prime minister is offered, alongside Lord Hartington and Gordon himself, as evidence that the national character at this time combined in equal measures eccentricity and conventionality, "matter-of-factness" and romance (246). Whereas some of these qualities might predominate in one figure or another—so that Gordon's eccentricities could be ranged against Hartington's conventionality—they converge in the persona of Gladstone. He is said to invite "the clashing reactions of passionate extremes"—to have been equally worshipped and despised—and it is Strachey's view that neither response was really wrong: "It might have been supposed," he comments, "that one or the other of these conflicting judgments must have been palpably absurd, that nothing short of gross prejudice or willful blindness, on one side or the other, could reconcile such contradictory conceptions of a single human being. But it was not so." The immediate explanation for this is that, like Gordon and the period itself, Gladstone is "a complex character," but Strachey goes on to note a further level of complexity in him: while his speeches might reveal "the ambiguity of ambiguities" and thus baffle listeners who would analyze them to understand his true personality and beliefs, "[i]n spite of the involutions of his intellect and the contortions of his spirit it is impossible not to perceive a strain of *naiveté* in Mr. Gladstone." Thus, as ironically representative of a time that saw itself as solid and honest even when it failed to satisfy such ambitions fully, the prime minister might be subjected to intensive scrutiny and close reading, only to reveal beneath his surface ambiguities an underlying simplicity: a "singularly literal" faith in a limited range of principles, a "simple-minded" egoism, "uncritical" views on religion, and no sense of humor (307–8).

Camp Stylistics

For Strachey, this last quality may have been Gladstone's most serious flaw, as well as the key to his contradictory appearance. Leonard Woolf describes his friend's method of thought as follows: "he had developed a protective intellectual façade in which a highly personal and cynical wit and humour played an important part. It was very rarely safe to accept the face value of what he said; within he was intensely serious about what he thought important, but on the surface his method was to rely on 'suggestion and instruction derived from what is in form a jest—even in dealing with the gravest matters'" (*Sowing*, 151). In this, he is both like and unlike his subjects in *Eminent Victorians*, especially Gladstone: deeply committed to

36 principles and beliefs, yet superficially ambiguous or contradictory. The difference is that Strachey self-consciously employed this as a strategy, one we now readily associate with camp. Citing Susan Sontag's influential definition of a modern gay sensibility working through the deliberate production of incongruity and exaggeration, Barry Spurr has labeled Strachey's literary style as "Camp Mandarin," and he provides a catalogue of its rhetorical techniques: indirect meaning, pastiche, the use of quotations and clichés for ironic purposes (and often revised for the sake of antithesis or bathos), a reliance on aphorisms and epigrams, and so on.[34] In camp, we can see the willed production of insincerity and a playful delight in contradiction, two qualities that seem for Strachey to be the unwanted or unconscious by-products of the Victorian age, even though they were widespread enough to be present in some of its leading figures.

As Spurr suggests, its camp style helps to explain the lasting reputation of *Eminent Victorians* as the work of a "contemptible sniggerer."[35] By focusing on its humorous effects, however, the book's critics neglect its other side, that aspect of Strachey's thinking that Leonard Woolf calls being "intensely serious about what he thought important." In this aspect, Strachey's most influential forerunner is clearly Wilde, a figure whose notoriety nonetheless rendered him largely taboo for Bloomsbury modernism, as Ann Ardis has shown; indeed, it was largely as a *stylist* that Wilde could be spoken about in the early twentieth century, given the general prohibition against discussions of his sexual politics.[36] In his important analysis of Wilde, however, Jonathan Dollimore has usefully remarked of his political project that it is focused on "a parodic critique of the essence of sensibility as conventionally understood," which includes for him those same qualities—truthfulness, sincerity, authenticity, and depth—that Strachey exposes as the mythological characteristics of nineteenth-century Britain.[37] Just as his method is to reveal the immanent tensions and contradictions within the self-presentation of his Victorian subjects, relying on their firsthand testimony as his symptomatic evidence, so Dollimore suggests that a subversive strain of camp "undermines the depth model of identity from inside, being a kind of parody and mimicry which hollows out from within, making depth recede into its surfaces."[38] This is a radically different project from the work of sustained opposition to "Victorianism" that Leonard Woolf outlines in his memoirs, which (as we have seen) consisted of pinning down the supposed essence of the period and then substituting antithetical values and qualities in its place.

The difference is very similar to one that has been developed in critical theory between a deconstructive practice on the one hand and simple strategies of inversion on the other. Bloomsbury's oppositional attitude toward the nineteenth century can be seen, from this perspective, as a form of carnivalesque reversal, in which the supposedly dominant or valued qualities of the past—a society structured by convention and class relationships, say, or placing a priority on active "doing," especially in the political sphere—are replaced by their polar opposites: the "civilized" individual and the introspection of "feeling" as the cornerstone of cultural practice. As we shall see throughout this study, the problem with such an approach is that it leaves the initial characterization in place rather than unsettling it, so that "the Victorian" hardens as an analytical concept the more it comes under attack; it is thus available, in turn, as a reference point or rallying cry for forces of reactionary counterinversion, as we shall see in the cases of Evelyn Waugh in chapter 2 or Margaret Thatcher in chapter 4. The effect is reminiscent of what some critics have identified as the weakness in Bakhtin's theory of the carnivalesque, where the licensed misrule and excess of a public holiday like Mardi Gras perversely serves to train its participants in a more efficient and productive use of their "regular" work time.[39]

Deconstruction, by contrast, considers the strategy of inversion to be only the first—but nonetheless a crucial—step in dismantling the hierarchies of power. Like Strachey, it insists that the dominant is never a coherent entity but instead contains contradictory elements and ambiguities; indeed, to the extent that what it opposes is inherent within it as a constituent aspect of its own identity, the dominant might be imagined as something like Strachey's General Gordon, a figure consisting of "intertwining contradictions." The intervention of a deconstructionist reading consists, in this account, of an active foregrounding of those contradictions, which pushes fixed definitions to the point of collapse or chiasmus, when one term of the binary inevitably entails its supposed opposite. The aphorisms of Oscar Wilde are exemplary here, because what seems on the surface to be a simple reversal—"If one tells the truth, one is sure, sooner or later, to be found out," for instance[40]—in fact works to delink habitual associations (of truth with transparency, or falsehood with exposure) and undermine the basis for a strict separation of terms. Strachey's sympathetic portrait of Cardinal Newman, committed to a complex casuistry that is simultaneously propelling him toward and resisting a conversion to Catholicism, provides us with a perfect instance of the inseparability of characteristics that would be conventionally thought of as antithetical: "The idea of deceit," Strachey suggests, "would have been abhorrent to him; and indeed it was owing to his very desire to explain what he had in his mind exactly and completely, with all the refinements of which his subtle brain was

38   capable, that persons such as Kingsley were puzzled into thinking him dishonest. Unfortunately, however, the possibilities of truth and falsehood depend upon other things than sincerity. *A man may be of a scrupulous and impeccable honesty, and yet his respect for the truth—it cannot be denied—may be insufficient"* (32–33; emphasis added).

His point here is not, I think, that Newman is anything as simple as a hypocrite, who pretends to particular public qualities (honesty, moral purpose, or heroism) in order to cover up real, private ones that suggest the opposite (deceit, confusion, or the intimidation of the weak). It is rather that the period itself, and possibly any period, makes contradictory demands upon its subjects: as a result, even—or especially—for these "eminent Victorians," piety produces fanaticism just as an overriding emphasis on personal duty is shown to generate massive egos and rampant self-glorification.

At an immediate level, then, we can conclude that "Victorianism" does not exist except as an amalgamation of such contradictions or as a retroactive construction that necessarily neglects half of the picture. More significantly, the period itself comes to signify the very opposite of the stolid, one-dimensional entity imagined by Bloomsbury. The effect of Strachey's rhetorical strategy is accurately described by Dollimore when he writes of Wilde's "transgressive aesthetic" that it illustrates the case where inversion "is not just the necessary precondition for the binary's subsequent displacement, but often already constitutes a displacement, if not directly of the binary itself, then certainly of the moral and political norms which cluster dependently around its dominant pole and in part constitute it."[41] What emerges from this is not the simple reversal of polarities that might claim that the modern is somehow better—truer to its convictions, say, or more complex—than the Victorian, but the larger question of whether we can fully the distinguish the Victorian from the modern, especially given the former's capacity for self-contradiction.

Strachey seems to have had something like this in mind when he opened his essay on Cardinal Manning by presenting his subject as nominally opposed to the spirit of his age, in the style of a General Gordon, and yet also one who—far from experiencing the disappointments and frustrations of the latter—personally thrived within it: "born in the England of the nineteenth century," he writes of Manning, "growing up in the very seedtime of modern progress, coming to maturity with the first onrush of Liberalism, and living long enough to witness the victories of Science and Democracy, he yet, by a strange concatenation of circumstances, seemed almost to revive in his own person that long line of diplomatic and ad-

ministrative clerics which, one would have thought, had come to an end
with Cardinal Wolsey. In Manning, so it appeared, the Middle Ages lived
again" (3).

The paradox can be resolved in any of three ways. It is possible, although unlikely given Strachey's methodology, that the "great men" theory of history applies here, in which case the "dominating character" of
Manning has "imposed itself upon a hostile environment." Or the opposite
explanation might apply, that his is in fact a less forceful personality, capable of being "supple and yielding" when necessary—though still driven, as
we have seen, by an overarching ambition and a ruthless sense of *Realpolitik*
in his dealings with Newman and the Vatican. Most interesting for my purposes is the hypothesis that is briefly considered in between these two,
which involves a reconsideration not of Manning but of the age with which
he appears to come into conflict: "was the nineteenth century, after all,"
Strachey wonders, "not so hostile? Was there something in it, scientific
and progressive as it was, which went out to welcome the representative of
ancient tradition and uncompromising faith?" (4). Evidence presented in
the rest of the text would suggest that this indeed might be so, and that
the century's attitudes toward the spiritual and the material in particular
might need to be rethought.

It is to this same end, of revising what we think we know of the nineteenth century to accommodate an understanding of some of its leading
figures, that Strachey approaches the issue of the Victorian zeitgeist in the
essay on Gordon. The recent past is first actively defamiliarized, so that his
readers are able to catch "a vision of strange characters, moved by myste-
rious impulses, interacting in queer complication, and hurrying at last—so
it almost seems—like creatures in a puppet show to a predestined catas-
trophe." But if this might seem like modernist condescension, marking its
own palpable distance from the past, what follows works to collapse the
gap by insisting that such odd personalities are nonetheless "curiously English" and defined by their capacities for self-contradiction: "What other
nation on the face of the earth," Strachey asks, "could have produced Mr.
Gladstone and Sir Evelyn Baring and Lord Hartington and General Gordon?
Alike in their emphasis and their lack of emphasis, in their eccentricity and
their conventionality, in their matter-of-factness and their romance, these
four figures seem to embody the mingling contradictions of the English
spirit" (246).

In answering his own question in this way, I would suggest, Strachey
implicitly poses others. Can a nation be said to be animated by a defining

40 spirit if part of what defines it are those "mingling contradictions" that he has noted throughout *Eminent Victorians*? If so, and if it can be represented by eccentrics like Gordon just as successfully as by establishment figures like Gladstone and Manning, then isn't the search for a distilled essence— of the nation or the age—a pointless one? At the very least, Strachey's view of the Victorian period as necessarily and definitively self-divided high- lights the inadequacy of the larger Bloomsbury orthodoxy, which pre- ferred to define the past as one-dimensional and the present as marked by complex ambiguities. If we take *Eminent Victorians* at face value, there is no benefit that accrues from such attempts to pin down the past, except the illusory consolation of feeling that it is really and truly *over*, and it seems equally unproductive to debate, as we shall see others doing throughout this study, whether one is for or against the Victorians.

CHAPTER TWO

The Politics of Nostalgia
Conservative Modernism, Victorian Kitsch,
and the English Country House

When pressed by the kind of deconstructive reading that I outlined in chapter 1, Lytton Strachey's *Eminent Victorians* can come
to seem shot through with ambiguities about the nineteenth
century, and thus to break ranks with the more orthodox
Bloomsbury attitudes exemplified by Clive Bell or the Woolfs.
In this chapter I want to focus on a more explicit ambivalence
toward the past that we can see in the works of E. M. Forster
and Evelyn Waugh, two novelists on the fringes of British
modernism and (in the case of Forster) also of Bloomsbury. It
is a sign of the pervasive influence of anti-Victorianism in the
first half of the twentieth century that neither exactly admitted
to an overt nostalgia for the nineteenth—although Waugh was
a figure in a kitsch revival of interest in elements of Victorian
style and furnishing at Oxford in the 1920s. I shall return to
that moment at the end of this chapter, seeing it as significantly contributing to a binary thinking about the Victorians
and avant-garde modernism that reduces both to simplified
fashion statements. My prime focus, however, is on Forster's
Howards End (1910) and Waugh's *Brideshead Revisited* (1945), two
texts that are redolent with a longing for some of the supposed
values of the past, at the same time that they also stage self-
reflexive discussions of the benefits and dangers of nostalgia.

The most immediate context for these discussions is war:
the world war that Forster can already foresee breaking out four
years later, and about which he astutely comments that "the

42 remark 'England and Germany are bound to fight' renders war a little more likely each time that it is made, and is therefore made the more readily by the gutter press of either nation";[1] and its successor, a conflict in which an aging Waugh (by then in his forties) still hoped to participate as he hastily composed *Brideshead* in 1944. As Patrick Wright has written, wartime consistently generates an image for Britons of what he terms a "Deep England" under threat, one that is typically figured through a pastoral language that describes a transhistorical landscape worth fighting and dying for, and thus a perceived connection to the national past. "To be a subject of Deep England," he notes, "is above all to have *been there*—one must have had the essential experience, and one must have had it in the past to the extent that the meaningful ceremonies of Deep England are above all ceremonies of remembrance and recollection. More specifically one must have grown up in the midst of ancestral continuities and have experienced that kindling of consciousness which the national landscape and cultural tradition prepare for the dawning national spirit."[2]

These same terms and values—experience, recollection, continuity, tradition—are the ones that we shall see endorsed in *Howards End* and *Brideshead Revisited*, even as both novels are keenly aware of the ways in which such sentiments are open to manipulation and outright falsification, operating as they do at a level that is felt to be collective and subconscious. This means that they often exist in tension with the sovereign individual as championed by Bloomsbury and with elements of a modernist stylistics, in particular ironic narration.

The best term for what these novels end up articulating is offered by Alison Light, who identifies a paradoxical strain of "conservative modernity" in the literature of the interwar years—although she suggests that the period itself might need to be expanded and thus could encompass a precursor text such as *Howards End*. Such writing, she argues, is "Janus-faced": it "could simultaneously look backwards and forwards; it could accommodate the past in the new forms of the present; it was a deferral of modernity and yet it also demanded a different sort of conservatism from that which had gone before."[3] As such, I would add that it carves for itself a different relationship to the past than that adopted by either Bloomsbury progressivism or the regressive nostalgia at the heart of traditional conservatism. While hesitant to argue for a full-fledged Victorian revival, except in such limited areas as fashion and furnishing, it sought to redefine the complex dialectic between heritage and the modern, and in the process began to rethink the characteristics by which we identify the nineteenth century: as Light suggests, it is on issues typically associated with the personal and domestic (and therefore the "feminine") that this contradictory discourse marks its distance from Bloomsbury, by associating the past with a sense of connectedness—to the land, the nation, and each other—instead of with abstract impersonality and the machinery of systematic analysis.

Forster: The New Economy and the Old Morality

In a radio broadcast recorded in 1946, Forster offered a retrospective balance sheet of his late-Victorian upbringing—he was born in 1879—from the vantage point of the postwar world. "I belong," he noted, "to the fag-end of Victorian liberalism . . . an admirable age" in many respects. Viewing the first half of the twentieth century much as Orwell would, as defined by the politics of instrumental power and by social divisions along racial and class lines, Forster looks back favorably on that earlier phase of liberalism as one that "practised benevolence and philanthropy, was humane and intellectually curious, upheld free speech, had little colour-prejudice, believed that individuals are free and should be different, and entertained a sincere faith in the progress of society."[4] Indeed, it is only on this last point that he now has reservations, recognizing that the national prosperity that underwrote this belief in progress was achieved only by "exploiting the poor of our own country and the backward races abroad." As a result, the broadcast outlines the sort of "Janus-faced" compromise that Alison Light describes, arguing that "we must manage to combine the new economy and the old morality" (57).

From the Victorians, then, Forster wants to retain a belief in the individual, but he proposes to delink it from its economic corollary of laissez-faire capitalism, which simply "will not work in the material world." That failure, he goes on to suggest, argues strongly for the forms of centralized planning that can only be done by the state, and which emerged around the turn of the century (as I shall discuss in chapter 4) precisely to address the inherent weakness of the laissez-faire model. "We must have planning and ration-books and control," he maintains, "or millions of people will have nowhere to live and nothing to eat," but the problem then becomes where to set the limits on planning so that it does not impinge upon the rightful territory of the individual; echoing Orwell, Forster fears that "if you plan and control men's minds you stunt them, you get the censorship, the secret police, the road to serfdom, the community of slaves" (55). What the essay outlines is a careful compromise that depends upon a demarcation between economics and morality in which the former should operate

44   with a twentieth-century emphasis on state regulation and planning and the latter according to a nineteenth-century faith in the sovereign individual. In the process, we might note here another transvaluation of Bloomsbury thinking, so that it is the private sphere of personal relations that becomes the hallmark of the Victorians, rather than the public sphere of impersonal politics.

Forster is aware that the compromise he calls for is a hard one to enact, raising persistent problems of divided loyalties and conflicting principles. To illustrate the difficulty, he offers a personal anecdote about town planning that seems very pertinent to *Howards End*, a novel he had published thirty-six years earlier. "I was brought up as a boy," he writes, "in one of the home counties, in a district which I still think the loveliest in England. . . . It must have always looked much the same," he continues, sounding the note of transhistorical continuity that Patrick Wright associates with recollections of "Deep England," and "I have kept in touch with it, going back to it as to an abiding city and still visiting the house which was once my home" (56). The values of permanence and rootedness form one side of the equation, then, the one that Forster identified with Victorian liberalism and the individual; on the other side is the reality that the area has recently been commandeered by the Ministry of Town and Country Planning, with the announcement "that a satellite town for sixty thousand people is to be built" (58). Where his conservative side bemoans the inevitable loss, the progressive thinks instead of "working-class friends in north London who have to bring up children in two rooms." In this case, the former wins out, with the conclusion that "I cannot free myself from the conviction that something irreplaceable has been destroyed, and that a little piece of England has died as surely as if a bomb had hit it" (59), but that dominating sentiment is presumably not inevitable in every such instance. Indeed, if the story is offered to illustrate the need for a balance between the new economics and the old morality, it seems instead to highlight the near impossibility of achieving it, given that the benefits on either side are so uneven as to appear incommensurable.

The difficulty has generated considerable critical discussion about the nature and depth of Forster's commitment to liberalism, including Lionel Trilling's influential assessment that while "all his novels are politically and morally tendentious and always in the liberal direction . . . he is deeply at odds with the liberal mind."[5] In approaching *Howards End*, the problem is compounded by the appearance at the turn of the century of the so-called New Liberalism, which sought to revise its orthodox Victorian predecessor by arguing for a more active intervention on the part of the state—for 45 what Forster terms "planning" in the 1946 broadcast. The liberal tradition is thus bifurcated between a modern, progressive tendency on the one hand and an older form that inevitably seems conservative in comparison. As David Medalie notes of this split, "when liberalism is associated with the past rather than the future, when it is the subject of elegies rather than ambitions, it has become a spent force," while its more progressive off-shoot is tarnished by its capitulation to many of the negative effects of modernity.[6] In that sense, the contradictory space Forster wants to occupy, positioned somewhere between an embrace of the modern and a nostalgia for the past, is one that he shared with liberalism itself during the early years of the twentieth century.

If, as Medalie suggests, *Howards End* is the text where Forster "sets up and evaluates many of the ingredients of the New Liberal programme,"[7] then it is the character of Leonard Bast, a clerk seeking to advance himself through a self-taught course in cultural appreciation, who acts as the novel's test case. As the subject of a discussion among a group of cosmo-politan intellectual women, including Margaret and Helen Schlegel, a phan-tom Leonard is the target of a wide range of supportive efforts that sum-marize the debates at the turn of the century concerning what to do for the poor: thus, for instance, in an echo of the late-Victorian argument that charity would "de-moralize" him, "his conditions must be improved without impairing his independence," while another proposal offers the more con-descending solution of "a Twin Star, some member of the leisured classes who would watch over him ceaselessly"; more Arnoldian suggestions in-volve "a free library" or "a third-class ticket to Venice,"[8] and it is only late in the conversation that Margaret argues for simply giving him money that he can spend on whatever he thinks he most needs.[9] That last position is not intended to represent simply a materialist solution, however, but also one that is grounded in a concern for the individual Leonard in place of an abstract rendering of him: as the narrative tells us of Margaret, "[o]thers had attacked the fabric of Society—Property, Interest, etc.; she only fixed her eyes on a few human beings, to see how, under present conditions, they could be made happier" (101).[10]

Such efforts on the part of Margaret and her sister are, however, disas-trous for the flesh-and-blood Leonard, who loses his job, gets evicted, and is finally killed on their account—a fate for which it seems a cruel consolation that his illegitimate son ends as heir to Howards End. In a sense, Leonard never really functions as anything other than a pretext for discussions that

46   take place elsewhere, and he struggles to elevate himself above the status of a character type: "You must keep that type at a distance," says Henry Wilcox on first meeting him, and while Margaret objects to the characterization here ("he isn't a type. He cares about adventures rightly"), she later seconds it, writing to Helen, "The Basts are not at all the type we should trouble about" (115–17, 191). Leonard is first introduced through the statistical categories that were favored by late-Victorian sociology, when we learn that "[w]e are not concerned with the very poor," and we can infer from this that he belongs instead to the adjacent category of the lower middle class that so concerned urban reformers: those, like him, who while "not in the abyss . . . could see it" (36). If culture is his chosen vehicle for elevation, it is significant that his preferred authors are of the kind that Bloomsbury modernists (or the Schlegel sisters) would reject as passé Victorians: Ruskin, Borrow, Meredith, Stevenson. "Oh, to acquire culture!" he thinks to himself when meeting the Schlegels, but "it would take one years. With an hour at lunch and a few shattered hours in the evening, how was it possible to catch up with leisured women who had been reading steadily from childhood?" (32). In such moments, we can recognize Leonard as a sympathetic variation on Virginia Woolf's Edwardian novelists, a figure who lags so far behind the cutting edge of the artistic avant-garde that he seems doomed to a perpetual Victorianism.

Leonard is also associated with the Victorians in a more complicated way. As part of his credentials to stand in for a social type, his family background is repeatedly rehearsed, so we recognize the accreted social history that is contained in the description of him as "the third generation, grandson to the shepherd or ploughboy whom civilization had sucked into the town; as one of the thousands who have lost the life of the body and failed to reach the life of the spirit" (91).[11] It seems appropriate, in this sense, that his reputation among the Schlegels as a seeker after adventures is founded on a nightlong walk in the woods around London, an occasion on which, he tells them, "I wanted to get back to the Earth." The only problem—and it is one that illustrates the distance between him and his grandfather—is that he does so on the inspiration of Meredith's *The Ordeal of Richard Feverel*, thereby reversing what the Schlegel sisters have presumed to be an admirable prioritizing of Nature over Culture (93). If this scene is played out for ironic effect, though, Forster elsewhere expresses a more direct sympathy with the desire to reconnect with nature, even if he sees a generalized environmental consciousness as unlikely to emerge within the immediate context of turn-of-the-century modernity: "The Earth as an artistic cult has had its day," he writes, "and the literature of the near future will probably ignore the country and seek inspiration from the town. One can understand the reaction. Of Pan and the elemental forces, the public has had a little too much—they seem Victorian, while London is Georgian—and those who care for the earth with sincerity may wait long ere the pendulum swings back to her again" (86). The image of the pendulum implies that the model of progress that is now dominant in the capital is capable of revision or outright rejection, but also that a wholesale return to the past and nature is currently unlikely. Forster is characteristically coy, however, about whether he would identify himself with such a desire or with the urban modernism of the Georgians.

Toward the end of the novel, we revert to a language of social types to address this question of the future. Leonard Bast is walking toward Howards End, a location that has been proclaimed from the outset to be an intermediate space between city and country, combining the superficiality required by businessmen with "hints of local life, personal intercourse" (13). He recognizes that "Here men had been up since dawn," although the narrator checks their idealization by interjecting that only "the sentimentalist" would assert that they "were men of the finest type" (255). Having thus identified Leonard, even in such a diminished form, with his own rural ancestors, Forster has his killer pass him in a motorcar, one of the novel's recurring metaphors for a modernity that maintains a polluter's disregard for nature. Charles Wilcox is labeled as "another type whom Nature favours— the Imperial," and the ensuing description reinforces the connection: it "breeds as quickly as the yeoman" and also "hopes to inherit the earth," yet such ambitions will be thwarted, we are told, because the imperialist only "prepares the way for cosmopolitanism" (256). As a type, the cosmopolitan has been associated throughout the novel with the Schlegels, and through them with artistic modernism and progressive politics, which makes it difficult to draw the conclusion that inheriting Howards End represents the pendulum's swing back from culture to nature. Indeed, since Leonard's son is also the descendent of Helen Schlegel, we might just as plausibly argue that he represents the ultimate triumph of cosmopolitan modernism.

The novel is, of course, less interested in the rural population than it is fixated on the rivalry between the imperial and the cosmopolitan, as set out in a series of stark contrasts that readily map onto Bloomsbury's larger distinction between past and present. As representatives of the imperial type, for instance, the Wilcoxes value "the outer life" (22), "the manner of the committee-room" (78), and the elimination of "the personal" (152), whereas

48   the cosmopolitan Schlegels prioritize "personal relations" (22) and "the imagination" (101), upholding "the priority of the unseen to the seen" (83). If neither emerges fully triumphant from the novel, this again suggests Forster's own distance from the Bloomsbury orthodoxy; what we get instead, as Margaret Schlegel increasingly feels that "there was something a little unbalanced in the mind that so readily shreds the visible," is a series of attempts at bridging the perspectives of "the business man who assumes that this life is everything, and the mystic who asserts that it is nothing" (152). The novel is famously ambivalent about how far she is successful in this endeavor, since their integration is proposed at what Terry Eagleton terms "a merely formal level" synthesizing "the abstract qualities of one party with the abstract qualities of the other."[12] The ending strains after some such affirmation by describing a cohabitation—however provisional—between Helen Schlegel and Henry Wilcox under the supervision of Margaret. On the one hand, it points toward the pastoral permanence that is fetishized in evocations of "Deep England," noting how "little events" like blossoming poppies or wheat-cutting "would become part of [Margaret] year after year" (265). Balancing this optimism, however, is Helen's caution that "London's creeping," with the most promising projection being the kind of *longue durée* suggested in the earlier image of the pendulum: "Because a thing is going strong now," Margaret reasons, "it need not go strong for ever. . . . This craze for motion has only set in during the last hundred years. It may be followed by a civilization that won't be a movement, because it will rest on the earth. All the signs are against it now, but I can't help hoping, and very early in the morning in the garden I feel that our house is the future as well as the past" (268).

The stress upon motion is one that the novel associates with the energy of the imperial type, possessed (as Margaret says of the Wilcoxes) of "those public qualities" of work and service without which "there would be no trains, no ships to carry us literary people about in, no fields even" (138). Yet if the novel depicts her breaking ranks with the orthodoxies of the cosmopolitan in coming to recognize the value of this other "type," it also reveals the basis of its energy to lie in an emptiness at its very core and a restlessness that uses the excuse of public service to disguise a collective self-loathing: "Though presenting a firm front to outsiders," we read, "no Wilcox could live near, or near the possessions of, any other Wilcox. They had the colonial spirit, and were always making for some spot where the white man might carry his burden unobserved" (161). The overseas ambitions of the family, exemplified by their work for the Imperial and West

African Rubber Company, are in this sense a convenient outlet for escaping each other and thus an extension of their restless moving between houses—Helen at one point counts eight Wilcox homes, from Howards End to "a hut in Africa" (134)—and an equally pathological insistence on speeding between them. The family is emblematized by its motorcar, which we first encounter producing a "cloud of dust" in the village of Hilton, and its instrumental use is illustrated by the later characterization of Henry as one who drove "so quickly through Westmoreland that he missed it" (156).

The Wilcox constitution, which contains within it a hereditary strain of hay fever, seems to be allergic to the pastoral pleasures of Deep England, which means in turn that it is destined to forge no lasting connection to the land: "It is not their names that recur in the parish register" of Oniton, we learn, having "swept into the valley and swept out of it, leaving a little dust and a little money behind" (197). The family's deficiency is most obvious in its attitude toward Howards End, the house that comes to bear so much significance at the end of the novel as "the future as well as the past." If we recall the test case through which Forster focused his 1946 call for a compromise between "the old morality and the new economy," the preference for the transhistorical continuities of rural life over the disruptive change brought about by urban planning, it is possible to read what happens to Howards End itself in similar terms. Ruth Wilcox's horror at the idea that "people mayn't die in the room where they were born" stands, in this sense, in opposition to the restless motion of the rest of her family (66). When she leaves the house to Margaret, who only belatedly comes to feel the same connection to Wickham Place once it is threatened with demolition, Ruth identifies her as the one person who might desire and value the sense of connection that Howards End figures in the novel. For the family to disregard her wishes in the matter is thus to act entirely in character, true to the belief that "Howards End was a house: they could not know that to [Ruth] it had been a spirit, for which she sought a spiritual heir" (79).

As Jon Hegglund points out, though, if the house seems to signify "a pure, natural construction of England, the narrative ultimately shows that Howards End is already infected by the mass culture it seeks to exclude."[13] To begin with, we have seen that it is located in an indeterminate contact zone, somewhere between the country and the city, while Helen's concluding warning that "London's creeping" suggests its inevitable absorption by the forces of urban planning. But Hegglund makes a strong argument that such a process is already well under way and may not be an entirely

50　　negative process. The political correlatives to Ruth Wilcox's solid connection to place are a series of reactionary or naïve views, ranging from her
lack of interest in the issue of suffrage—"I sometimes think that it is wiser
to leave action and discussion to men" (62)—to a mild rebuke to her husband's accumulative obsessions when she questions why "people who have
enough money try to get more money" (71). As the novel insists, Ruth represents a "gentle conservatism" that represents only half of Forster's ideal
compromise; the other seems hinted at by Margaret's suggestion that the
countryside "left to itself . . . would vote Liberal" (212), but it would do so
only if released from the ossifying tendencies to close down discussion and
deny change that Ruth stands for. As Hegglund argues, her absolute identification with her house, and "the timeless, transcendent, and natural" elements with which it is associated, in effect "makes social participation almost
impossible."[14] For that to happen, the novel suggests, something else—
whether the energies of an imperialist or the progressive politics and culture of the cosmopolitan intellectual—is required.

By itself, then, Howards End cannot embody the future as well as the
past; to do so, it needs to engage with what Margaret views in the last
chapter as "the battle against sameness" (267), which can presumably come
in a temporal form (of living the same way through history) as well as an
environmental one (of identical suburban homes, for instance). In reality,
the house has already experienced some modernization, having managed
to absorb the novel's ultimate symbol of modernity, the motorcar, with the
installation of a garage "in what used to be the paddock for the pony" (57).
The Wilcoxes, in their constant dissatisfaction with stasis, imagine other
improvements to it: the enclosure of the meadow for a rockery, "a small
park, or at all events shrubberies," with the house being rebuilt "farther away
from the road" (162). As we shall see from the novels of Evelyn Waugh,
such projects of architectural refashioning and landscaping were occurring
in the early years of the twentieth century, as efforts to retain some sem-
blance of traditional country-house living in a reconfigured economic and
social climate. Hegglund suggests that something similar might be not
only the inevitable future of Howards End but also its past. Beginning from
Helen's first description of the house as "old and little, and altogether delightful—red brick" (3), he notes how this echoes the stylistic preferences
of the Arts and Crafts movement in vogue at the turn of the century, and
speculates that Forster in fact "constructs this house *as* a representation
using the materials of a specifically Edwardian architectural fashion that
fetishized an idea of 'old England' through its skillful simulation of past

styles."[15] Howards End might, in other words, *already* be modern, not least
in its careful imitation and evocation of timeless tradition.

It is not necessary to insist upon this alternative reading of the house to recognize that the novel is critical of efforts to artificially preserve or simulate the past as a purely aesthetic spectacle. Simpson's restaurant, where Henry delights in the "thoroughly Old English" fare of mutton and cider, is for instance "no more Old English than the works of Kipling" (120–21) and thus seems to anticipate the revival of interest in kitsch Victoriana that I shall discuss later in this chapter. Such faddish efforts would presumably function for Forster by preserving only the outer shell of the past without its animating spirit, and be underwritten by the vacillations of fashion just as much as Mr. Eustace Miles's, where Margaret proposes to take Henry for a return engagement: there, she explains, "it's all proteids and body-buildings, and people come up to you and beg your pardon, but you have such a beautiful aura" (122). Once more, the novel insists upon its own ambivalence at such moments, by offering as alternatives to such triviality images of the past that can be faked or (just as dangerously) be the real thing in an ossified form.

In their proper place and context, we have to conclude, even the attitudes and artifacts most associated with the Victorian period must have some value, as we can see from Margaret's first impressions of Henry's interior decoration at Ducie Street:

> The dining-room was big, but over-furnished. Chelsea would have moaned aloud. Mr. Wilcox had eschewed those decorative schemes that wince, and relent, and refrain, and achieve beauty by sacrificing comfort and pluck. After so much self-colour and self-denial, Margaret viewed with relief the sumptuous dado, and frieze, the gilded wall-paper, amid whose foliage parrots sung. It would never do with her own furniture, but those heavy chairs, that immense sideboard loaded with presentation plate, stood up against its pressure like men. . . . Even the Bible—the Dutch Bible that Charles had brought back from the Boer War—fell into position. (129)

This is a stage in her imagining of a compromise with Wilcoxian utilitarianism, of course, but it also offers an implicit self-criticism of her own fashionable Chelsea milieu, which has sacrificed comfort entirely for aesthetic effect. Margaret's momentary delight in the recherché spectacle of such outmoded furnishings is, we recognize, overdetermined, and quickly

52   undercut by the narrator's insinuation that she is "keen to derive the modern capitalist from the warriors and hungers of the past" (129). But in that case, the false imposition of continuity originates with her, not with Henry. Whatever we might think about his tastes, they are at least genuinely Victorian, rather than the mocked-up simulacrum of Simpson's. Later in this chapter, we shall see how the Oxford undergraduate circle around Evelyn Waugh in the 1930s attempted a similar revaluation of nineteenth-century furnishings and architectural tastes, and how that revival was undermined by the same tendency toward ironic deflation that we can detect in the commentary of Forster's unnamed narrator. As is the case with Margaret here, it is ultimately unclear whether we can (or *should*) prefer Victorian solidity and function to modernist aestheticism. If a synthesis is being proposed, as *Howards End* insistently suggests, the precise basis upon which such a project might be attempted is equally unclear.

The First Time as Farce: Waugh's Early Satires

Evelyn Waugh's novelistic output seems designed to reverse Marx's famous dictum (from "The Eighteenth Brumaire of Louis Bonaparte") about history repeating itself "the first time as tragedy, the second as farce," as the early satires on the "Bright Young Things" of the twenties give way to a portentous tone of high moral seriousness in later works like *Brideshead Revisited*.[16] It is customary to see Waugh's conversion to Catholicism as the turning point, when a young insider's mockery of modernity's pretensions makes way for a full-blown adult conservatism, but I want to suggest instead that we view the two sides or phases as dialectically linked, in much the same ways that Forster simultaneously affirmed and critiqued contemporary culture and its nostalgic longings for the past. By looking first at how architecture is represented in Waugh's novels and then at his involvement from his Oxford days in the promotion of a revived Victorian style, I hope to identify him with the schizophrenic incoherence of a conservative modernism that was never fully able to jettison its first critical instincts. If, for Waugh, the past starts out as an inauthentic refuge from the horrors of modernity, it remains just as suspect in *Brideshead;* what seems different is the depth of longing (or, alternatively, of his *loathing* of the present), which means that the insistent nostalgia of the later novel is strong enough to withstand even the satirist's own insistence that the past we cherish is one that we retrospectively construct for ourselves.

My focus is on three of Waugh's novels—*Decline and Fall* (1928), *A Handful of Dust* (1934), and *Brideshead Revisited* (1945)—that all address, with

an increasing emphasis and seriousness, the plight of the English country
house. Its decline, as Robert Hewison shows in *The Heritage Industry*, had
multiple causes, including an agricultural depression in the last quarter of
the nineteenth century that reduced the value of country estates, the increasing expense of heating and maintenance (and the offsetting costs of
modernization, including the conversion to electricity), the introduction
of death duties in 1894, and the deaths of estate heirs in World War I. The
Society for the Protection of Ancient Buildings, and especially the National Trust (a renaming of 1865's Commons, Open Spaces, and Footpaths
Preservation Society, with a concurrent shift from landscape to architecture), offered the best solution for penurious landowners, especially after a
1931 Act of Parliament allowed them to provide land or buildings to the
Trust in lieu of death duties, while continuing to live on the property in the
meantime. "In exchange for often quite limited rights of access to the public," Hewison concludes, "the owner was able to continue his life very
much as before, without the financial burden of maintaining the house in
which he lived."[17]

The problem of residential maintenance is one that Waugh satirizes in
the appropriately titled *Decline and Fall*, a novel in which one character offers domestic architecture as a metaphor for life itself, suggesting that "It's
the seed of life we carry about with us like our skeletons, each one of us
unconsciously pregnant with desirable villa residences. . . . We are just potential home builders."[18] The Pastmasters' ancient seat of King's Thursday
in Hampshire, where "[f]or three centuries the poverty and inertia of this
noble family had preserved its home unmodified by any of the succeeding
fashions that fell upon domestic architecture," serves as the vehicle for the
novelist's satire when the house suddenly becomes fashionable after having been "considered rather a blot on the progressive county" (152–53).
The major families of the area accordingly make a pilgrimage to a house
where "[r]ushlights still flickered in the bedrooms long after all Lord Pastmaster's neighbours were blazing away electricity," before returning "in
their big motor cars to their modernized manors" with the thought that
they "seemed to have been privileged to step for an hour and a half out of
their own century into the leisurely, prosaic life of the English Renaissance" (152–53). Encumbered by the cost of assuaging his neighbors' guilty
consciences in this way, however, in a period when "[m]odern democracy
called for lifts and labour-saving devices," Lord Pastmaster decides to sell
up, a decision that is met with "something very like consternation . . . not
only in the Great Houses, but in the bungalows and villas for miles about"

54   (154). If, as this suggests, there is a nascent sense that such an "unmodified" location might have some claim on the collective interest of the region or the nation, others are not yet willing to share either the cost or the physical inconvenience that comes with it, except in their roles as casual weekend tourists.

A marked contrast is provided by the building that comes to take its place, a modernist extravaganza designed by the (Bloomsbury-residing) Professor Silenus, who takes the factory as his model and aims for "the elimination of the human element" (159). On approaching it for the first time, the novel's gullible antihero Paul Pennyfeather, who is later offered character-building work in a prison's Arts and Crafts workshop, hears "the spirit of William Morris" whispering to him (165), but he finds instead a Bauhaus show home seemingly constructed entirely from aluminum, glass, pneumatic rubber, and malachite. Waugh's parable about the horrors of modern life and fashion seems complete when he terms this rebuilt estate a "newborn monster to whose birth ageless and forgotten cultures had been in travail," yet it is unclear at this point whether he feels, as he would later in life, that it is King's Thursday, in its pristine, expensive, and inefficient state, that should still stand in its place (183).

Decline and Fall's scattershot satire mocks all the possible alternatives, from doing nothing to doing anything else. If we lean toward leaving the past as it is, we have to be cautious of a commercial motive that seeks to package a quaint but false way of life for a tourist audience. Later, in order to illustrate the danger, we track Paul to a Parisian slum, the kind of cliché that might have been constructed "at Hollywood itself for some orgiastic incident of the Reign of Terror," but the caustic commentary suggests that its English equivalent "would have been saved long ago by Mr. Spire and preserved under a public trust for the sale of brass toasting forks, picture post cards, and 'Devonshire teas'" (202). If, instead of preservation, we favor some form of modification that keeps old buildings up with the times and thus renders them viable both as investment properties and living spaces, we have to consider the bad faith that accompanies Pastmaster's neighbors in their visits to King's Thursday, or the source of their need to imagine having spent the afternoon "just as the very-great-grandparents of their host might have talked in the same chairs and before the same fire three hundred years before, when their own ancestors, perhaps, slept on straw or among the aromatic merchandise of some Hanse grotto" (153). By the same token, partial modernization brings with it the potential for glaring anachronism, which might only be revealed in hindsight, as is the case with Llanabba Castle, a Georgian country house with a medieval front grafted onto it that is the result of its enlightened owners wanting to find work for unemployed millworkers. Rejecting the past entirely for the present is, of course, Silenus's road to modernist monstrosity.

Does this mean that whatever the landowning aristocracy does is wrong? In a sense, yes, but we might equally conclude that no action is fully subjected to critique, either. The detachment of the satirist dictates, as Michael Gorra suggests, that "Waugh's terms are not moral but descriptive, and so he does not have to commit himself" to any particular position.[19] It is this fundamental undecidability that lends his early novels their air of urbane cynicism, for which Waugh and his friends are just as much the butt of the joke as their elders, and a longing for meaningful continuity is just as bankrupt as cutting-edge fashion. As Terry Eagleton argues, however, this evenhandedness cannot help but excuse the aristocracy themselves. When Pennyfeather is jailed as a scapegoat for a white slavery scheme concocted by Margot Beste-Chetwynde, the owner of the modernized King's Thursday, he comes close to outright condemnation of the outdated code of conduct that demands self-sacrifice from him, thinking that "there was something radically inapplicable about this whole code of ready-made honour that is the still small voice, trained to command, of the Englishman all the world over"; and yet he is forced to concede her son's sense of "the *impossibility* of Margot in prison" and thus the reality that the law functions differently for her than for him (252–53; emphasis in original). As Eagleton concludes, the moral force of the former observation is overriden by the second's "sense of taste and stylistic fitness, which leads to the endorsement of an *Ubermensch* morality for the rich, but not in a way which involves a direct stand on snobbish privilege."[20]

The same paradoxes and limitations recur in *A Handful of Dust*, which moves the dilemma of the country-house owner from the peripheral subplot of King's Thursday to the very heart of the narrative. Tony Last is heir to Hetton and hopes his son John "will be able to keep it on after me."[21] Like its forerunner, the house is "not altogether amenable to modern ideas of comfort" (13), forcing its owners to spend fortunes on what Brenda Last enumerates as "fifteen servants indoors, besides gardeners and carpenters and a night watchman and all the people at the farm and odd little men constantly popping in to wind the clocks and cook the accounts and clean the moat." Without it, Brenda figures, they "should be quite rich" (45), and Tony is in no position to argue: "almost every penny goes on the estate" (206), he complains when she seeks a sizable divorce settlement, while

56 even the modest improvements he earlier envisaged could only take place "as soon as the death duties were paid off" (13). This seems a clear case of wanting to preserve a traditional life that no longer makes economic sense, in an age in which (as Brenda's brother tells Tony) "[b]ig houses are a thing of the past in England I'm afraid" (206).

In fact, though, the standing structure of Hetton is not all that old, having been demolished and rebuilt "in the Gothic style" in 1864 and thus "now devoid of interest" (13). It owes its affect to the medieval revival of the nineteenth century, which explains the absurd Pre-Raphaelite inflections through which Tony understands the life he is losing when the divorce comes: "there was now no armour, glittering in the forest glades, no embroidered feet on the greensward; the cream and dappled unicorns had fled" (209). What this language seeks to mystify, however, is a set of empty rituals and social conventions that Waugh condemns as being entirely Victorian in their origin and appeal, the transhistorical past as filtered through the paternalistic pretensions of bourgeois *arrivistes*: thus Tony feels that his son should "be considerate to people less fortunate than you, particularly women" (25), while Sundays require a routine visit to the local church—at which the vicar still honors "our Gracious Queen Empress" (39)—to be followed by sherry in the library, "rather solemnly" drunk. When Brenda teases him for "posing as an upright, God-fearing gentleman of the old school," Tony is forced to acknowledge the truth of the accusation (35–36).

The central plot of *A Handful of Dust* raises the same questions that are implied far more obliquely in the minor episodes of *Decline and Fall* that revolve around King's Thursday. Is Tony's deep attachment to Hetton and the lifestyle he thinks it requires of him comical only because the house itself is a Gothic revival restoration rather than the real thing? In which case, would his insistent affirmation of the rituals and conventions that define that lifestyle be appropriate if he belonged to a truly ancient family with an unbroken residence in an authentic country house—or would he then be faced with the even greater economic problems faced by the Pastmasters? Waugh is seemingly ambivalent here, just as in his earlier novel, about how to answer such questions, but his evasions take a different form, injecting a tone of wistful regret into the shrill laughter of farce. As before, we see a clear contrast in modernism's tendencies toward a decontextualized style, in which objects are divorced from their intended use and historical period, which means that a belief in progress and the new can offer nothing by way of an alternative. Perhaps the most obvious example of the latter is the flat furnished by Brenda's London neighbor, the Princess Abdul

Akbar, in an anticipation of postmodern kitsch and "with a truly Eastern disregard of the right properties of things," so that (among a long list of anachronisms) "swords meant to adorn the state robes of a Moorish caid were swung from the picture rail; mats made for prayer were strewn on the divan"; and a radio is constructed "in fumed oak, Tudor style" (156). By comparison, the replacement of Hetton with a nineteenth-century facsimile seems a minor crime, especially given Tony's devotion to the lifestyle and ideals that he believes should accompany it.

We can recognize the princess's furnishings as the stock of the curiosity shop run by Mrs. Beaver, who tries to sell Brenda a similarly eclectic mix of the modern ("an electric bed warmer") and the ancient ("an antique grandfather clock"), all "grouped in the shop for her as a 'suggestion'" (73). In a classically modernist note of cynical despair, it is Mrs. Beaver who finally appears to a delirious Tony Last in Brazil, at the moment he recognizes that the mythical lost City he has been seeking—essentially "a transfigured Hetton," similarly "Gothic in character" (222)—is a mirage: "There is no City. Mrs. Beaver has covered it with chromium plating and converted it into flats" (288). A version of the new, or the old reconfigured for new and unintended uses, is what we see triumphing in the final chapter, with Hetton itself getting another overhaul as a scaled-down but profitable fox farm under Tony's nephew, Richard: "the dining hall and the library were added to the state apartments which had been kept locked and shuttered; the family lived in the morning room, the smoking room and what had been Tony's study. Most of the kitchen quarters, too, were out of use; an up-to-date and economical range had been installed in one of the pantries" (304). While this may seem a practical accommodation to what Forster termed "the new economy," suggesting that one way in which the aristocratic living to which Tony ascribed will continue to signify is through the residual pastime of foxhunting, it is hard not to sense a pathos at the end of the novel that is absent from *Decline and Fall.* Waugh is either honest or cynical enough to insist on puncturing the Hetton ideal, yet he also regrets that it is unrealizable in a modern context, when it is clearly superior to the progressive alternatives on offer. As Michael Gorra astutely concludes, Waugh's "classical insistence upon the inadequacies of Tony's attempt to understand the present through a romantic conception of the past ensures that while the novel contains the religious impulse toward transcendence, it cannot offer the possibility of transcendence itself."[22] In that sense, *A Handful of Dust* is situated in a transitional space, somewhere between the earlier farces and the tragic mode of *Brideshead Revisited.*

If Waugh's conversion to Catholicism at the age of twenty-six is conventionally offered to explain the difference between his earlier satires and a more mature emphasis on the abiding value of tradition, it must be pointed out that this event had already occurred five years before the publication of A Handful of Dust. Explaining the change in a 1949 essay on conversion, Waugh denied that it was the aesthetic or ritualistic aspect of Catholicism that appealed to him, pointing out that in England religious spectacle and tradition—"[t]he medieval cathedrals and churches, the rich ceremonies that surround the monarchy, the historic titles of Canterbury and York," and so on—are all on the side of the Church of England, "while Catholics meet in modern buildings, often of deplorable design." What defines its superiority for Waugh is instead the absolute authority of Catholicism as a transhistorical institution, one that is embodied in a simple line of reasoning asserting that, assuming "Christian revelation was true, then the Church was the society founded by Christ and all other bodies were only good so far as they had salvaged something from the wrecks of the Great Schism and the Reformation."[23] In this way, the basis of Catholicism's greater claim can be seen to rest on tradition after all, but one that is defined as spiritual rather than architectural or cultural in its nature and is thus capable of being embodied in a "deplorable" modern building just as easily as a medieval cathedral.

This explanation seems difficult to square with the increasingly negative attitude toward contemporary life that we find in Waugh's work. Even his successful satires of his own age ultimately come to signify modernity's inherent emptiness, with the ironic mode representing merely another attitude that needs to be transcended. As Gorra suggests, it is Catholicism's historical continuity—as testified to by its "ability to withstand the ridicule of nineteen hundred years"—that stood for Waugh as "a test of its truth," but a key measure of that truth is its imperviousness to "his own laughter and the forces that were making the other beliefs of his society dissolve."[24] Its suitability to fill the space of the transcendent that is left empty in A Handful of Dust is thus guaranteed by its resistance to the author's own satirical reflexes; they might successfully lampoon Tony Last's need for a set of beliefs rooted in history and paternalistic authority, but not Waugh's own—especially with Catholicism signifying a more durable tradition than even the English country house. Ancient buildings can be faked, rebuilt, or devoted to schismatic Protestantism, we might conclude, but they can serve an authentic function (one that can withstand irony) only with the added 59 element of Catholic belief.

This, at least, would seem to be the implication of the ending of *Brideshead Revisited*, with its culminating image of a "small red flame" in a copper lamp that its narrator, Charles Ryder, finds in a disused Catholic chapel at Brideshead—an artifact "quite remote from anything the builders intended" and transcendently transhistorical, the same flame "which the old knights saw from their tombs."[25] The figure is a belated (and perhaps forced) reconciliation of the twin beliefs in Catholicism and the country house that run through the novel, and it is necessary because both otherwise seem subject to the satirical deflation and mockery that characterized the earlier novels. As Terry Eagleton argues, the optimism of *Brideshead*'s frame and ending, which reduce the bulk of the text to a series of flashbacks and thus subordinate it to the mature Charles's reacquaintance with the house, feels inconsistent with the implications of the earlier scenes: if the purpose "is to make out a defense of the social order which the Marchmains of Brideshead symbolize, in the face of the vulgarity and commercialism which are undermining it," Eagleton points out, "the responsibility for the Marchmain decline lies, not with conspiring invasions from the outside, but with the Marchmains themselves."[26] If that is the case, then the presumption of a break between Waugh's early and late work would be less certain, with the latter not exempt from the leveling ironies that characterize the former.

What is distinct in *Brideshead*, though, especially in contrast to its handling in *Decline and Fall* and *A Handful of Dust*, is its use of the country house as the anchor of that traditional social order, which is no longer instantiated—or, at least, not *only* instantiated—through empty rituals and blind adherence to convention but is instead underwritten by its author's religious beliefs.[27] The novel's depiction of Catholicism by itself is an unsuitable vehicle for his message, one that Eagleton terms "a way of hinting at a level of experience which cannot be directly articulated because to do so would be to run the risk of a dull, Brideshead-like moral earnestness."[28] Its clearest embodiment comes in the final conversion of the agnostic Lord Marchmain and its acceptance by the equally skeptical Ryder, who kneels in prayer as the dying man makes the sign of the cross; and yet it is hard to see this newfound piety as definitively canceling out Charles's earlier suspicions of the church's deceit in appearing "now, when his mind's wandering and he hasn't the strength to resist, and claim[ing] him as a death-bed penitent" (324). What gives the gesture meaning in the novel is its location, as the exiled landowner returns home to his estate and, in a final delirium, mentally

60   reconnects with a line of "barons since Agincourt," each "called by the name his fathers bore" (332).

Lord Marchmain singles out a fountain, "old before it came here, weathered two hundred years by the suns of Naples," as an architectural corollary of that genealogical continuity, which significantly reverses its previous use as an emblem of imperial plunder. When Charles first sees the grounds, his view is dominated by the same fountain, such "as one might expect to find in a piazza of Southern Italy, such a fountain as was, indeed, found there a century ago by one of Sebastian's ancestors; found, purchased, imported and re-erected in an alien but welcoming climate" (81). This earlier passage equates it with an inauthentic facsimile of antiquity like the Gothic revivalist Hetton, and indicts the nineteenth-century Marchmains as the prototypical purveyors of a form of cultural tourism that Waugh negatively associates with the Victorians elsewhere in the novel: indeed, a page earlier, Sebastian had replied to Charles's question about the dome at Brideshead by upbraiding him not to "be such a tourist" (80), while the odious Mr. Samgrass is referred to as "the Victorian tourist, solid and patronizing, for whose amusement these foreign things were paraded" (110). Mr. Samgrass's claim to "love the past" is merely a cover for a self-aggrandizement that depends upon a superficial cultural knowledge, as exemplified by the tedious photographic slide show of the Middle East that he inflicts upon the family. At other moments, however, such an attitude is associated with the Canadian Rex Mottram, described by his wife Julia as "something absolutely modern and up-to-date that only this ghastly age could produce" (200), most notably in a scene when he visits Charles, who is now an art student in Paris. When they have dinner, in a place chosen by Charles that he imagines Rex would consider the "sort of place you could pass without looking at," competing cultural competencies enter into an unspoken dialogue: on the one hand, Rex eats caviar with chopped onion because a "[c]hap-who-knew told me it brought out the flavour" and ends the meal with bad brandy in a glass "the size of his head," poured from a "mouldy old bottle they kept for people of Rex's sort"; on the other hand, Charles can serve as the embodiment of an unquestioned good taste, dismissing ostentation and pretension for the sake of simplicity and savoring a burgundy "serene and triumphant, a reminder that the world was an older and better place than Rex knew" (173–77).

The scene is stacked so that Rex can only be wrong and Charles right, but the criteria for defining good taste are entirely occluded. Age by itself is no guarantee; otherwise, Rex's brandy would doubtless trump the better

one Charles orders, "in a bottle free from grime and Napoleonic cyphers"
and "only a year or two older than Rex" (177). Nor is the source of Charles's
cultural capital ever really spelled out, given that for most of the novel he
plays the role of the uninitiated ingenue in relation to the Marchmains. He
might be said to triumph as Rex's cultural superior on the grounds that his
suitability for the role is simply unquestioned, depending (as it seems to)
on an occulted knowledge that he possesses by right on account of his English upbringing and cultural heritage. Like the Catholicism that is affirmed
with Lord Marchmain's conversion, Charles's taste somehow manages to
elude the accusation that it is arbitrary, manipulative, or merely absurd;
like the reconstructed fountain, it can signify equally as the embodiment
of an "older and better place" and as a counteracting refusal to value archaic artifacts like the Napoleonic brandy simply for their own sake. This
is not a knowledge, though, that Charles possesses from the outset, when
he can say of the chapel at Brideshead that "it's a remarkable example of its
period. Probably in eighty years it will be much admired" (92); he clearly
needs to abandon such relativizing judgments (and indeed, periodization
itself) to come to recognize the transcendent value of the "small red flame"
contained within it.[29] To do so, he must renounce both the dictates of fashion—which are associated in the early Oxford chapters, as we shall see,
with Bloomsbury-style modernism—and the point of view of the tourist.

It is another of the novel's central ironies, though played entirely
straight in the text, that this process brings Charles to the point where he
(and not any of the Marchmain family) can come to seem the rightful heir
to the estate. His desire for it is obliquely signaled when, having identified
his youthful relationship with Sebastian as a "forerunner" for a more mature
relationship with Julia, he shares her assessment that she might equally
function as a placeholder for an even deeper attachment (303); the erotics
of his relationship to the house are made more explicit when Lord Marchmain raises the prospect of leaving it to him and Julia, and Charles questions whether "I [need] reproach myself if sometimes I was rapt in the vision" (322). By this stage, the house is already in a downward financial
spiral, one that Rex correctly predicts during the Parisian dinner by describing the family as people "who aren't *using* their money," with "no rents
raised, nobody sacked, dozens of old servants doing damn all, being waited
on by other servants" (174–75; emphasis in original). The crisis takes the
form diagnosed by Robert Hewison in *The Heritage Industry*, and so does the
preferred solution: already, by the time of Lord Marchmain's death, we
read of the so-called Chinese drawing room that "one could not normally

62   go further into it than a small roped area round the door, where sight-seers
were corralled on the days the house was open to the public" (315). It is
hard to tell whether the novel regrets such pandering to the needs of the
tourist industry or simply recognizes it as the one last hope for preserving
ancient estates.[30]

In a similar ambiguity, Charles puts his Parisian art training to use as
an "architectural painter" who directly benefits from the progressive modernization that threatens such estates. He is commissioned to make sketches
of them before they are demolished, thereby seeking to preserve or even
enhance the cultural capital they possess—as opposed to their dwindling
economic capital—by converting them into aesthetic artifacts, with what
David Rothstein terms a "fetishistic realism."[31] Charles himself offers the
strongest defense of this work, declaring in an editorializing narrative
commentary that "I loved buildings that grew silently with the centuries,
catching and keeping the best of each generation, while time curbed the
artist's pride and the Philistine's vulgarity, and repaired the clumsiness of
the dull workman. In such buildings England abounded, and in the last
decade of their grandeur, Englishmen seemed for the first time to become
conscious of what before was taken for granted, and to salute their achieve-
ments at the moment of extinction" (226–27). In such a passage, his sensi-
tivity to the nuances of Deep England, as signified by the country-house
tradition, would seem to qualify Charles as its ideal interpreter; and yet he
recoils when he hears such sentiments from the mouth of his wife ("I see
everything through his eyes. He *is* England to me," for instance) and has
to agree with the stuttering Anthony Blanche's dismissal of his paintings as
merely charming, like "a dean's daughter in flowered muslin," but on that
score "t-t-terrible t-t-tripe" (268, 272; emphasis in original).

When we consider that the novel is, in a sense, simply a textual ana-
logue of Charles's painting, this looks like another example of Waugh having it both ways, satirizing even those preservative actions that the novel
seeks to affirm. Introducing a new edition published in 1959, he clouded
the issue even further, claiming that he "piled it on rather, with passionate
sincerity," in order to draw attention to what he foresaw as being the inevitable "decay and spoilation" of the ancient aristocratic estates; given "the
present cult of the English country house" in postwar Britain, he now recognized, "Brideshead today would be open to trippers, its treasures arranged
by expert hands and the fabric better maintained than it was by Lord
Marchmain."[32] As we have seen, *Brideshead Revisited* had already anticipated
this solution in 1944, so we must conclude that the threat it describes was

deliberately overblown, presumably to incite the public conscience. In the process, though, an imaginary projection comes to substitute for a less dramatic reality, in a process that the novel—through the narrative mediation of Charles Ryder—simultaneously cautions against and endlessly repeats.

Waugh announces as he begins the final section of the text that "[m]y theme is memory" (225), an assessment that seems self-evident when we consider its structural organization as a series of embedded flashbacks and Charles's persistent return to the experiences of the past. And yet, it is not clear exactly what the novel wants to *say* about the topic. On one level, memory is highly unreliable and subject to conscious and unconscious manipulation, with the result that how we recollect the past is always clouded by present preoccupations. Looking back at his underdeveloped tastes when he first arrived at Oxford, for instance, Charles cautions himself that "It is easy, retrospectively, to endow one's youth with a false precocity or a false innocence; to tamper with the dates marking one's stature on the edge of the door" (27). Anthony Blanche similarly explains how such projections can come to take the place of reality in discussing a scene in which he parades in the Mercury fountain before an audience of hostile undergraduates. On hearing Boy Mulcaster declare, "Anyway, we *did* put him in Mercury," Blanche predicts the lasting power of the fabrication when "in thirty years' time . . . they're all married to scraggy little women like hens and have cretinous, porcine sons like themselves, getting drunk at the same club dinner in the same coloured coats, they'll still say, when my name is mentioned, 'We put him in Mercury one night'" (50; emphasis in original). In such passages, the text is acutely aware of the editing function of memory, the ways it can retroactively reshape past events in the service of a fictional image of youth.

In *The Country and the City*, Raymond Williams describes a collective tendency toward such idealizations within pastoral literature through the image of a moving escalator, dictating that each generation views itself in terms of a decline from a supposed "golden age," often one that is located "in the childhoods of their authors."[33] He concludes that one person's youthful paradise is always another's debased present, with the implication that all such projections are equally suspect, and the same inference might be drawn from the opening of Waugh's novel. As Charles looks out—from the perspective of a soldier preparing for World War II—at an ugly modern world that he characterizes as "the homogeneous territory of housing estates and cinemas" (3), a chance re-encounter with the Brideshead estate acts like "a conjuror's name of such ancient power" to return him mentally

64   to his arrival at Oxford (15). On "a cloudless day in June" of 1923, he re-calls, "[i]n her spacious and quiet streets men walked and spoke as they had in Newman's day; her autumnal mists, her grey spring-time, and the rare glory of her summer days—such as that day—when the chestnut was in flower and the bells rang out high and clear over her gables and cupolas, exhaled the soft vapours of a thousand years of learning" (21). As Williams reminds us, however, one act of nostalgic remembrance only begets an-other, with the result that Charles's idealized world of his own youth im-mediately clashes with the view of his scout, Lunt, for whom "things could never be the same as they had been in 1914" (22)—and we could presum-ably continue the sequence by imagining a figure from that prewar period longing nostalgically for the Oxford of Ruskin and Pater.

    The difficulty of reading *Brideshead*, though, is that its self-awareness of the falsifying nature of memory does little to diminish its insistence on the actual superiority of the past: thus, the relativizing commentary of Lunt does nothing to invalidate Charles's own nostalgic recollection, and for every passage warning against "endow[ing] one's youth with a false pre-cocity or a false innocence" there is another bemoaning "[h]ow ungener-ously in later life we disclaim the virtuous moods of our youth" (62). In such a context, memory itself becomes another unstable thematic element of the novel (like Catholicism, good taste, or the country house) that seems capable of surviving in the face of its author's own—admittedly muted—satiric impulses. While each is clearly open to the scrutiny of the skeptical intellect, their power is seemingly derived from another source and remains impervious to the forms of ironic deflation that the young Waugh had perfected. In part, we need to ascribe the difference to a criti-cal self-examination that intensified his abhorrence of modernity, which had supplied the framework as well as the subject matter for his earlier satires. Looking back in 1949 at his own life in the 1920s, he highlighted the limits of that ironic attitude and suggested the basis for *Brideshead*'s more tragic mode, commenting that "[t]hose who have read my works will perhaps understand the character of the world into which I exuberantly launched myself. Ten years of that world sufficed to show me that life there, or anywhere, was unintelligible and unendurable without God."[34] In the process, as we have seen, an entire ideology, rooted in the supposed continuities of ancient buildings and traditional tastes, can also come to be affirmed as a meaningful refuge from what Waugh saw as the horrors of modern life.

Kitsch Victoriana

It is worth asking the question: where are the Victorians in *Brideshead Revisited*? For all of its concerns with family, heritage, and historical continuity, it is hard to isolate a coherent position on the nineteenth century from the novel as a whole. As I have suggested, the term "Victorian tourist" is used in a derogatory sense in relation to Mr. Samgrass, and nineteenth-century Marchmains are responsible for plundering and relocating Brideshead's imposing fountain—but the novel works hard to naturalize that action by the end, especially in contrast to its callous abuse by Ryder's modern-day soldiers, who deposit cigarette butts and the remains of sandwiches into it. If, for Waugh, the past seems intrinsically superior to the present, little direct evidence shows that he feels a particular nostalgic longing for the nineteenth century, with the exception of an oblique hint about the aesthetic tastes and preferences of the Oxford undergraduates.

In one of his reflections on the distorting effects of memory, Charles acknowledges the ease with which we can edit our own past: "I should like to think—indeed I sometimes do think—that I decorated those rooms with Morris stuffs and Arundel prints and that my shelves were filled with seventeenth-century folios and French novels of the second empire in Russia-leather and watered-silk. But this was not the truth." What follows is a listing of what the fashionable undergraduate of the 1920s would prefer, with hindsight, to forget: a reproduction of Van Gogh's *Sunflowers*, "a screen painted by Roger Fry with a Provençal landscape," "a porcelain figure of Polly Peachum" ("most painful to recall"), and a bookshelf that included Fry's *Vision and Design*, *Eminent Victorians*, Housman's *A Shropshire Lad*, and volumes of *Georgian Poetry* (27). If these last titles denote the outdated nature of Charles's literary tastes, we should also pick up on his adult regret at an earlier fondness for what would have passed for a Georgian avant-garde: the eye-catching names on this list of Fry and Strachey, as well as Clive Bell, whose aesthetic theory is reduced to a childish naïveté by Sebastian a moment later, when he reads aloud Bell's rhetorical question "Does anyone feel the same kind of emotion for a butterfly or a flower that he feels for a cathedral or a picture?" and answers with a simple "Yes. *I* do." This moment, and not the overly serious Mr. Collins's painstaking dissection of the theory of significant form, is when Charles claims "my eyes were opened," presumably to the bankruptcy of Bloomsbury (28; emphasis in original).

66   That realization leads to his search for a new theory or set of artistic tastes, which will ultimately cohere in his acquired reverence for the country house. If Sebastian provides this initial impetus, though, it is worth dwelling on his own domestic furnishings, which represent an eclectic mélange of arbitrary styles and objects: "a harmonium in a gothic case, an elephant's-foot waste-paper basket, a dome of wax fruit, two disproportionately large Sèvres vases, framed drawings by Daumier—made all the more incongruous by the austere college furniture and the large luncheon table" (31). Waugh scholars have readily identified this as a fictional echo of the consciously retro taste for Victorian artifacts initiated by Harold Acton, who arrived at Oxford in 1922, the same year as Waugh.[35] This evidently became quite the fashion among Waugh's friends, who also included Brian Howard (the model for Anthony Blanche) and Robert Byron, before whom (according to Acton) stood always "the vision of a 'large-limbed, high-coloured Victorian England, seated in honour and plenty.'"[36] Examples of the undergraduate fad for Victoriana include a fancy-dress party held at the "Hypocrites Club" in Oxford, with Byron as the queen and "significant scenes of Victorian history" painted on the walls, and a proposed exhibit of "Early Victorian domestic ornaments" that was banned by the Oxford proctors (124, 127).

It is not obvious why this fashion for Victorian ephemera should have caught on as it did, nor why it proved so dangerous to the Oxford authorities. One answer is Michael Bracewell's, that for "decadent wit" the best way to confront the Victorians was "to fetishize their culture."[37] Acton and Byron seem to have thought otherwise, however, with the former explaining his interest by suggesting that "[t]he Early Victorian Era, trying to recover from the Napoleonic War, was closer to us than the 'nineties, that 'Twilight of the Gods' succeeded by the Age of Muddle. We wanted Dawns, not Twilights" (118). This statement suggests a more serious engagement with the nineteenth century, a potential parallel for the renewed optimism that was briefly felt in the interwar years. It also implies that the appeal of a Victorian revival should be assessed in relation to not only Bloomsbury but also the 1890s, when Oxford had last been a center of youthful fashion; indeed, Acton's own rebellion had been catalyzed by an encounter with a throwback "aesthete" whom he considered "sterile to the core" (111). His return to the Victorians as an inspiration for domestic furnishings and dress (a bowler hat, side-whiskers, the pleated trousers that became known as "Oxford bags") thus can come to seem like another Oedipal rebellion on the part of youth against the prevailing tenets of the previous generation:

as Waugh himself noted later, it was the familiar "wish to scandalize parents who had themselves thrown out the wax-flowers and woolwork screens which we now ardently collected."[38] The other available option, as Humphrey Carpenter notes, was "to become pure modern," as the Auden circle at Oxford would a few years later, but the shadow of Bloomsbury clearly continued to haunt Acton and his friends.[39]

For Robert Byron, the closest to a "true believer" among these Victorian revivalists, Bloomsbury represented the reigning orthodoxy as well as an exclusive cultural elite, against which he sought to position a revived Victorianism as part of a more populist backlash. Having settled after Oxford in Paddington, he wrote to Acton championing the area as "the symbol of all that Bloomsbury is not. In place of the refined peace of those mausolean streets, here are public-houses, fun-fairs, buses, tubes, and vulgar posters" (*Memoirs*, 155). Acton and Brian Howard, conversely, saw the return to the Victorians as consistent with a camp sensibility and with avant-gardist artistic practices, and thus in no sense contradicting their support of T. S. Eliot, the Sitwells, or Lytton Strachey: we might read a gentle mockery into Acton's proposal to play the author of *Eminent Victorians*, taking notes from beneath a sofa, in a "Queen Victoria ballet," but he also invited Strachey to write the introduction to an illustrated catalog that was to have accompanied his planned exhibition of Victorian domestic ornaments (127). Neither position adequately summarizes Waugh's own stance with respect to the Victorian revival, however, something to which he seems simultaneously less committed than some of his contemporaries (especially Byron) but also seriously devoted—even much later in life, when his contemporaries had all moved on to other interests.

The issue of period revival is one to which Waugh repeatedly returned in his journalism during the 1930s, by which point the passing of time seemed great enough to accommodate a renewed interest in the *fin de siècle* as well. In a short essay from *Harper's Bazaar*, evocatively titled "Let Us Return to the Nineties, but Not to Oscar Wilde" (1930), Waugh commented that "[t]he early Victorian tide in which, before luncheon, we paddled and splashed so gaily has washed up its wreckage and retreated, and all those glittering bits of shell and seaweed—the coloured glass paper weights, wax fruit, Rex Whistler decorations, paper lace Valentines, which we collected— have by late afternoon dried out very drab and disappointing and hardly discernible from the rest of the beach."[40] Waugh's wave metaphor acts as the reverse of Raymond Williams's moving escalator, so that as one period revival grows stale, or proves less significant than anticipated, we simply move forward in time to the next: "Any period," he notes accordingly, "acquires a certain glamour after twenty-five years or so" (21).

The need to raid the past stems from what Waugh sees as the unendurable strain of trying to stay forever modern (with Jean Cocteau and Bloomsbury cited as examples of why such an effort is ultimately futile), but if the 1890s should inevitably be the next decade to occupy prime place in the wheel of fashion, he nonetheless feels it is possible and necessary to distinguish between better and worse figures through which to represent the period: thus, a return to Wilde, for him, connotes a clinging on the part of "fashionable people in London" to an outmoded idea of the centrality of art to life and a narcissistic view of themselves as a contemporary cultural elite. Instead, we might celebrate more prosaic aspects of nineties life, such as "the cult of the safety bicycle" or technological innovations such as the telephone or the airplane. "Let us by all means return to this splendid, fashionable decade," the essay concludes, but the icons it name-checks are Edison, Kipling, General Kitchener, and the cricketer W. G. Grace, and not Beardsley or Wilde (21–22).

Such examples seem deliberately chosen to represent the unfashionable underside of the 1890s, putting Waugh's revisionism in agreement with Robert Byron's populist championing of the vulgar and quotidian in contemporary life.[41] But we can also see Waugh's essay as engaged in a serious exercise of zeitgeist analysis, beginning to open up a larger reevaluation of the nineteenth century itself that takes the facetious humor of the Oxford days in new directions. As we have seen, Waugh's early fiction is acutely sensitive to the ways in which architectural revivals in particular can reify style at the expense of substance, producing in the process a distortion that is the equivalent of assuming Wilde to be the exemplary embodiment of his time. A 1938 essay from *Country Life* makes this point about what he saw as an ill-advised return to eighteenth-century design, which—like an earlier fashion for Elizabethan half-timber architecture—threatened to produce only ornamental anachronism, with past elements being "re-erected . . . with scant regard for propriety." Interestingly, given the delight in Victorian ephemera that was predominant at Oxford, Waugh uses the term "bric-à-brac" to define the resulting negative effect, a proto-postmodern pastiche that throws together assorted objects, each of which was originally "designed for a specific purpose in accordance with a system of artistic law."[42] Respecting such principles of function and form would presumably mean, for Waugh, coming closer to the kind of spiritual essence of objects and houses that he looks to celebrate in *Brideshead Revisited.*

He seems less sure, however, that the Victorian zeitgeist could be ac- 69
cessible at a relatively short distance in time and more prepared to indul-
gence his own youthful delight in its bizarrerie. An essay from the same
year on "The Philistine Age of English Decoration" from *Harper's Bazaar,* for
instance, offers at best an ambiguous—and perhaps entirely tongue-in-
cheek—endorsement of mid-Victorian architecture as "prosaic, nonde-
script, and as slavishly functional as any 1920 theorist could demand. . . .
It is the only period of English architecture that cannot be said to have any
style of any kind at all." The one unqualified advantage it has over inauthentic imitations of eighteenth-century columns or Elizabethan half-
timber construction is that the proximity to the present guarantees that
Victorian artifacts are never counterfeit: "What looks mid-Victorian today
is mid-Victorian. The collector's art is to select what was most extravagantly
representative of the period."[43] That last oxymoronic phrase, which it is
tempting to call "Wildean," points to Waugh's reluctance to abandon the
playful humor of his Oxford days, as well as to the attraction of Victorian
ephemera mostly for its shock value; it might also suggest a Stracheyean
struggle to define or take seriously the idea of the representative when applied to the mid-nineteenth century, as opposed to the 1890s, for which
Waugh can readily supply examples of the nonexotic and everyday.

What seems to be emerging here is a glimpse of the author on the
brink of taking his own joke seriously, yet still pulling back from outright
sincerity. Even though Waugh took Wilde as his target in his essay on the
1890s, they share (especially within their respective Oxford circles) a fascination with camp appropriation and bricolage, as well as a penchant for
the art of the pose. In his memoirs Harold Acton describes his friend as not
only failing to abandon his public enthusiasm for the Victorians when its
shock value wore off (as Acton himself evidently did) but also extending it
so that it became an all-encompassing character trait. In Hollywood to discuss an aborted effort to film *Brideshead* in the late 1940s, for instance,
Waugh appeared to Acton as "defiantly Victorian" in his anti-American
pronouncements and his romantic attachment to "hierarchical traditions."[44]
A subsequent rendezvous in 1950 (again in California) finds Waugh "[c]lad
as an Edwardian country gentleman" and resorting to "such Victorian drugs
as bromide and chloral" (2:310–12); later still, he is reported as having
"pretended to be deaf" and in need of an ear trumpet (2:373). There is, perhaps not surprisingly, a virulently conservative politics that complements
this bizarre public image, but even that seems to have its roots in Waugh's
desire to shock at Oxford, where Humphrey Carpenter describes him as

70   uttering "some of the most outrageous reactionary sentiments the Union had ever heard" but being treated "as a comic turn."[45]

Interestingly, Waugh is not alone in seeming uncertain about just how seriously to take his taste for the Victorians, and in growing into a character in later life that he only pretended to when younger. Malcolm Muggeridge's memoir of life in the 1930s charts a general course in which the Victorian period (as represented by its furniture and bric-a-brac), once "so confident of its own greatness and solidity, had been regarded successively with horror, sniggering amusement, and now with romantic esteem."[46] Carpenter offers the parallel example of John Betjeman, who came to Oxford in 1925 and thus caught the tail end of the Victorian revival, noting that his early experiments in poetry included such pastiches as "For Nineteenth Century Burials." If, according to Carpenter, the writer had "no wish to tarnish his comic mask by appearing in public as a serious poet," the same went for his professed love of ancient country houses, with his journalistic writing on the subject appearing "invariably frivolous."[47] In the late 1930s Betjeman published a study of English architecture that termed Victorian examples "repulsive" and "unfortunate," yet he later emerged as a great admirer of it—though only (in Carpenter's view) "because in the meantime modern architecture had dropped to such a low standard that even the grotesqueries of the late nineteenth century seemed attractive beside it."[48] It seems appropriate to read this movement as the equivalent of the one I trace in Waugh's later novels, where an enthusiastic endorsement of aristocratic Catholicism can emerge only after it has withstood the author's persistent attempts to mock it. In that sense, the Victorian era could take its place as an imagined golden age only when the external signifiers of the time—especially its architecture, but also its dominant styles of ornamentation and design—adequately represented what Waugh and Betjeman took to be its animating spirit.

A class dynamic is also at work here, one that influenced the way they struggled to reshape how the previous century was recalled. Like Leonard Woolf, both Betjeman and Waugh were born outside of the traditional English aristocracy, the former as the son of a London-based manufacturer and the latter as part of an upper-middle-class family of clergymen, lawyers, civil servants, and publishers. Humphrey Carpenter diagnoses Waugh's background as affording him an insecurity, beginning at Oxford, that could be partially assuaged through "pretending to a Victorian certainty of his position" and ridiculing anyone he saw as beneath him.[49] As I suggested in chapter 1, Woolf's efforts to elevate himself into the upper class, partly on the grounds of intellect, involved a reflexive demonization of the "Victorian bourgeois," and we can presumably see the continuation of the connection that Bloomsbury made between the two terms in Harold Acton's decision to wear a bowler hat, the perfect symbol (as René Magritte's paintings of the 1920s emphasized) of prosaic middle-class conformity and work. Waugh's ear trumpet represents a very different image of the Victorians, however, one drawn not from its ascendant middle class but from its declining aristocracy.

Both symbols reveal compacted attitudes toward the previous century, with important class valences in either case. Yet their immediate use and shock value depended upon a perception that particular artifacts of the past had been removed from their ordinary contexts and recombined in a bricolage effect that foregrounded anachronism and dissonance. In the process the Victorian came to be refashioned as a *style*, one that could be adopted through the wearing or display of particular artifacts—henceforth, "Victoriana." On witnessing the first signs of this transformation after World War I, Roger Fry was amazed at the rapid revaluing of nineteenth-century furnishings such as the ottoman or the "Whatnot," which seems, from Waugh's own account of it, a kind of display space consisting of trays set at a series of levels.[50] "I, alas! can remember the time when the Ottoman and the Whatnot still lingered in the drawing-rooms of the less fashionable and more conservative bourgeoisie," Fry wrote in 1919, "lingered despised, rejected, and merely awaiting their substitutes. . . . And now, having watched the Whatnot disappear, I have the privilege of watching its resurrection. I have passed from disgust, through total forgetfulness, into the joys of introspection."[51] Here, Fry sounds suspiciously like Waugh (who singled out the Whatnot for praise in his essay on "The Philistine Age of English Decoration"), and it is hard to take him at face value. In fact, Fry takes this example as illustrating a process by which we come to confuse past objects and artifacts that "become symbols of a particular way of life" with our aesthetic response to them. To consider the Whatnot as an *objet d'art*, regardless of whether the impulse is a sincere or satirical one, is thus to detach it from the lifestyle it once represented—still, for Fry, that of the Victorian bourgeoisie—and thus to begin forgetting what was so horrific about it in the first place.

This presumes a sufficient gap of time, which Fry notes has not passed since the late Victorians—and we recall, in this context, that Waugh endorsed a return to the 1890s only in 1930: "We have just got to this point with the Victorian epoch," Fry notes (presumably thinking of mid-century), and "[h]ow charming and how false it is, one sees at once when one reflects

72   that we imagine the Victorians for ever playing croquet without ever losing their tempers. It is evident, then, that we have just arrived at the point where our ignorance of life in the Victorian period is such as to allow the incurable optimism of memory to build a quite peculiar little paradise out of the boredoms, the snobberies, the cruel repressions, the mean calculations and rapacious speculations of the mid-nineteenth century" (529). We can read in this passage a note of Bloomsbury defensiveness concerning a revisionary process that Fry sees as pernicious but also inevitable. By all means, he concludes, we should feel free to "amuse ourselves by collecting Victorian objects of art," although he cannot help but restrict that inclusive "we" to "those of us who have the special social-historical sensibility highly developed," presumably in the hope that the (negative) symbolism of Victoriana is not entirely lost. What is most crucial, however, is that such artifacts are never treated aesthetically, with beauty being confused with "the more spirited and disinterested feelings" (530). Whatever we might come to think of the nineteenth century, with the increasing passage of time, it can never be as an age of beauty.

    This central question, about whether we can detach some positive manifestation of Victorian art or thought from its general context and view it as useful or beautiful in its particularity, has recurred throughout the past century. In chapter 3, I look at what is perhaps the most recent instance of it, the debate over so-called heritage culture (specifically adaptations of literary works for film and television) with its attendant question of whether the past is being selectively edited and beautified for public consumption. The fact that this discussion was shadowed by a larger one I address in chapter 4, concerning the Thatcher government's efforts to promote a return to so-called Victorian values, shows Roger Fry's concern—that the passage of time would entirely erase the political and social dimensions of nineteenth-century life—to be unfounded. What does seem accurate is his premonition that our historical understanding of the period would henceforth be bound up with the shifting currents of style and fashion.

    In *Theatres of Memory*, Raphael Samuel documents another revival of Victorian style in postwar Britain that precisely repeats the logic in operation at the beginning of the twentieth century, replacing the "forward-looking and progressive" fashion of the 1950s with one that had previously signified the ugly, old-fashioned, and out-of-date.[52] Among instances of what he terms "retrofitting," Samuel lists a renewed interest in William Morris wallpaper, conservatories, velvet, cobblestones, cast-iron door knockers, and street lamps. Much of this, he stresses, is really "modernization in disguise" (75) and predicated on twentieth-century conveniences such as central heating and double-glazed windows. It also participates in a wider trend of "retrochic" that does not especially privilege the Victorians, but instead simply allots them an appropriate position in a much larger cycle of fashion in which items from any period—not excluding "Oxford-bags, and . . . the seriously reactionary, *Forsyte Saga–* or *Brideshead*-derived three-piece suit" (89)—can take their turn. These revivals are clearly susceptible, as Samuel acknowledges, to the charges of "'commodifying' the past, instrumentalizing it for the purposes of commercial gain, exploiting the sacred in the interests of the profane," but they might just as fairly be praised for "animating the inanimate" as a contribution to the awakening of a historical consciousness in the public (113). As a social historian, Samuel could only view such a development as an (admittedly qualified) positive.

It is harder to make this case for heritage adaptation, which is less able to defend itself against the accusation of commodification, especially since its own aesthetic style depends upon the production of history as spectacle. It stands at the opposite pole from the active and tactile recontextualizing of past objects that Samuel praises, opting instead to reverse what he sees as the transformation of the sacred into the profane. Not coincidentally, some of the most celebrated heritage adaptations have been drawn from novels by authors like Forster and Waugh, including *Howards End* and *Brideshead Revisited*. The latter, in its reincarnation in an eleven-part television miniseries, even helped continue the revival of the English country house that Waugh himself already noted after World War II, by encouraging a new tourist fashion for visiting National Trust buildings. It is fitting, in that sense, to think of such adaptations as seeking to restore to such buildings their presumptive status as sacred objects of the national heritage, accessible only through the limited vision of the tourist's gaze, which can hope to see but never touch (or enter into dialogue with) the past.

Victorian Vision and Contemporary Cinema

The Visual Inheritances of Heritage Culture

CHAPTER THREE

If *Brideshead Revisited* and *Howards End* together indicate a strain of modernist writing with a marked ambivalence toward the nineteenth century, the adaptations of those novels for television and film—in Granada Television's 1981 serialization of Waugh in eleven episodes and Merchant Ivory's 1992 film of Forster—have generally been read as uncritical celebrations of the high culture of the past. Writing of *Brideshead*'s successful broadcast on *Masterpiece Theatre* in the United States, for instance, Spencer Golub has argued that "Waugh's nostalgia for manor-house architecture and life, amid the aesthetic and moral confusion of modern history, reawakened a ghost-limb Englishness not only in England but in the world."[1] In the context of the Thatcher government's endorsement of a return to so-called Victorian values in the 1980s, which I will examine in more detail in the next chapter, the success of the serialization prompted critics to coin the term "heritage cinema" to characterize the nexus of conservative politics and aesthetics that the moment signaled, while Tana Wollen remarked that *"Brideshead* for all its *noblesse oblige* is a truly Thatcherite text."[2] Such arguments have been extended to cover similar adaptations on film, most notably those from the team of director James Ivory and producer Ismail Merchant, often assisted by screenwriter Ruth Prawer Jhabvala, whose films have been rou-

tinely denounced for colluding with a Thatcherite agenda: Cairns Craig,   75
for instance, argues that they "reflect the conflict of a nation committed
to an international market that diminishes the significance of Englishness
and at the same time seek to compensate by asserting 'traditional' values,
whether Victorian or provincial" (quoted in Higson, 70).

It was under Thatcher's leadership that the Department of National
Heritage—subsequently renamed the Department of Culture, Media and
Sport by the more modernizing Blair government—was formed, with an
explicit agenda for filmmakers: one secretary of state at the department,
Virginia Bottomley, urged them to "promote our country, our cultural heritage and our tourist trade. . . . This is what films like *Sense and Sensibility* did
as well as the BBC's *Pride and Prejudice*. If we have got the country houses and
the landscapes, they should be shown on film, particularly as we approach
the millennium" (quoted in Higson, 54). Extending the work of the National
Trust, and encouraging the continuation of the "cult of the country house"
that Waugh himself noted with satisfaction as emerging in 1959, Thatcher
oversaw a growth industry in preservation and new building based on old
designs. As Robert Hewison noted in his 1987 study *The Heritage Industry*,
"The campaign on behalf of the country house has been so successful that
it is more flourishing now than at any time in the last century," in spite of
routine predictions of its imminent decline; in reality, as he goes on to
argue, "it turns out that, far from the country house disappearing, more than
200 new ones have been built since the war."[3] That construction boom,
and an attendant rise in visits to country estates, was undoubtedly encouraged by the successful adaptation of Waugh's novel (Hewison's chapter is
titled "Brideshead Re-Revisited"), but it is difficult to isolate a parallel line
of influence between the values encoded in his or Forster's texts and those
flagged for revival by the Thatcher government: hard work, self-reliance,
self-respect, national pride, and so on.

This is where the issue of period setting becomes more complicated.
The leading critic of heritage cinema, Andrew Higson, struggles to define
exactly what moment in the past it celebrates, suggesting first that "more
than a quarter" of the films concern "the exploits of the English upper
classes and upper middle classes in the late Victorian period or in the early
part of the twentieth century, between 1880 and 1940. . . . While there are
just as many set in the nineteenth century," he continues, "there are far
fewer set in earlier periods," with the noted exception of the Regency (26).
It is hard to make sense of Higson's categories here, as the nineteenth century is first compared with a later period that includes its last twenty years

76   and then to an earlier one that occurred within it. What may explain his confusion is an unwillingness to acknowledge that whatever term we settle on for the preferred temporal setting of heritage cinema, "the Victorian" seems—despite its satisfying echo in Thatcherite ideology—to be an unlikely candidate. The same conclusion might be drawn from a study of literary adaptations on *Masterpiece Theatre* during thirty-one seasons stretching back to its debut in 1971–72: of the authors that have most frequently provided source materials, Dickens is the most common (with eight novels adapted, including two twice), followed by Shakespeare and George Eliot (four each), Hardy and Austen (three), then Wilkie Collins, Conrad, Flaubert, Ibsen, James, and Trollope (each with two). The list certainly highlights the nineteenth century, but the stress falls disproportionately on the end of the century—as with Higson's initial category—and on those authors we might consider as writing at the cusp of modernity: Hardy, Conrad, Ibsen, James. As I shall argue later, what is partially revealed by such a survey is a stylistic preference for source texts that emphasize an impressionistic narrative form, which is surprising given film's difficulties with replicating literary devices of internal monologue and subjective perspective. Given the formal properties of film, adapting texts such as *Jude the Obscure*, *The Secret Agent*, *The Golden Bowl*, or *A Passage to India* is no easy task.

To briefly return, though, to the presumed Thatcherite agenda of heritage culture, we might remark, with Higson, that it seems less the confidence imputed to high-Victorian triumphalism that we are viewing on screen than its ebbing away at the *fin de siècle*: "In so many ways, for all their elegance and allure," he proposes, "heritage films seem very often to deal with the last of England, or at least the last of old England. . . . The idea of heritage implies a sense of inheritance, but it is precisely that which is on the wane in these films" (28). If that is their explicit emphasis, then we clearly need to rethink how serviceable such films were for a conservative politics that sought to restore a sense of national pride and to uncritically celebrate the old-fashioned values that supposedly undergirded a now lost empire. As chapter 2 showed, authors such as Forster and Waugh provide the occasion for a thorough examination of the costs—as well as the appeal—of such nostalgic longings, addressing not only the goals and uses of conservative retrospection but also its psychic effects. How, then, can we see filmed versions of *Brideshead* and *Howards End* as posthumously endorsing and encouraging such thinking in contemporary British culture? In this chapter, I begin by considering this paradox in relation to these particular authors and texts, then I extend my focus to the central debates

concerning realism, narrative perspective, and cinematic technique that have
concerned filmmakers and critics in the twentieth century; at the same time
I work back into the Victorian period to consider the ways in which those
debates are themselves the result of an unfinished argument about photography and the artistic and mimetic capabilities of the new visual culture.

Heritage Stylistics: Adapting Literary Modernism

There is, as I have suggested, a clear disconnect between the texts of
Forster and Waugh as they were published and received in the first half of
the twentieth century and the response to their visual adaptations in its
closing decades. In part, the problem is intrinsic to the historical process
itself. If, after all, the novel *Howards End* seeks to distinguish between Wickham Place as it has existed as a family home for the Schlegels and the modern flats that will take its place after it has been demolished, the problem
for a contemporary audience is that *those* homes would now register as historic buildings in need of preservation. Within a visual aesthetic that prizes
fidelity to the original location, it is difficult to capture that historical
transformation on film in a way that does not make both architectural sites
equally desirable as aspects of the national heritage; indeed, Higson offers
this example as evidence that Merchant Ivory's film adopts a pastiche of
styles, quoting the cinematographer's remark that in order to "suggest it
being encroached upon by huge blocks of flats, they're matting in other
buildings from other parts of London onto our prime location," a Georgian
square near Buckingham Palace (152). Contemporary London would certainly furnish its own examples of the supplanting of the old by the new,
of course, but not this precise displacement of the even older by the merely
old that had to be recreated through digitally juxtaposing different locations in a single shot.

   This is quite literally a local problem for a televisual genre that ob-
sesses to distraction about finding "authentic" locations, as I shall discuss in
a moment; it does, however, reflect a larger difficulty of narrative perspective in texts like these—and Waugh's especially—that depend for their impact on recognizing the distorting effects of temporal distance. As I discussed in chapter 2, the prologue and first chapter of *Brideshead Revisited*
provide a textbook illustration of Raymond Williams's "moving escalator"
of regressive nostalgia, as we are transported back from a middle-aged
Charles Ryder's unhappy sighting of Brideshead (now seconded for military purposes) to the idealized Oxford of his youth, only to hear that for
Lunt "things could never have been the same as they had been in 1914"

78   (*Brideshead*, 22). Film has at its disposal the perfect technique for capturing this backward movement, the dissolve, in which the images are momentarily superimposed as one fades in and the other out—a technique that the Russian film theorist Sergei Eisenstein once detected in prototype form in the closing chapter of Dickens's *A Tale of Two Cities*.[4] The television adaptation of Waugh's novel makes full use of the technique, holding on a close-up of Charles (Jeremy Irons) as he first views Brideshead and dissolving to a panoramic view of the gleaming spires of Oxford, then giving us a second, embedded flashback as he recalls meeting Sebastian (Anthony Andrews) while they pause en route to the house. As with the Wickham Place example, however, this idealized past is being contrasted with a more recent past within living memory of many of its viewers, that of World War II—a period that has itself been the focus of considerable nostalgia. This wartime Britain is inevitably recalled when Lunt complains somewhat vaguely of changes occurring "on account of the war" (*Brideshead*, 22).

The problem of film is that whatever it shows us assumes the status of a tangible material reality unless specific techniques cue us otherwise, and this inevitably compounds the difficulty faced by the novel's adapters. The novelist John Mortimer, who wrote the adaptation of *Brideshead*, addresses the inherent difficulty of the project by insisting that Waugh's novel "saw the past in a roseate glow . . . which may never have been apparent at the time." If it therefore "throws less light on our past than on our present situation," the same would have to be said of the television series, which was produced (Mortimer asserts) "at a time when the world may appear to [have been] in an even more desperate plight than in 1944 . . . the simple optimism that looked forward to a just and equal society seem[ing] to have vanished in bitterness and despair." As an avowed socialist and atheist, he admits to being out of step with Waugh's conservative Anglo-Catholicism and to have problems in particular with the novel's negative depiction of the 1926 General Strike and with Charles's evident snobbery.[5] Such political differences are not, however, noticeable in watching the adaptation, and Mortimer seems to acknowledge the more conservative appeal of his work, noting after its first screening that "British viewers have just relished, in unexpectedly large numbers, looking back in nostalgia on a writer looking back in nostalgia."

The difficulty, he acknowledges, is partly one of "solving technical problems" that arise from the novel's own backward glance. How, for instance, to recreate the passage in the opening chapter of the Oxford section, when an older Charles reflects that "It is easy, retrospectively, to endow one's youth with a false precocity or a false innocence," before confessing that he decorated his room with a reproduction of Van Gogh and was still reading the likes of Strachey and Roger Fry? Television can show us the *Sunflowers* print on the wall but not the embarrassed gaucherie that the older and wiser Ryder feels in hindsight when recalling such a clumsy attempt to appear modern. Besides the print and the Polly Peachum statue, we get to see, rather incongruously, a promotional poster for the London Underground on Charles's wall, and in a key scene he returns from lunch with Sebastian to remark on a "jejune air" in his rooms; with the room filled with flowers, he remarks that "nothing but the golden daffodils seemed to be real" as he takes down the *Sunflowers*, but he simply puts the picture to one side while handing Lunt a printed screen to put away in storage—perhaps to avoid offending television viewers who might also have a Van Gogh reproduction on their walls. In any case, the painting cannot signify equally to viewers in the 1980s and readers in the 1940s, for the same reasons that Sebastian's own eclectic furnishings—including its resurrected Victoriana— will register differently at a further historical distance. As we saw from chapter 2, Waugh's novel looks to capture a precise moment, when Bloomsbury modernism and postimpressionism were becoming passé and the Victorians first acquired a retro-kitsch appeal, but that time is inaccessible to reconstruction and largely unreadable for the television audience.

Beyond the simple problem of temporal distance, this points to a larger difficulty in the adaptation that presents itself in terms of a form/content dichotomy. Heritage filmmakers seem drawn to literary source texts that are characterized by narrative impressionism and also by what Higson terms an "edge . . . of satire or ironic social critique," including (as we have seen in both cases under discussion here) a critique of social pretension, of the fetishizing of wealth and possessions, and of the reification of material objects as the bearers of value. The difficulty arises when efforts are made to reproduce that critical edge on film, especially as it interfaces with the filmmakers' desire to display "authentic" period settings, costumes, and props. The result, as Higson concludes, is that "that which in the source narratives is abhorrent or problematic often becomes prettified, elegant, and seductive in the films. Even those films which develop an ironic narrative of the past often seem to end up celebrating and legitimating the spectacle of one class and one cultural tradition and identity at the expense of others through the discourse of authenticity, and the obsession with the visual splendours of period detail" (80).

80   Film, as this suggests, finds it difficult to convey an ironic narrative voice—though Spencer Golub argues that the *Brideshead* serialization attempts a similar kind of distancing effect through its deployment of Charles's voice-over, marked by a "flatness and numbness [that seem] to be telling his ear and ours to refrain from enthusiastically embracing or even passively accepting the beauty that the eye sees."[6] If so, it is a caution that seems doomed to go unheeded, forgotten as soon as the voice itself fades and we leave the frame of World War II from which it emanates for the past into which it effortlessly dissolves. That voice-over, repeating warnings from the text about the dangers of nostalgic wallowing, seems ill-matched against an array of filmic techniques that encourage us to do precisely that.

  Among these, the most prevalent is heritage cinema's conspicuous display of elements of the mise-en-scène—by which term film studies denotes features inherited from theater, such as costume, setting, lighting, or props—often at the expense of narrative logic or a conventional emphasis on character and dialogue. Most crucially, these adaptations emphasize the importance of *place*, just as the press materials and commentaries by which they are promoted insistently remark on their use of "authentic" locations: Yorkshire's Castle Howard doubling for the fictional Brideshead, for instance, or Ottoline Morrell's Peppard Cottage for Howards End.[7] The *Brideshead* series set the tone and standard here, transforming a country-house location that had actually been largely rebuilt after a fire during World War II into one of the National Trust's prime tourist destinations. The choice was an inspired one, though for reasons that the filmmakers may not have considered. Just as the novel makes clear that Brideshead itself had been rebuilt, and included features like a looted Italianate fountain, so (as Golub notes) was its stand-in "built and altered in stages between 1700 and 1737. . . . Perched majestically above a 10,000-acre estate, it is neither a real castle nor a splendid country seat but rather a dramatic façade before an interior jumble of small rooms." Waugh himself visited it once and was impressed with its central dome (prominently displayed in the television series) as well as its south-facing fountain.[8]

  We can see the filmmakers' desire to display this location to full effect in an early sequence dramatizing Charles's second visit, to nurse a supposedly ailing Sebastian. As he arrives in the car with Julia (Diana Quick), we first see Brideshead (in a shot that is repeated throughout the adaptation) at a considerable distance, seen from across a river and yet framed to face the camera square on.

Fig. 1. Brideshead as we first see it, at a distance. From the 1981 TV production of
Brideshead Revisited (Granada/Acorn Media).

We then cut to an angle inside the main hall, with the camera positioned centrally so that the doors will open in perfect symmetry—there is
even a dog, placed on the center line, which Julia bends to pick up as she
and Charles enter.

Fig. 2. Charles and Julia entering Brideshead. From the 1981 TV production of
Brideshead Revisited (Granada/Acorn Media).

82   The classical symmetry of the shot carries over into the next, which frames an almost identical doorway, only this time with two busts positioned on either side and a view through to the fountain in the background. A servant wheels in the injured Sebastian, who takes up a position at the precise center of the frame, looking directly at the camera from the same distance that Charles and Julia had occupied in the previous shot.

When we then cut back to them, we see this as a point-of-view shot from Sebastian's perspective, and we can mentally construct the filmic space as a narrow hallway with two facing doors. In retrospect, we understand that the second shot (of Sebastian) was from the perspective of Charles and that the sequence follows the conventional Hollywood logic of a shot/reverse shot pattern. What, though, can we say about the previous shot, which emanates from a space that Sebastian has not yet come to occupy? Its framing seems to be dictated not by the logic of character interaction, which has yet to begin, but by a logic of visual design in which the key "character" is Brideshead itself—or its synecdoche here, the centered doorway that replicates in miniature our straight-on view of the house.

Moments later, we dissolve from an interior of a hothouse garden to an exterior long shot of the house in the distance, with the viewer's atten-

Fig. 3. Reverse shot: Sebastian. From the 1981 TV production of *Brideshead Revisited* (Granada/Acorn Media).

Fig. 4. Sebastian and Charles, dwarfed by the reconstructed Italian fountain. From the 1981 TV production of *Brideshead Revisited* (Granada/Acorn Media).

tion drawn to the two elements of Castle Howard that survived from Waugh's own time: its imposing dome in the background and the fountain that occupies the front right of the frame.

The voice-over helps to smooth over the shot transition, and it is only gradually that the eye is drawn to the tiny human figures of Charles and Sebastian at the extreme left of the frame, rendered insignificant by the scale and grandeur of the house and fountain. Appropriately, they begin to discuss Charles's reaction to Brideshead, with Sebastian's remark "Oh, Charles, don't be such a tourist! What does it matter when it was built, if it's pretty?" ironically just at the moment—one of many—when the television viewer has been offered the tourist's detached viewpoint. Charles looks up at the dome seconds later, in a point-of-view shot that is sandwiched between two nearly identical shots in which he wheels Sebastian, again in the exact center of the frame, in a straight line running first from the fountain toward the camera—which is thus presumably positioned in or near the house—and then back again, in a long take in which the camera slowly tracks back to reveal the house behind them. In all of these shots, either our attention is drawn away from the characters to their surroundings

84   or we see them from what we might describe as Brideshead's point of view, so that the house possesses from the outset the attributes of a character that it gradually comes to possess in Waugh's novel.[9]

A central difference between these novels and their adaptations can be stated in this way: while the source fictions focalize our relation to narrative space through the perceptions of a character, stressing the subjective experience (for instance) of Venice as viewed by Charles while he is "drowning in honey," the filmed version can only offer us Venice itself, indistinguishable from the one that Cara has in mind when she tells Charles a few sentences earlier that "We will become *tourists,* yes?" (*Brideshead,* 100–101; emphasis in original).[10] In Andrew Higson's reading of the visual and narrative logic of heritage aesthetics, "[s]tory-situations and character psychologies may cue emotional engagement, but the richly detailed and spectacular period mise-en-scène also cues the distanced and therefore more detached gaze of admiring spectatorship." If part of Waugh's purpose is to maintain a tension between engagement and detachment, so that the evident partiality or naïveté of Charles's subjective perception cautions us against sharing his rose-tinted vision of the social world of the Marchmains, the series has trouble distinguishing between them, in spite of the added voice-over: the "admiring gaze," as Higson concludes, "will often become entangled with the discourse of authenticity, especially at the level of production and promotion," even at those moments when the text explicitly cautions against it (41).

This can be illustrated by the adaptation's dramatic expansion and reorienting of a key scene in Waugh's novel, in which Sebastian uses the excuse of the Brideshead hunt to escape his family's watchful eyes and go in search of alcohol. On television, the audience saw the vast majority of its weekly installment devoted to showing the hunt itself, complete with the lavish helicopter shots that are needed to display it as a panoramic spectacle, whereas it is only a pretext for Sebastian's actions in the novel, the kind of scripted and empty social ritual that he can exploit because the family are reluctant to air their problems in public. The gap Waugh delineates between private dysfunction and public appearance—so well emblematized by the social drinking they cannot curtail, like the port that gets passed round after dinner—thus disappears from the filmed version, as the background event becomes foregrounded for the television audience.

The characteristic cinematic style of Merchant Ivory films follows the same pattern as *Brideshead,* though of course lacking the opportunities for narrative expansion that come with television serialization. Elements of the mise-en-scène are similarly emphasized by a series of cinematographic and editing techniques that collectively enhance the ostentatious spectacle on display. Editing is spare and unobtrusive, relying on unusually long takes between cuts—Higson estimates the average shot length in *Howards End* to be 8.92 seconds, against a typical average of 5–7 seconds (172). The camera is thus allowed to glide through space in languorous tracking shots, with the motivation for the movement and reframing often disconnected from character point of view and instead seemingly designed to showcase the view itself; in interior scenes especially, the camera keeps a distance from the actors, relying mainly on medium and long shots—so that Higson can conclude that "there's not a single shot in [*Howards End*] that would normally be described as a close-up" (172). This seems an exaggeration, but the close-ups we get are far more frequently of things than people. In one montage sequence, for instance, a scene that we hear about only in retrospect in Forster's novel, we see the unpacking of the Schlegel possessions as they are moved into Howards End: a grandfather clock, a carpet that is unrolled before us, a bust placed on the mantel, books (shown close enough that we can recognize them as a set of Dickens), the father's sword. Minutes later we get a similar series of close-ups, this time of portraits hung at Henry Wilcox's house at Oniton Grange: as Higson notes, this montage is "only retroactively anchored in the narrative by a subsequent shot of Margaret Schlegel (Emma Thompson) looking at the paintings" (173), but it is even more significant that she then asks, "Are these all Wilcoxes?"—to which Henry (Anthony Hopkins) replies, "No, I bought the place lock, stock, and barrel . . . I'm told some of these are pretty good—what do you think?" The exchange works in the context of their relationship, counterposing his interest in the material commodities to her aesthetic taste and focus on their familial significance, yet the order of the shots presumes in advance that the paintings *are* significant before we are asked to consider how; in the process the spectator is denied the necessary time in which to ponder Henry's question.

Another brief sequence suggests how the film works against its thematic content, seeming to celebrate material wealth and possessions even at those moments when the narrative most pressingly questions their importance. In a scene we see repeated on a number of occasions, as both a flashforward when he is reading and as a flashback when he is walking to his final doom at Howards End, Leonard Bast (Samuel West) spends the night walking in the woods and later recounts the experience to an audience of Schlegels. The scene moves from the dinner table to the front parlor while

86 the camera lingers behind to show the maid cleaning up the table and putting out a candle with her fingers, in a literal example of what Higson has in mind when he says of the film's meal scenes that "the camera will often stay with a scene longer than might be strictly necessary for the purpose of presenting a narrative action or event" (171). We open again with a close-up on Leonard's hand, fingering the handle of the sword in a clear foreshadowing of its role in his death. The camera then zooms out toward a space in the room occupied by the Schlegel sisters, as the question "Why did you do it?" emerges from this same offscreen space, so that by the end of the shot Leonard is seen in a medium-long shot, positioned to the right of the frame.

This decentering is significant in a film that relies so heavily on balanced composition, and it allows us to see a large portrait and a bookcase on the left side of the frame—and later Tibby. As Leonard reveals his inspiration in Meredith's *The Ordeal of Richard Feverel*, we cut to a medium two-shot of the sisters, who together recite the relevant passage. They laugh as they do so, but not necessarily, as in the novel, at Leonard or his regressive Victorianist tastes. In the reverse shot of Leonard (even farther off to the right now), we see Helen enter the space left open and take the book from the shelf, setting the stage for a two-shot of her and Leonard together that cements their association for the spectator.

As with the close-ups of Henry's bought paintings and the Schlegel possessions, the framing here deemphasizes the person of Leonard in favor of the commodities he wants but cannot afford. Even the Meredith novel takes its place in this richly composed mise-en-scène, whereas Foster has Helen near exasperation at the repeated mention of literary (pre)texts and

Fig. 5. Leonard Bast, framed by other people's possessions. From the 1992 film of *Howards End*, directed by James Ivory (Merchant Ivory Productions).

Fig. 6. Helen and Leonard. From the 1992 film of *Howards End*, directed by James Ivory (Merchant Ivory Productions).

pleading to hear "about your road" rather than "another beautiful book" (*Howards End*, 94). The novel's ambivalent critique of wealth and material goods—"the warp of civilization" against which Leonard sets the woof of "walking at night" (103)—is occluded here, along with the preference for "something far greater" that Helen reads into Leonard's story (95). Indeed, their subsequent discussion of his case leads Margaret to feel that "[i]t is sad to suppose that places may ever be more important than people," and yet this is a conclusion that it is tempting to ascribe to the filmmakers, who insistently foreground the former (103). The novel is hard to pin down on a precise answer to this question: its response would perhaps be closer to Orwell's George Bowling in *Coming Up for Air* (1939), who answers the rhetorical question of whether one "oughtn't to prefer trees to men" by asserting that "it depends what trees and what men."[11] As with the "modern" Georgian flats and the cherished houses like Wickham Place that they supplanted, the film has trouble making such value distinctions: places in general are shown to be important, whatever they might have represented in Forster's novel.

The film's interpretive choices are best analyzed in relation to its final scene, adapting the coda to the novel, which takes place fourteen months after the close of the main action. As I suggested in chapter 2, the text is carefully poised between the conservatism associated with the pastoral— the "little events" that would "become part of [Margaret] year after year" (265)—and the need to respect and foster difference: on the one hand, "the battle against sameness," but on the other a rearguard action against "London's creeping" and the desire for a future civilization "that won't be a movement, because it will rest on the earth" (267–68). If Howards End

88   itself represents these ambiguous desires, it undergoes a change here at the end by passing into Margaret's hands, yet one that is also a kind of restitution, respecting Ruth Wilcox's original wishes; again, this seems both a conservative and "natural" gesture and also a disruptive one, especially given Margaret's stated desire to pass it on in turn to the illegitimate child of Helen and Leonard Bast. Her discovery that the house had always been hers by right is signaled by a physical gesture—"Something shook her life in its inmost recesses, and she shivered"—and then by a conciliatory dismissal of Henry's concerns at keeping the information from her: "Nothing has been done wrong," she tells him, in an inclusive passive voice that would seem designed to wipe all slates clean (271).

The film's conclusion opens with an intertitle announcing a shift in time to "THE FOLLOWING SUMMER." The scene signals its focus on the issue of the house by beginning with a shot of the property and concentrating on the discussion between the Wilcoxes concerning the estate. As they leave, the camera shows us a pastoral cliché of a farmer mowing his fields, with Helen and her child framed by this natural landscape that he is set to inherit; in this representation, the counteracting sense of a progressive movement is indicated only by the negative image of the Wilcoxes, driving away in their loud and obtrusive vintage car. After Henry explains his decision to keep his former wife's wishes from his new one, Margaret seems to stumble a little to register the shiver of the novel and grips his arm tighter, in Garrett Stewart's perceptive reading, "as if she were taking another light blow from the unknown, taking it and making do." For him, the lack of a response to Henry's question ("Didn't do wrong, did I?"), and the film's excision of the passive construction of the novel's own answer, implicitly criticizes both a kind of "spiritual force field associated with Mrs. Wilcox" (whose wish is finally granted here) and an imperialist attitude that the impersonality of the passive voice helps to shield. "Almost inevitably," Stewart concludes, "the story's contemporary treatment cannot help but sabotage the celebration of landed privilege and bourgeois continuities that, in the novel, survive even the critique of Henry's Imperial and West African Rubber Co. and all that its owner blindly embodies."[12]

And yet, it can do so only, as Stewart acknowledges, by having the camera leave them at this point, climbing up and away in a crane shot that reconnects them to the larger question of who should inherit Howards End. Crossing a stone wall and a road, along which we now see the Wilcoxes' motorcar belching out fumes, the camera reframes Helen, her child, and the farmer in an aerial long shot, leaving us with what Higson describes as

Fig. 7. "A final Constable-like image": the last shot of Howards End. From the 1992 film of *Howards End*, directed by James Ivory (Merchant Ivory Productions).

"a final Constable-like image of a green landscape bordered by trees and the ancient cottage" (148).

In the process, Henry's question is rendered irrelevant, along with Margaret's truncated response: it is *this* continuity that matters far more than one associated with Henry or his class, the film suggests—the land itself and not merely "landed privilege." The polluting Wilcoxes can appear on this reading as temporary aberrations and illegitimate landowners not through a process of restoring the house to its "rightful" possessor but through a more abstract celebration of the English countryside as a transhistorical space, belonging at once to all and none. Within such a framework, the film leaves us with the comforting thought that the debates about property ownership, marriage, and progress that have consumed its characters are ultimately beside the point, in comparison to this enduring and mythic spectacle of what Patrick Wright termed "Deep England."

Photo-Realism

While Higson is right to link this particular vision of the countryside to the iconographic influence of Constable's paintings, the visual aesthetic of heritage cinema has a more immediate history in photography and film, with key examples dating in each case from the earliest forms of these respective media. Writing of the photographs that we most readily associate with the Victorians—portraits of the royal family, Alice Liddell, Thomas Carlyle, and others, picturesque views of pastoral landscapes as well as vanishing urban sites, theatrically staged images, *cartes de visite*—Jennifer Green-Lewis has argued that they present another retroactive reconceptualizing of the period. Its key features, she notes, would include an interest in outdoor scenes "reflect[ing] the elevated viewpoints of the landed gentry at home . . . or the colonial traveler abroad"; a sentimentalizing of the rural poor, as a counterbalance but also a complement to the privileging of upper-class life; and an "elegiac . . . invitation to look back" at scenes that might already have been disappearing from view.[13] There were certainly alternative currents at work, as I shall suggest later in sketching a kind of countertradition in art photography and film; but if Green-Lewis is right, we can begin to associate the heritage aesthetic with artistic tendencies inherited from the Victorians themselves and (more importantly for my project) with a retrospective rereading of that period in terms of selected examples of its visual culture.

In particular, we can locate in early discussions of photographic technique the same emphasis on the authenticity of the object being shot as opposed to the interpretive perceptions of the person behind the camera. A good example here is William Henry Fox Talbot, the inventor in 1841 of the calotype process, which shortened the time required to expose the latent photographic image by changing the way it was developed. Fox Talbot's central metaphor for photography, which he used as the title for his first published collection of images, was "the pencil of nature," by which he indicated the evaporation of human agency from the artistic process: instead, he claimed, the photographs were "impressed by Nature's hand, obtained by the mere action of Light upon sensitive paper. They have been formed or depicted by the chemical means alone, and without the aid of any one acquainted with the art of drawing. It is needless, therefore, to say that they differ in all respects, and as widely as possible, in their origin, from plates of the ordinary kind, which owe their existence to the united skill of the Artist and the Engraver."[14] Such ideas did not go uncontested, as we shall see, especially when the relegation of the status of the photographer to a secondary role was enshrined by the Great International Exhibition of 1862, which classified photography as a form of machinery that was, by logical extension, operated by a mere mechanic.[15]

Even after the calotype process drastically reduced the period required for sitters, the early works of Fox Talbot tended to focus largely on architectural views rather than portraits. Of the two dozen images reproduced in "The Pencil of Nature," for instance, none feature human subjects: ten are of buildings (including three of his own Lacock Abbey) while another three depict outdoor scenes of rural life; of the rest, almost all are close-ups of artifacts in the domestic space, including busts, prints, books, glass and chinaware, fruit, and lace.[16] Discussing the most famous of Fox Talbot's

Fig. 8. William Henry Fox Talbot, "The Open Door," from *The Pencil of Nature* (1844)

images, "The Open Door," Nancy Armstrong argues that it "detaches the object from the symbolic economy in which it had a practical role to play," thereby providing the viewer with "indications that it is on the verge of perishing."[17]

For Armstrong, this preservationist impulse speaks to the complex function of photography, which—in tandem with disciplines like folklore and travel literature—celebrated and also mourned the vanishing of rural life in the mid-nineteenth century, and in this twinned sense anticipated a similarly conflicted impulse in heritage culture. Thus, if a broom can serve as a synecdoche for an entire way of living, as it seems to in Fox Talbot's photograph, this is only because of the absence of the human form and the labor that the artifact is used to perform. Already at the point of becoming an object in a museum, it can simultaneously suggest the preservation of the obsolete that is the hallmark of the photographic medium (since everything it captures is, in a sense, dead to its presumed audience, the freezing of a past moment in time)[18] and a deep continuity that presumes that viewers will still connect with it across time (since it requires no explanatory information or situating context).

Fox Talbot's own accompanying notes make no reference to when, where, or why the picture was taken but instead reference Dutch realist

92   paintings of "scenes of daily and familiar occurrence" to justify its content. Modifying that earlier emphasis on seeing nature itself as the artist, he now accords himself some creative agency, noting how "[a] painter's eye will often be arrested where ordinary people see nothing remarkable. A casual gleam of sunshine, or a shadow thrown across his path, a time-withered oak, or a moss-covered stone may awaken a train of thoughts and feelings, and picturesque imaginings."[19] In fact, as Larry J. Schaaf comments, it seems likely that the image was "refined by Talbot in several stages [in response to] the critical comments of his friends,"[20] and yet this labor is occluded in his own account, which continues to represent the scene itself as preconstituted before him. Elsewhere, he extended the central metaphor of "the pencil of nature" to bestow agency on the object being photographed, writing of Lacock Abbey in 1839 that "I believe [this building] to be the first that was ever yet known *to have drawn its own picture.*"[21] In such passages, we see a central forerunner of the Merchant Ivory aesthetic, with its tendency to represent buildings as characters and to use the camera to give the viewer something like an architectural point of view.

We can locate a figure like Fox Talbot, in this sense, at the beginnings of a history of photo-realism, a technical and aesthetic discourse that would recognize what John Tagg calls "the transparency of the photograph" as also "its most powerful rhetorical device," from the earliest experiments with daguerreotypes through to the amateur photographer with a Kodak.[22] I will explore an alternative trajectory, beginning with art photography, in the next section, but first I want to stress the ways in which other elements of the visual style of heritage cinema—especially its use of long takes and deep focus and its reluctance to use close-ups—are part of that same history of photo-realism; indeed, they form an ensemble of techniques that directly link the work of a Fox Talbot with a realist tradition in film that includes such major figures as the Lumière brothers, Jean Renoir, and Orson Welles. In film studies the most articulate spokesperson for this tradition is the critic André Bazin, who noted in 1945 that "[p]hotography and the cinema . . . are discoveries that satisfy, once and for all and in its very essence, our obsession with realism." Extending Fox Talbot's description of the photographic process, Bazin goes on to argue that "between the originating object and its reproduction there intervenes only the instrumentality of a nonliving agent." Unlike all previous art forms, it makes "an image of the world . . . automatically," deriving for the first time "an advantage" from the absence of the human subject from the process. All film adds, on this account, is the ability to place that image in motion.[23]

On this basis, Bazin rewrites the history of early film to deemphasize
the coming of sound as its pivotal event: instead of silents/talking pictures,
the key distinction in his schema falls between those directors (both before
and after the coming of sound) "who put their faith in the image and those
who put their faith in reality."[24] In the former category we find filmmakers
who make expressionistic use of elements of the mise-en-scène (through
stylized acting, exaggerated costuming, or chiaroscuro lighting effects)
and those for whom the juxtaposition of images through editing represents
the epitome of cinematic achievement. The latter category, in contrast, includes for Bazin such filmmakers of the silent and sound eras as F. W. Murnau, Erich von Stroheim, Renoir, and Welles. Writing of Murnau, he claims
that "[t]he composition of his image . . . adds nothing to the reality," just
as in Stroheim's films "reality lays itself bare like a suspect confessing under
the relentless examination of the commissioner of police"; in each case under
consideration, he concludes, "the image is not evaluated according to what
it adds to reality but what it reveals of it" (27–28).

If such claims rehearse those made for photographic realism a century
earlier, the filmic techniques through which such a revelation presents itself also anticipate those that Andrew Higson and others have identified as
the hallmarks of heritage cinema. First, editing is kept to a basic minimum,
with the camera kept running in long takes that aim to capture the reality
of a scene in its totality, rather than in discrete fragments: here, the ideal
for Bazin would be for the film to be "capable once more of bringing together real time, in which things exist, along with the duration of the action, for which classical editing had insidiously substituted mental and
abstract time" (39). A corollary of this emphasis on experiencing the action in "real time," moreover, is that viewers have a complementary understanding of the physical location of the scene, a "verisimilitude of space in
which the position of the actor is always determined, even when a close-
up eliminates the decor" (32). As we have seen, heritage aesthetics dis-
penses with close-ups wherever possible, preferring to keep the camera at
an appropriate distance to be able to situate the characters within their visible surroundings. This goal can best be accomplished through deep focus
cinematography, in which all the planes of action from foreground to
background are simultaneously in focus. Describing Welles's celebrated
use of this technique in *Citizen Kane* (1941), Bazin notes approvingly how
"whole scenes are covered in one take, the camera remaining motionless.
Dramatic effects for which we had formerly relied on montage [editing]
were created out of the movements of the actors within a fixed framework"

94 (33). As a result, the viewer is encouraged to attend to character action and dialogue without sacrificing an understanding of the overall space in which it occurs—an understanding that, as we have seen, is crucial in cases where the locations and visible props are required to serve important narrative functions, in addition to contributing to the overall effect of the cinematic spectacle.

Bazin's argument for a cinematic realism, while subject to challenges, has remained massively influential in the history of film studies. Its usefulness here is that it helps develop a consistent ontological and aesthetic position that, as he himself suggests, begins with the earliest debates about the uses and limits of photography. By denying the crucial historical break that had been posited with the coming of sound technology, he sought to reconnect postwar cinema to its earliest forerunners in a chain of influence that can thus be imagined as stretching back, via those first film realists, into the nineteenth century. As Nancy Armstrong has argued, what we have come to think of as the triumph of realist modes of representation in the nineteenth century is one that relies upon a distinctly new visual regime that was ushered in by photography, within which "the so-called material world to which the Victorians were apparently so committed was one they knew chiefly through transparent images."[25] Only with a bank of images of people, places, and things could they come to recognize who and what they were, as well as what they were not, in a process that we can see continuing in contemporary heritage culture: films that provide us with a view of "authentic" locations and props, for instance, only make sense within a regime of realism that dictates that it is through photographic representation that we can recognize the genuine objects of the past.

If the Victorian image bank taught its users to recognize themselves from among a range of character types and poses, heritage films position their viewers through a similar play of identification and difference, offering forms of historical continuity as well as a measure of our distance from the past on display. A site such as Castle Howard can indicate the former through its sheer persistence, not simply as an image but also as a place that we can see for ourselves if we need to verify its material existence; yet its conversion from stately home to tourist destination also means that it stands as a synecdoche for a way of life that is now over with, just as surely as Fox Talbot's photograph of a broom. If, as I suggested earlier, it has been hard to accept heritage cinema as "Victorian" in terms of its content or source material—and easier, in many ways, to see it as the exact opposite, to the extent that it has consistently restaged the breakdown of the social formation that dominated nineteenth-century Britain—then the stylistic inheritance I have been tracing here might offer a different proposition: that such films adopt what we might think of as a "Victorian" realism even when they are not telling Victorian stories per se.

Photomontage

What, though, of the alternative? As I have already suggested, a striking feature of heritage cinema is its attraction to a number of turn-of-the-century authors—including Forster, Conrad, James, and Hardy—who collectively might be taken to have undermined the claims to transparent realism that photography had helped validate earlier in the century. In that sense, the desire to film their texts from within the aesthetic tradition of photo-realism that I have outlined seems a perverse one, in which (as Andrew Higson suggests) form and content are plainly set at odds. To propose this approach is not, however, to replay the narrative of a decisive modernist break with the Victorians that I recounted in chapter 1, or to see these films as a contemporary version of the Edwardian novels of Bennett or Wells. In many respects, as Armstrong argues and an essay such as *Mr Bennett and Mrs Brown* makes clear, modernism is "no less dependent upon a visual definition of the real than Victorian realism."[26] Virginia Woolf's experiment in that essay presupposes, after all, that a more accurate depiction of Mrs. Brown becomes possible as soon as the novelist ceases to fixate on the details of external life and learns to focus on the person instead.

In the same way, it is tempting but ultimately misguided to identify an antirealist or avant-garde tradition in photography and film within which a "better" heritage cinema might take its place; to the extent that I see the figures in this section as operating differently from a Fox Talbot or a Bazin, it is important to emphasize their shared commitment to a realist project. At the same time, it is worth noting that somebody like the photographer Oscar Gustave Rejlander has tended to be marginalized in accounts of nineteenth-century visual culture, which generally assume, as Jennifer Green-Lewis suggests, that the Victorians were "humorless realists about to be shattered by modernism and the cubist war."[27] The situation is different, however, when we come to early cinema, a medium that was in many ways born within modernism itself. It has been standard practice in film history and criticism, at least since the publication in 1960 of Siegfried Kracauer's *Theory of Film*, to identify an internal fault line separating two main stylistic traditions: in film's earliest years, the realism of the Lumière brothers versus the illusionism of Georges Méliès, and at a later date, the formal techniques

96   championed by Bazin versus those advocated by the revolutionary Russian school of montage cinema, with its alternative emphasis on discontinuity and juxtaposition.[28]

One of the most perceptive accounts of the early history of film, Keith Cohen's *Film and Fiction*, situates the new medium at the intersection of two contrasting impulses in late-nineteenth-century fiction, naturalism and impressionism, seeing it as simultaneously building upon a realist aesthetic and its opposite. In common with the former, as a critic like Bazin would agree, film displays a consistent interest in representing the world as it is, being in effect merely a further development of the photographic apparatus that aims to capture a reality that is relatively unmediated, especially in comparison with painting. In this way, Cohen suggests, early documentaries "represented the complete reduction of external events to mechanically gathered data," but he goes on to suggest that whatever film contains of "'art' would depend more and more on the ways in which the camera was manipulated and the shots assembled."[29] As with photography, what distinguishes the film from external reality are the framing of its subjects, the camera distance, and the angle of vision—as well as the additional ability of the movie camera now to travel through space. Noting the contemporaneous experiments in painting to suggest a three-dimensional space, as undertaken by impressionism and cubism in particular, Cohen argues that film "did not simply endow the still photo with motion: it raised to a new, decidedly visual level the investigation of change and mobility, which, with more or less urgency, had preoccupied the European mind since the end of the Renaissance" (41). Decisively, the fixed spectatorial position around and toward which conventions of perspective had been developed (the so-called Renaissance perspective) was now replaced by a mobile positioning allowing for multiple viewpoints and angles.[30]

Considered in this light, we might be able to rethink heritage cinema's interest in novels of the same period by Forster, James, or Hardy, which fixate on similar problems of narrative unreliability and the limits of subjective vision. Along with Bazin, we could see the preference for long takes, deep focus, and mobile framing as offering one set of possibilities for capturing the totality of the filmed space, in which the camera is detached from a limited character in order to move freely in space. As Cohen argues, however, the same problematic can also be addressed by going in the opposite direction, toward a cinema of montage that works through fragmenting vision into discrete units and then reassembling them in a whole that can claim to be greater than the sum of its parts:

An object had to be presented from more than one viewpoint in   97
order to suggest its total contour and, in certain cases, its direction
of movement. The distance and angle of vision between the object and the camera further attenuated the establishment of anything resembling a fixed or authoritative point of view. So long as
the simultaneity of multiple viewpoints was impossible (and cubism was accomplishing this in other arts), an object or action had
to be rendered in discontinuous fragments that only in sequence
and hence through time could be fully apprehended. (80)

Such a cinema, as we shall see, dictates the exact opposite in terms of
its preferred techniques: discrete images, usually filmed from fixed camera
positions, rather than the mobility of long takes; shallow focus and close-
ups that isolate the object in space, drawing attention to the particular
angle of vision; and especially a privileging of the editing process rather
than cinematography as the source of meaning, which is now constituted
through the juxtaposition of montage fragments rather than being somehow revealed by reality itself. For Cohen, though, the purpose would not be
to provide the spectator with a feeling of disjunction, because the emphasis falls not on the fragmented parts but on the ways in which continuities
and connections are made between them: "When two shots, mutually illogi-
cal, unconnected, or even contradictory, are brought together in the film,"
he notes, "the automatic and relentless flow of images forces at least the
appearance of sequence" (81).[31] Once again, we see that the goal of a representing a comprehensible and coherent understanding of the visual space
before the camera might be approached by sharply divergent means.

Reading back into the early history of photography, we find the same
central debate about how best to employ the technology to convey the
fullest sense of the real. As we have seen, a pioneer such as Fox Talbot
sought to deemphasize the agency of the photographer (at least in theory)
in favor of an idea of nature as the creative force, with the camera apparatus functioning as a mere recording device. At the same time, a school of
art photography adopted a position closer to the one that Cohen associates with montage cinema, in which what emerges from the self-consciously
interventionist manipulation of the photographic process is a reality that is
supposedly "superior" to the one that the human eye can see. A representative example of this lesser-known strand of Victorian photography is
Oscar Rejlander, whose most famous image—1857's "The Two Ways of
Life"—demonstrates the process of combination printing, in which multiple

Fig. 9. Oscar Gustave Rejlander, "The Two Ways of Life" (1857). With permission of the Science and Society Picture Library, London.

individual images (thirty in this case) are rephotographed in an early form of photomontage.

The resulting image was conceived in terms of a visual allegory, similar to Hogarth's engravings illustrating the paths of "Industry and Idleness," in which two young men are presented with starkly opposed trajectories in life to the right and left of the frame. In this sense, it fits the retrospective image of the Victorians as didactic moralists, of course, and the image clearly succeeded in those terms: it formed the centerpiece of the 1857 Art Treasures Exhibition in Manchester, for which a special building was erected that (as Beaumont Newhall claims) "rival[ed] the Crystal Palace of London"; and although the use of nude models provoked some controversy—"only the righteous half . . . was shown at the annual exhibition of the Edinburgh Photographic Society," according to Newhall—it received the ultimate seal of approval when Queen Victoria herself purchased a print.[32]

It was the technique of combination printing itself that proved most controversial, as it posed a clear challenge to the relegation of early photographers to a secondary status as mechanical technicians. Rejlander ridiculed such an idea, asking hypothetically in 1866 "if my maid of all work, after I have posed myself before the looking-glass, takes off the cap of the lens when I cough, and replaces it at my grunt, has she taken the picture?"[33] Shot composition and the postproduction masking and editing of the individual "takes" become, on Rejlander's account, the fundamental tasks of the photographer, even if such efforts ultimately are placed in service of a realist ambition. In an 1863 lecture to the South London Photographic So-

ciety promising "An Apology for Art-Photography," Rejlander explained his   99
first experiments with what he termed "double-printing" as arising "through
sheer vexation, because I could not get a gentleman's figure in focus, though
he was close behind a sofa on which two ladies were seated."[34] This statement raises the possibility that what he was working toward is the equivalent of deep focus photography for Bazin: by posing each group of figures
in "The Two Ways of Life" and shooting them separately, Rejlander en-
sured that all were in focus, whether in the fore- or background. By contrast, a photo-realist such as Sir William Newton argued for the necessity
of shallow focus by insisting that compositions "a little *out of focus*" were
therefore "more *suggestive* of the true character of nature."[35]

Such arguments placed art photographers like Rejlander on the de-
fensive. Writing in 1859 to Henry Peach Robinson, a kindred spirit who
came in for his own share of controversy, he complained with bitter irony
that "I am tired of Photography for the public, particularly composite pho-
tos, for there *can be no gain* and there is no honor but cavil and misrepre-
sentation. The next Exhibition must, then, only contain Ivied Ruins and
landscapes forever besides portraits—and then stop."[36] The debate looks
very different in hindsight, however—and in many ways it foreshadowed
that which dominated during the early years of film criticism and aesthetics. While his emphasis on a consistent focus would align Rejlander with a
critic like Bazin, he seems in other respects much closer to one of the latter's primary interlocutors, the Soviet filmmaker and theorist Sergei Eisenstein. In particular, the Russian emphasis on the individual shot as a montage unit (or "cell") suggests that the aim is—like the allegorical meaning
intended in "The Two Ways of Life"—to produce something greater than
the sum of its individual parts: using the example of the Japanese hiero-
glyph as a parallel (showing, for instance, that signs for "dog" and "mouth"
combine to signify "to bark"), Eisenstein argued in an early essay from
1929 that the goal of cinema involves "combining shots that are *depictive,*
single in meaning, neutral in content—into *intellectual* contexts and series."[37]

Such an approach also involves a dialectical emphasis on juxtaposition,
so that the discrete montage units act upon each other as thesis and antithesis in order to produce a composite meaning that would not emerge
from the individual shots or their simple addition (as the hieroglyphic example might suggest). So that the content of each shot was clearly comprehensible, Eisenstein preferred that images be both in close-up and shallow focus, as opposed to long shots or deep focus, which allow the viewer's
eye to wander. The emphasis, he notes here and elsewhere, is on "conflict"

100 and "collision" between successive shots, which can occur in a variety of ways: graphic conflicts of scale, volume, or mass within a single image, for example, as well as across images when a close-up procedes a long shot, or motion in one direction is juxtaposed with a contrary movement in the following shot. Interestingly, we find something like this happening in Rejlander's 1860 double-exposure print "Hard Times," which he labeled "a Spiritistical Photo."

Inspired by Dickens's industrial novel, the image dramatizes the dilemma of the textile worker Stephen Blackpool, who is seen as simultaneously turned away from a woman and child lying in bed (thereby demonstrating Eisenstein's graphic conflict of frame direction) and also—less distinctly—as facing another woman, whose head is superimposed over his; while neither is identified as such, these would presumably signify the drunken wife and the lover, Rachael, between whom Dickens's Stephen remains torn.

In the novel, though, this problem is intended to connect—in rather uncertain terms—to Stephen's internal division on the issue of trade unionism, as he similarly finds himself positioned between his fellow workers and management, as well as to a more immediate political critique of Victorian marriage laws that refused him on economic grounds the divorce that could readily be obtained by the wealthy.[38] It is difficult, even with prior knowledge of the text, to read any of this larger context into Rejlander's photograph, as Eisenstein's dialectical method would dictate that we should. The problem, as Nancy Armstrong argues, is that the photographic process has the tendency to abstract figures from their social context. Discussing Henry Peach Robinson's defense of combination printing as allowing the photographer to maintain a consistent focus on all the different parts of the image, Armstrong notes that its advantage was "to suppress the relations among the various elements supplying the photographer's subject matter and to resituate them in a relationship determined by the sense and symmetry they might achieve within the photograph"; in the case of "The Two Ways of Life," then, "the effect of detaching images from the social relations governing their subject matter was to create a new set of distinctions between light and shadow, foreground and background, high and low, nature and culture. Inequities among and between the various subgroups of Victorian society were reinforced as they were turned into visual information and accordingly assigned to one of several social spaces" (147). Again, this suggests that the same montage techniques that for Eisenstein were designed to reveal and critique dominant social relations can instead tend

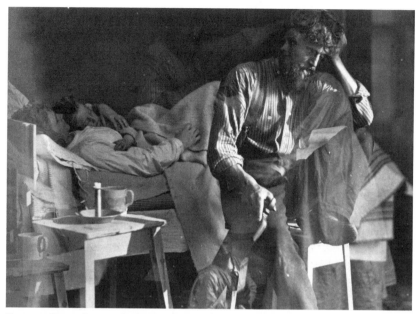

Fig. 10. Oscar Gustave Rejlander, "Hard Times" (1860). With permission of George Eastman House, Rochester, NY.

to evaporate them, with the result that the explicit political or moral conflict within the image becomes reified as a purely formal one.

The same might be said, of course, of Fox Talbot's "The Open Door," which works in different ways to suppress the social contexts within which a broom might signify something other than an aesthetic object. It is notoriously difficult, as this survey of opposed tendencies in photography and film might suggest, to read off political or social effects from particular techniques or to align formal stylistic choices with either the content of the images or artistic ambitions. An effect of deep focus composition, for instance, might be achieved through composite printing by Rejlander and through a naturalistic cinematography by Orson Welles; and it might equally be said to advance either an allegorical meaning or a mimetic transparency. The stylistic preferences of photo-realism (for long takes, a moving camera, and few close-ups, in particular) have clearly dominated in heritage cinema, but they have no a priori connection to the source texts or the periods in which they are set—often, as I have suggested, at a time during the turn of the century when seemingly contradictory artistic styles coexisted in fiction and film. To privilege one over the other does not, in and of itself, make these films conservative or necessarily "Victorian" in design

102   or effect. Nor does the stylistic choice necessarily follow from the selection of texts for adaptation or the heritage genre as a whole, as I hope to show in examining a recent group of "metacinematic" heritage films that collectively stage and comment on the history of Victorian visual aesthetics. In the process they denaturalize our habitual associations of the period with the techniques of photo-realism and suggest some of its ideological presuppositions and blind spots.

The Metacinematic Heritage

A small group of recent period films has resisted the attraction of heritage aesthetics, offering instead a metacritical viewpoint on the relationship between form and content in the heritage genre. In doing so, they suggest that the question of how to portray the nineteenth century is conditioned not only by how we view the Victorians but also by the visual aesthetics we inherit from them. For example, Karel Reisz's 1981 film of John Fowles's *The French Lieutenant's Woman*—a novel that works in part by highlighting what remains irretrievable or unrecognizable when we try to comprehend the past—adopts the metacinematic device of cutting between the nineteenth-century story and scenes from its filming, with actors (in particular Meryl Streep and Jeremy Irons) performing double duty. This technique enables the film to suggest the contemporary moment's difference from the past it is recreating as well as its parallels. Fowles's novel, first published in 1969, conveys the distance we have traveled through an omniscient narrative voice that is simultaneously aware of the events it describes and of those that have taken place in the interim—so an early passage insists, for instance, that "Charles knew nothing of the bereaved German Jew quietly working, as it so happened, that very afternoon in the British Museum library; and whose work in those somber walls had yet to bear such bright red fruit."[39] Fowles also uses epigraphs from Victorian authors (most commonly, Tennyson, Arnold, Clough, and Marx) as well as—less frequently— from twentieth-century commentators.

Two of these, from E. Royston Pike's *Human Documents of the Victorian Age*, help to suggest a modern critical distance from the past by acting in counterpoint to other quoted passages: chapter 2's epigraphs, in particular, contrast a West Country folk song ("I'll spread sail of silver and I'll steer towards the sun / And my false love will weep") with Pike's statistical analysis of the population at midcentury, which concludes that "if the accepted destiny of the Victorian girl was to become a wife and mother, it was unlikely that there would be enough men to go around" (11). As we have seen,

a conventional heritage aesthetic strains to include such critical commen-   103
tary, even in the relatively mild form of Charles Ryder's cautions about the
dangers of retrospective nostalgia in *Brideshead Revisited,* which aired on television the same year in which Reisz's film was released; Harold Pinter's
screenplay for *The French Lieutenant's Woman,* however, accomplishes this with
the simple device of having similar information being read by the modern-
day actors as they research their roles in the costume drama. Thus, Anna
(Streep) reads to her lover, Mike (Irons), a set of statistics that seem to
originate in a source like Pike's book: "In 1857 it's estimated that there were
80,000 prostitutes in the county of London. Out of every sixty houses, one
was a brothel. . . . At a time when the male population of London, of all
ages, was one and a quarter million, the prostitutes were receiving clients
at a rate of two million per week." This produces a predictably gendered
response: Anna hopes to use the passage to better understand the limited
choices facing her character (that "hundreds of the prostitutes were nice
girls like governesses who'd lost their jobs"), while Mike is content to calculate the percentages, figuring out that "outside of marriage, your Victorian gentleman could look forward to 2.4 fucks a week."

While a scene like this tries to incorporate the critical distance from
the Victorians that Fowles's narrative voice and structure open up, its presumption of a modern-day superiority is not sustained by the film's conclusion, which duplicates the complicated double ending of the novel. In
an echo of Virginia Woolf's thought experiment in *Mr Bennett and Mrs Brown,*
Fowles's narrator makes an appearance at a pivotal moment in the novel,
when Charles Smithson has broken his engagement and is in turn abandoned by his lover, Sarah, to observe his own creation sitting in a railway
carriage. In a text that represents duplicity as the hallmark of the Victorians, and ambiguity as a state of being that they most avoided,[40] the narrator appropriately imagines two possible endings, after first noting that "the
conventions of Victorian fiction allow, allowed no place for the open, the
inconclusive ending" (317). According to the first (with priority decided
by a imaginary coin toss), Charles eventually finds Sarah after years of
searching, now working as an amanuensis and model for Dante Gabriel
Rossetti, and reunites with her after discovering the existence of a child; the
second follows a similar pattern, except that he leaves her without ever recognizing the child to be his.[41]

The adaptation splits these endings, so that we first see a title announcing "Three Years Later" in the period film. In this more positive ending, we
see Sarah working as an artist herself, declaring that "[i]t has taken me this

104 time to find my own freedom"; there is no evidence of a child, but she and Charles argue and reconcile, as in the first version in the novel, with one final glimpse of them sailing away from the camera in a rowboat. The alternative ending is reserved for the present-day story line, as Anna and Mike fail to connect at a wrap party to celebrate the end of filming. We see her enter the house and look at herself in the makeup mirror, as if to disconnect finally from the character of Sarah, and we hear her car drive off as Mike comes to look for her, finally shouting "Sarah" after her in a gesture that suggests that he cannot so easily disentangle past from present. Considering these two endings, it is hard to agree with Steven Gale's assessment of them as "indicative of their respective societies" or as reflecting "the constraint of the Victorian and the license of the modern."[42] The resumption of an affair that has already cost Charles his social reputation hardly represents an affirmation of nineteenth-century "constraint," with their shared rowboat instead functioning as a fairly clichéd image of liberation. By the same token, the failure of the modern affair between Mike and Anna, and his seeming desire to remain in the past of the film they are shooting, surely work to deflate what Michel Foucault termed the "repressive hypothesis" that we have somehow escaped Victorian sexual constraint for a brave new world of liberatory "license."[43]

In a generally negative assessment of Pinter's screenplay, Shoshona Knapp argues that it ruled out "Victorian *facts*" and ends up offering in their place "a distanced perspective without a background of knowledge," but this presumes that we know which "facts" would provide us with an adequate context for its Victorian story.[44] If, in place of such certainty, it instead reveals what Knapp—commenting on Anna and Mike's discussion of prostitution—terms "the fallibility of a generalization that may not apply, as well as the limits of the modern characters' attempts to reach back into an age they do not know" (66), this seems more consistent with Fowles's project. Rather than simply judging the past by the standards of the present (as Foucault argues we do in the case of Victorian sexuality), both the novel and the film aim to keep open the question of the relationship between them. While Reisz's adaptation generally conforms to the conventions of heritage film aesthetics, the interplay between historical moments undermines the fiction of an authentic past for its audience to inhabit. Indeed, the very first scene of the film punctures this illusion as a shot of Sarah walking in the town is instead revealed to be the production of the film-within-the-film, with a diegetic director offering Anna offscreen instructions and the request for "Track" signaling the imminence of one of heritage film's trademark moving camera shots.

At such moments, we might see the film as straining against not only the commonplace assumptions about the Victorians that seem to have been recycled by critics of the film but also an emerging consensus about how such film adaptations should be shot. Francis Ford Coppola's *Bram Stoker's Dracula* (1992) also engages this question by reminding us that the novel itself was a contemporary of the earliest screenings by Méliès and the Lumière brothers; indeed, given Stoker's position as the manager of the Royal Lyceum, it is not a fanciful suggestion to speculate (as Ronald Thomas does) that he might have witnessed the cinematographic demonstrations in London theaters that began the year before *Dracula's* first publication— including a two-minute vampire film, *Le Manoir du Diable*, by Méliès.[45] Coppola's film dramatizes the simultaneous invasion of London by Dracula and the cinema, staging the vampire's first meeting with Mina Harker (Winona Ryder) inside one such theatrical demonstration. The effect of the sequence is to reverse conventional readings of the vampire as an archaic holdover of the premodern and to see him instead as fascinated by the possibilities of the cinematic apparatus, one through which he has now managed to live on for more than a century.

Coppola's meditation on late-nineteenth-century film technology extends to the formal look of his film, which rejects computer-generated special effects in favor of those that would have been available to the earliest filmmakers who were Stoker's own contemporaries. Paying homage to Méliès in particular, he reprises a variety of in-the-camera effects by means of mirrors and front or rear projection, multiple exposures, running the film backward, shooting upside down, and so on. The opening of the sequence with Mina begins with a long shot of Dracula (Gary Oldman) on a London street, filmed with an old camera from the Pathé Frères film studios that dominated the export market in the early years of the twentieth century. The shot, in sepia tint, is accompanied by the sound of a camera cranking and an offscreen promoter's voice encouraging the city's residents to "see the amazing cinematograph, a wonder of modern civilization, the latest sensation." The scene dissolves into color just as Dracula spots Mina in the crowd, one of many instances in which he seems able to control the filmic apparatus; as Thomas and Garrett Stewart have pointed out, his telepathic command to her to "See me, see me now" puts himself in the place of the cinematograph in the promoter's sales pitch, thereby reinforcing his connection to the technology of film.[46]

Once inside, Mina and Dracula witness a miniature highlight reel of early cinema, including footage of Victoria's funeral, pornographic scenes, and the Lumières' famous film of a train arriving at the station at La Ciotat,

106   which was exhibited in London in 1896 and which had—according to a
celebrated but disputed story[47]—caused its earliest French spectators to
scream in terror and possibly run from the theater. Taken together, these
clips offer a condensed history of early film: documentary footage of historical events alongside examples of what Tom Gunning has termed the
"cinema of attractions," sexual titillation and the threat of violence.[48] Mina,
whose typewriting skills help mark her as a New Woman in Stoker's novel,
is unimpressed, first chastising Dracula that "If you seek culture, then visit
a museum" and then responding to his rapturous delight in the projected
images—and his declaration that "there are no limits to science"—by pointedly asking whether Madame Curie would make such a comparison. As the
images on the screen morph into the puppet figures we saw at the beginning of Coppola's film, illustrating Dracula's own backstory, his connection
to the new technology is secured. As Thomas concludes, "Bram Stoker's *Dracula* arrives in London at the same time as the cinema, and his supernatural
powers are identified with the effects of that magic medium."[49]

   This metaphorical connection between the vampire and film seems to
counteract our conventional understanding of Stoker's novel, in which the
former's enemies are the ones armed with a range of modern technological innovations, from shorthand and phonographic recording to a Kodak
camera that Jonathan Harker uses to help seal Dracula's purchase of Carfax Abbey estates.[50] If, however, we see this as a use that accords with the
demands of photo-realism, with Harker's images of the abbey intended to
function as simple simulacra of the building itself, then Dracula seems, by
contrast, to be employing the alternative principles of photomontage, in
order to defy the laws of time and space.[51] In the text, trompe l'oeil effects
and morphing techniques depend upon forced juxtapositions and rapid
alternations, which repeatedly cause other characters to doubt their own
eyes even as they recognize that ocular testimony, however questiona-
ble, is the only evidence they have. On first seeing Dracula, for instance,
Harker records that "there appeared a strange optical effect: when he
stood between me and the flame he did not obstruct it, for I could see its
ghostly flicker all the same" (22), while Mina's sighting of him occurs as "a
fleeting diorama of light and shade," in which "it seemed to me as though
something dark stood behind the seat where the white figure [of Lucy]
shone, and bent over it. What it was, whether man or beast, I could not
tell" (112). In such passages Stoker might be said to be employing an early
language of cinema, in much the same ways that Eisenstein famously suggested of Dickens—though less in anticipation, perhaps, than through di-

rect reference to visual effects that he could have witnessed in the London
theaters.

In other places, characters describe Dracula in terms that suggest the cinematic technique of the graphic match, in which images are edited together on the basis of their shape rather than any narrative logic of cause and effect. Such descriptions interestingly occur at moments when Dracula's eyes function as a metonym for his body, with his power stripped down to a hypnotic stare that locks in his victims. Mina first describes his eyes as "like burning flames" but immediately dismisses it as an "illusion" (117), although the connection returns later in an extended metaphor when she thinks she sees a thick mist that "got thicker and thicker, till it seemed as if it concentrated into a sort of pillar of cloud in the room, through the top of which I could see the light of the gas shining like a red eye." That flame in turn "divided, and seemed to shine on me through the fog like two red eyes," by which point the movement between fire and eyes has become a reciprocal one, with the onlooker unsure of what she is actually seeing and what her mind might be substituting for it (309). Again, Coppola's film extends this uncertainty by highlighting a hypnotic connection between Dracula and Mina that proves useful in allowing the former's enemies to track him. It is noticeable that his association with the cinema ("See me now") first occurs when he fixes her in his sights, willing her to look in his direction, and the link is underscored in a brief series of shots that cut, in a careful graphic match, from Mina's photograph to her body lying in bed, having been hypnotized by Van Helsing (Anthony Hopkins). In between, a brief shot shows Dracula standing over her to illustrate his own mental connection with her, but the effect, as Garrett Stewart points out, is to suggest that "by insinuating itself into the seams and folds of narrative transition per se, supernatural agency has also lent its authority to the film mechanism."[52]

Coppola's film might be said to dramatize, in both form and content, the superiority of cinematic techniques that add to reality rather than merely reflecting it. Another recent film, Sandra Goldbacher's *The Governess* (1997), takes a similar position in relation to the founding debates about the uses of photography. The film imagines Rosina, a young Jewish woman from London (Minnie Driver), who is forced by her father's death to take a position as governess in the Scottish highlands, where her employer seems to be a surrogate figure for Fox Talbot. Charles Cavendish (Tom Wilkinson) has figured out how to capture camera obscura images on sensitized paper but not yet how to fix them permanently; the secret to the

108   invention of the calotype process is given to him by Rosina, who spills salt on one of his plates while conducting the ritual of the seder. Their collaboration is later destroyed by an affair, after which he excises her from the discovery process, telling an expert from the Edinburgh Royal Society that he succeeded through sweat, empirical endeavor, and happy accident. As her revenge, Rosina leaves a revealing nude portrait of Charles for his family and takes the camera back to London, where she sets up a portrait studio with her sister to capture images of the capital's Jewish population.

Intersecting with the romance plot is a pivotal debate about the possibilities of photography, which Cavendish, as a representative of mid-Victorian naturalism, sees only in terms of providing "a faithful and scientific record of reality." Rosina, by contrast, sees it as a "means of expression," an argument he dismisses as neither rational nor empirical in its basis. The debate is played out in terms of their choice of subjects: his are, predictably, the dead objects of nature (shells, bird's wings) or those associated with the formal exercises of the pictorial still life; she sees photography instead as an extension of baroque art and portraiture, and encourages him to shoot her in poses inspired by Queen Esther and Salome. Ultimately, it is a different kind of death that she wants to memorialize, those of what she pointedly terms (in a post-Holocaust context) a "lost people" that might be preserved by being captured on camera: "You've made it possible to capture the essence of people, to fix memory, fix people," she tells Charles, and one of the final shots in the film illustrates what she has in mind, as we pan across a series of portraits of Victorian Jews.

The paradox of this shot is that it is only the moving camera that allows us to see the totality of these images, out of which a "people" can emerge as the sum of discrete individuals. In that sense, Rosina's advocacy of extramimetic uses of the camera anticipates its later development in the cinema. This is distinct from the photo-realist argument of André Bazin, who sees film as simply putting still images in motion; to the extent that the composite representation of a people suggests a meaning that is inaccessible from any single photographic unit, it seems closer to Eisenstein's or Rejlander's emphasis on the power of juxtaposition. An earlier scene illustrates another difference between photography and film, as we see— through a kind of time-lapse effect of speeded-up film—the problem posed by the lengthy exposure time required by early photographers, which partially accounted for the preference for the still life or architectural view over portraiture. In the shot Rosina stands still in the center of the frame while the world moves around her at high speed, thereby revealing film's

considerable technological advance over photography, which allows it to   109
accelerate rather than having to slow down time.

As Lynette Felber has argued, the film's "embedding of photography within a motion picture creates both a visual juxtaposition and a historical anachronism," as it provides a solution at the level of its own style and technique to the technical problems posed within the narrative.[53] I would argue, however, that the disjunctive implication of such an embedding is lessened when we recover the neglected side of photography's own history and recognize that Rosina's arguments about its possibilities rehearse those made by early pioneers like Rejlander and Robinson. At the same time, Felber correctly asserts that *The Governess* seeks to rewrite that history in order to inscribe within it a modern feminist perspective, by representing Rosina not as a privileged photographic amateur (like Julia Margaret Cameron or Clementina Hawarden) but as a working woman. In doing so, she suggests, the film also enters into the debate within film studies initiated by Laura Mulvey's landmark essay from 1975, "Visual Pleasure and Narrative Cinema," which argued that the master code of cinema is that of a voyeuristic male gaze directed at a passive female object. If such a model is confirmed by Cavendish's photographic studies of Rosina, it is partially challenged by a reverse gaze when she photographs him while he is sleeping, and by a self-portrait of her own eyes that seems to represent the gaze itself, thereby drawing attention to a dynamic that (according to Mulvey) is effective because it operates at a deep structural level and is rarely thematized.

For Felber, this places *The Governess* in a small group of "turn-of-the-[twentieth-]century films [that] not only turn nostalgically to the past, but reinterpret it through a contemporary lens, purporting to recover subtexts about gender and sexual orientation that were unspeakable at the time" (27). In doing so, they operate along parallel lines with recovery projects and critical reevaluations of the nineteenth century, displaying a heightened self-consciousness about visual form that critiques the widely held assumption that an unproblematic realism is the appropriate style for representing the Victorians. As we have seen, such assumptions were contested in the period itself but have been reinforced by much of twentieth-century visual culture—and directly endorsed by most works of heritage adaptation. In that sense, it is possible to trace a direct line of influence back from Merchant Ivory through Bazinian cinematic realism to a pioneering photographer like Fox Talbot, but we can likewise identify comparable stylistic choices among Rejlander's art photography, Soviet montage cinema, and *Bram Stoker's Dracula*.

110   If this means that we need to complicate our understanding of Victorian visuality, we should be wary of falling back into the kind of simple binary thinking that was initiated by Bloomsbury modernism, within which some elements of the past (such as Rosina, Dracula, or Sarah Woodruff) can be valued for their anticipation of the following century's preoccupations yet are highlighted against a simplified background of Victorian conventionality. Recovery work always poses the problem that renewed attention to repressed or demonized elements of the culture—a process to which Janet Wolff has referred as "the politics of correction"—can also tend to reify our sense of its dominant characteristics.[54] It is just as important to interrogate the motives that subtend all such efforts at reevaluation, recognizing that they often involve powerful stakes and interests. In shifting focus from heritage cinema to the wider discourse concerning the national heritage, especially as it emerged during the Thatcher years in Britain, I hope to address these larger political questions, beginning with the issue of why anyone in the 1980s might offer the public a narrowly partisan definition of "Victorian values" and hope in doing so to secure their electoral support.

Victorian Values?

Neoconservatives and the Welfare of the Modern State

It seems a strange quirk of history that the Victorians would emerge as a key reference point for elections and legislative agendas in both Britain and the United States in the late twentieth century: first in the early 1980s, when Margaret Thatcher famously used the phrase "Victorian values" to describe one element of her reelection campaign, and then in the mid-1990s, when congressional Republicans led by Newt Gingrich searched for a convenient historical parallel to support the case for welfare reform. These moments represent something more than the simple oscillation I have been tracing between a forward-looking modernity and a retrospective nostalgia for the past, a structuring framework within which the Victorians have alternately moved in and out of fashion. In analyzing Thatcherism's ideology as one in which British society was disciplined into "a particularly regressive version of modernity by, paradoxically, dragging it backwards through an equally regressive version of the past," Stuart Hall would seem to position it as an updated version of what Alison Light termed the "conservative modernity" of the interwar years.[1] If, however, we recall E. M. Forster's formula from chapter 2, of uniting "the new economy and the old morality," we can immediately pinpoint a key difference: whereas Forster presumed the general worth of state-centralized planning as a brake on the excesses of

111

112 unfettered market forces, it is precisely those forces that Thatcherism sought to liberate. In that sense, British conservatism might have reworded Forster's slogan as a combination of the old morality with the old economy, seeking to replace the interventionist welfare state with a version characterized by a supposedly "Victorian" minimalism. As I shall be arguing, however (and as Hall already anticipates in describing it as simultaneously a process of modernization), this was never a case of simple nostalgia for the Victorian era, except insofar as that period could be redefined to suit a late-twentieth-century political agenda.

These political debates played out on the loaded terrain of moral values, as the capsule phrase associated with Thatcher's appeal suggests. As Elaine Hadley has argued, this discursive focus, in which values are coded as a measure of personal character, seems designed to shift discussion away from their strong correlation with class and property relations, a connection that was apparent (if in sometimes mystified forms) to most Victorian commentators; indeed, as I shall suggest later in my discussion of Matthew Arnold, it was the presumption that social values and voting habits directly flowed from one's class position that was seen as the critical problem, especially in the context of an expanding electoral franchise.[2] In contemporary politics, the term "values" nominally marks the opposite extreme from the political entity that is most squarely under attack, the state, with the implication that to be in favor of one is inevitably to oppose the other. Part of the paradoxical character of Thatcherism, however, was (as Hall noted) its combination of an aggressive "anti-statism" in relation to economic policy with a correspondingly "merciless use of the state as an agent of social regulation" on issues of morality that included abortion, homosexuality, sex education, and gender inequality: in that sense, he concludes, "on *social* questions, Thatcherism in power has been the most 'interventionist' government of the whole postwar period." This is not a question of the state's abolition, then, but of its "recomposition."[3]

That reorganization, I would argue, was itself predicated on the parallel project of recharting the definitive characteristics of the Victorians. As we have seen, Bloomsbury modernism was inclined to disparage the nineteenth century as a period marked by the action of impersonal forces or the insistence on constructing machinery for the purposes of systematic social analysis, each operating against the interests of the sovereign individual. In a published commentary on T. A. McInerny's *The Private Man*, Evelyn Waugh sought to defend the Victorians in the 1960s while still holding onto this thrust of the critique, by arguing that the deficiencies of

the period were not (as they had been defined by Morris, Ruskin, and others) the by-products of industrialization— "the regimentation of the poor
by avaricious employers," "the great private fortunes accumulated," or "the
physical hardships of the Victorian miner or factory-hand"—but instead
the associated moral evil of a "loss of independence and self-respect in the
new industrial conurbations. The new Gradgrind," Waugh concluded, "is
the State," thus implying that the real problem the Victorians created
would emerge only posthumously with the centralized bureaucracy of the
postwar period.[4] This sounds very much like the same shift that Thatcher
herself identified as beginning with the 1945 Labour government, which
sought to redress the perception of a national decline "along lines which—
whether we call them socialist, social-democratic, statist or merely Butskellite—represented a centralizing, managerial, bureaucratic, interventionist
style of government."[5] This line of argument rescues the Victorians (and
their morality) from even the modified criticism offered by Waugh, but only
through a revisionist compression of more than a century of history, during which the modern state had emerged. It presumably sounded less dras-
tic for Thatcher to propose to turn the clock back by a mere four decades,
instead of seeking a wholesale return to the early-Victorian minimalism
that would be championed by her American acolytes, for whom even the
1834 New Poor Law and its notorious workhouse system could serve as a
positive model.

The key transatlantic intermediary here is the conservative historian
and Victorianist Gertrude Himmelfarb, whose work—most notably *The
De-moralization of Society: From Victorian Virtues to Modern Values* (1994) and *One
Nation, Two Cultures* (1999)—has helped to translate what remained a
largely underdeveloped slogan of Thatcherism into a full-blown reinterpre-
tation of the nineteenth century, better suited to the neoconservative challenge to President Clinton that hardened into the Republican Congress's
"Contract with America" of 1994. Gingrich, who was then Speaker of the
House, was quick to credit her influence, telling the National League of
Cities that the Victorians "changed the whole momentum of their society.
They didn't do it through a new bureaucracy. They did it by re-establishing
values, by moral leadership"; when asked if similar tactics might work in
contemporary America, he replied, "Read Himmelfarb's book. It isn't that
complicated."[6] A 1995 *Newsweek* debate with Clinton about "What Good Is
Government" specified some of the lessons Gingrich took from the book:
for instance, that moral leadership involved "being willing to look people
in the face and say 'You should be ashamed of yourself when you get drunk

114 in public. You should be ashamed of yourself if you're a drug addict,'" and
that the Victorian model mobilized "a volunteer for every two poor people," with the result that "they actually knew the person they were willing
to help." While Gingrich does not explicitly pose this approach as an alternative to centralized welfare provision, these references nonetheless occur
in the context of thinking about the time "before the welfare state," when
poor immigrants could elevate themselves into "full citizens earning a good
living and moving to the suburbs" instead of being "trapped in poverty for
three generations."[7]

From this discussion, it seems clear that the neoconservative return to
the Victorians was inseparable from contemporary efforts to reform welfare,
and that it required a specific narrative concerning nineteenth-century attitudes toward poverty, welfare, voluntarism, and the state. In what follows,
I first focus on the political dimension of these debates in the 1980s and
1990s, before tracking back—through a critical analysis of Himmelfarb's
writing—to the Victorians themselves, who held a divergent set of opin-
ions on such issues yet seem (if anything) to lean toward an acknowledg-
ment of the necessity of a centralized welfare professionalism. On my
reading, the period gives little support to the Thatcherite position, which
demanded the return to a mid-Victorian minimalist state with strict priorities given to defense, domestic order, and the enabling of international free
trade; instead, what was increasingly enshrined in the second half of the
nineteenth century was the idea of an impersonal and bureaucratic state
as the only available option for dealing with large-scale social problems,
especially when the alternative options were private charity and a philanthropic moralism.

Margaret Thatcher's Victorians

Raphael Samuel has hypothesized that Margaret Thatcher "stumbled on
the phrase 'Victorian values'" almost "by accident" when she first used it in
a 1983 television interview.[8] It may be that this offhandedness helped condition the fierce debates that the phrase engendered during her reelection
campaign, including the future Labour leader Neil Kinnock's ineffectual
counterargument that "[t]he 'Victorian Values' that ruled were cruelty, misery, drudgery, squalor and ignorance." In response, the closest Thatcher
came to defining her own terms came in an interview with London's *Evening
Standard*, in which she enumerated the lessons learned from having been
"brought up by a Victorian grandmother": "we were taught to work jolly
hard. We were taught to prove yourself; we were taught self-reliance; we

were taught to live within our income. You were taught that cleanliness was next to godliness. You were taught self-respect. You were taught always to give a hand to your neighbour. You were taught tremendous pride in your country. All of these things are Victorian values. They are also perennial values."[9] Despite the specificity of this list, which predictably finds no overlap with Kinnock's, commentators have continued to insist that the appeal is in fact a coded endorsement of something else. In James Walvin's conclusion to *Victorian Values*, a study that grew out of a Granada Television series of the same name, he insists that "[h]er evocation was not really of what had happened" in the nineteenth century but instead just "of those worthy and virtuous elements of the past which seemed attractive and relevant to contemporary life."[10] Having gainsaid as much, though, considerable uncertainty remains about the precise elements of the modern agenda with which the phrase was intended to resonate: Peter Clarke, for instance, speculates that "[t]he enterprise culture was lauded as a return to Victorian values," while Joel Krieger feels that "[s]uburbanism is the experience and reality behind the catchphrase 'Victorian values.'" Samuel in turn reads it as a gloss for an insidious process of "modernization in mufti."[11]

Stuart Hall's analysis of Thatcherism's "regressive modernism" takes more seriously its stated interest in the past, positioning it (as we have seen) as simultaneously looking back and forward. On the one hand, then, it is "deeply regressive, ancient and archaic," because "[y]ou couldn't be going anywhere else but backwards to hold up before the British people, at the end of the twentieth century, the idea that the best the future holds is for them to become, for a second time, 'Eminent Victorians.'" On the other hand, it attempts a belated modernization that would finally transform outmoded (in fact "Victorian") industrial and political structures in order to halt Britain's century-long decline.[12] This helps explain some of the contradictions that Samuel seizes upon: that Thatcher maintained "a radical contempt for the antiquated and out-of-date," modeling her vision of an "enterprise culture" on high tech rather than heavy industry; that she sought "to put an axe to what is arguably the most substantial twentieth-century legacy of the Victorian era, the public service ethic," by associating it with bureaucratic inefficiency; or that she encouraged high levels of consumer debt, despite the importance of thrift as one of her cardinal virtues or the conceit of running government spending on the model of a household budget.[13] Samuel repeatedly accords the appeal to the past a primary meaning within the political theater of the imaginary, viewing it as creating "a metaphorical space for the expression of moral anxiety" or

116 undertaken "for purely symbolic rewards."[14] This presumes, however, that the connotations it sought to conjure through the example of the Victorians were already fixed in the popular imagination, in order for the reference to operate at a largely unconscious level.

I want to focus here on three such connotations, which together constitute an ensemble of interconnected beliefs about the period. First, the dominant image of the Victorians depicts them as moralists who sought to explain social problems primarily as the symptoms of personal failure. Recalling Newt Gingrich's invocation of the drunkard or drug addict in need of face-to-face shaming, we might add that a central presupposition was that direct encounters prove much more effective than intervention by the state, which sees only a statistic and not the individual. This line of thinking returns to the distinction underlying the New Poor Law, according to which it was necessary to separate the "deserving" from the "undeserving" poor. Connected to this view is a second image of the Victorian as entrepreneur, largely unfettered by government and prepared to take greater risks in the drive for greater rewards. On such a model, welfare (or even charity) is anathema to the principle of self-help and the Protestant work ethic; indeed, the de-moralization thesis of the late nineteenth century argued that the provision of such a safety net, whether publicly or privately funded, inevitably encouraged dependency among its intended recipients, sapping them of the vitality necessary for social advancement. Third, we have the image of the minimalist state, which combined a laissez-faire attitude toward business and trade with a core commitment to national strength and military superiority.

The first of these connotations is most noticeable in Thatcher's efforts to impose a moral etiology on deviant behavior, especially in situations where dominant sociological explanations typically suggest economic or political causes—an explanatory framework that, as we shall see, ironically originated in the Victorian period. Her 1993 autobiography, for instance, rejects Kinnock's insistence on ascribing rising levels of violence and intimidation during the year-long miner's strike of 1984 to "the social ills from which he claimed Britain was suffering," a phrasing designed to cast suspicion on the list of grievances she goes on to quote (from "long-term unemployment" to "loneliness, decay and ugliness") and thus to deflect blame away from her own policies.[15] The mounting problem of homelessness is also tied to a range of "behavioural problems" that she claims would not be solved "by bricks and mortar," with a proposed terminological shift to speaking instead of the "roofless" seemingly designed to deter any possible connection with the government's policies—most notably the priority afforded to selling public housing to tenants in order to advance the political vision of a home-owning society. The homeless have no place in such a vision, of course, and are accordingly pathologized in *The Downing Street Years* as "crowds of drunken, dirty, often abusive and sometimes violent men" that pose a threat to "ordinary citizens." But such a rhetorical denial of full citizenship to a segment of the poor can only work if the cause of their poverty is shown to lie with themselves and not with larger social forces, which explains why the central problem they raise is not one of policy (the rather vague suggestion being to enlist the help of "voluntary organizations to see what they rather than the state could do") but rather perception: "Unfortunately," Thatcher notes, "there was a persistent tendency in polite circles to consider all the 'roofless' as victims of middle-class society, rather than middle-class society as victim of the 'roofless.'" This is a clear case of blaming the poor for their poverty, especially when one way that threat to "ordinary citizens" manifests itself is through the simple aggregation of the homeless on London's streets, implying that their visible presence—whether violent and abusive or merely dirty—was sufficient "to turn central areas of the capital into no-go zones" (603–4).

In her perceptive analysis of the emphasis placed on personal character in neoconservative discourse, Elaine Hadley argues that it is explicitly designed to pose an alternative explanation for social problems to one rooted in concepts of class, and yet it does so only through a rhetorical sleight of hand. Ideals of respectability or good character, after all, presuppose an "equality of access" in order that the individual can choose whether or not to aspire to them, but that is in turn predicated upon social realities—most obviously, in the example above, having a roof over one's head. Those same realities also provided the basis for the very Victorian social classifications (such as those who will work versus those who won't, or the deserving and undeserving poor) that neoconservatives look to revive, and thus they set the preconditions for what can appear to be individualized moral judgments. As Hadley suggests of the welfare mother, another locus of right-wing condemnation, indices of class, race, and gender "have become—over time, with continual usage—marks of moral failure, naturalized signs of a person's inability to be a proprietary individual, and, in turn, a good character. Insofar, then, as a welfare mom is primarily classifiable by her receipt of welfare, insofar as she is most recognizable as a poor (and black) woman, she is decidedly not a liberal character."[16] The same goes for the homeless in Thatcher's example, posing a threat to

118   "ordinary citizens" because they are not ones themselves; in the process, a "character" trait such as dirtiness—an explicit repudiation of cleanliness, one of her core "Victorian values"—can be magnified into evidence of personal failure and by implication becomes the cause rather than a consequence of the person's homelessness.

One last example suggests both this inversion of sociological cause and effect and Thatcher's simultaneous insistence on laying blame at the door of the modern welfare state for creating the conditions for the emergence of collective character types. In the aftermath of a series of riots in largely minority (and high-unemployment) neighborhoods of Britain's major cities in 1981, she recalls having "been told that some of the young people involved got into trouble through boredom and not having enough to do" but then dismissing this explanation after having looked "at the grounds around those houses with the grass untended, some of it almost waist high, and the litter . . . They had plenty of constructive things to do if they wanted." Once again, environmental conditions that might be considered the logical consequences of economic deprivation instead appear as a kind of causal index of youth unemployment, the confirmation that the rioters each lacked "a sense of pride and personal responsibility." That pride, moreover, should ideally not arise only from individuals but also from a collective investment in "a sense of community," which in turn would ideally operate to constrain the antisocial behavior manifested in the riots (145). At this point, however, it is surely wishful thinking to expect unemployed individuals to emotionally invest in a community that invests so little (emotionally or economically) in them.

To anchor her appeal, Thatcher resorts to the familiar trope of an earlier golden age, although it seems less to the Victorians that she turns than a more recent past—as Raymond Williams might anticipate, one drawn from an idealized childhood overseen by her Victorian grandmother. After invoking a nostalgic image of "genuine communities" previously united through tradition and "common moral values," she is then able to focus on the disintegrative forces at work at various times throughout the twentieth century: some of these (like "the state") are long-standing, while others (like "large-scale immigration") are clearly designed to conjure the postwar period only, thus obscuring exactly when her Edenic communities last existed. Predictably, however, "welfare arrangements" are singled out as the major obstacle to their return, having "encouraged dependency and discouraged a sense of responsibility." Elements of "the surrounding culture" (especially television) have also worked to undermine the purported unity

of working-class communities and "immigrant families" alike (146)—although there is clearly no question of any unity *between* those two categories,
with the latter having appeared as a contributing factor in the breakup of
the former.

This analysis indicts individuals along gender lines, with the twin consequences of the breakdown of community values said to be "a steadily increasing rise in crime (among young men) and illegitimacy (among young
women)." At the same time, there are larger social and cultural forces, not
least of which is the state itself, that create the conditions within which
such asymmetrical and gendered behavior patterns can emerge. The composite picture is one of a closed loop of interaction between individuals and
society, with each feeding back into and helping to constitute the "failure"
of the other, and yet it is striking that the need for change is geared mainly
toward the personal and not the institutional: Thatcher sees no need, for instance, to reform or regulate television, which—besides supposedly contributing to the decline of common values—also gave participants the sense
that they "could enjoy a fiesta of crime, looting and rioting in the guise of
social protest." The charge to the state, besides enhancing its repressive apparatuses to combat a perceived "decline in authority" (more police, tougher
sentencing guidelines), is thus aimed at inculcating an individual sense of
responsibility while also reversing a culture of welfare "dependency" (147),
although it is unclear whether a diminished or strengthened state would be
required to accomplish this. Given that the rhetorical equivalent of the pregnant and unmarried young woman is the criminal male here, we might in-
terpret Thatcher's policy conclusions as pointing toward a redistribution of
the state's resources, from welfare provision to law enforcement.

In this sense, she seems prepared to rearticulate and update two principles of Victorian welfare policy: first, the need to distinguish between the
"deserving" and "undeserving" poor on the basis of their behavior—a willingness to work when it is available, to accept responsibility for one's lot
in life, and to resist looking to place blame elsewhere; and second, the belief that assistance, whether it originates from private individuals or the
state, can have the effect of de-moralizing the poor by encouraging a dependency on others. In this context, Joel Krieger cites an opinion poll conducted in 1983, the year of Thatcher's call for a return to "Victorian values,"
which offers mixed support for her campaign to reform the welfare system.
On the one hand, his data shows a general consent for the universal provision of major welfare programs in education, health, and pensions, with
current levels of funding in each case needing either to be maintained or

120   increased; on the other hand, the numbers diminish in cases of support given to public housing tenants, the unemployed, single parents, and children, with only a third of respondents describing child welfare benefits as a universal provision and the same number favoring a cut in state spending in this area. Krieger's analysis suggests that such figures identify a growing discomfort with the redistributive goals of welfare and a readiness to distinguish between different population groups that deserve benefits differently; in its most basic form, he notes, the level of enthusiasm for universal provision in particular instances "corresponds simply to a rank ordering of the respondent's expectation that she/he will be a beneficiary."[17]

Such thinking identifies a range of social groups to which the normative subject does not and ideally will not belong, in the process seeming to stigmatize those that do for lacking the symbols of social success: a job, a mortgage, a wedding ring. If what is at stake here is the state's commitment to try to make good that lack, we need to keep in mind that such programs still find considerable support: for instance, more than two-thirds of those polled still considered child benefits a necessary provision of the state, with similar numbers arguing that levels of funding should be maintained or increased, while even greater support was registered for unemployment and single-parent benefits. What is significant is that such agreement does not extend to the idea that these benefits should be provided *universally*, in isolation from considerations of who might actually need them, even as the high levels of support for each individual program represent a rejection of the incipient moralism that would identify such people as inherently irresponsible or less deserving. Another survey cited by Peter Clarke indicates that "in 1977, before Thatcher came to power, 35% of voters thought that, if people were poor, their own lack of effort was probably to blame; but by 1985 that figure had fallen to 22%, and 50% now blamed outside circumstances."[18] On this evidence, the public under Thatcherism would seem to have been reluctant to place the blame on the poor themselves, especially when other economic and social explanations (such as high unemployment or a widening income disparity) were available and seemed more likely.

Largely as a result of its heavy-handed moralizing, Thatcherism was only partially successful in securing popular consent for a reduced role for the state in welfare provision, with the subsequent New Labour administration of Tony Blair better able to negotiate a balance between individual and governmental responsibilities.[19] We need to recall, however, that Thatcher's policy goal was never really a return to the minimalist state of the early Victorians as much as a shift in spending priorities; when it needed to be,

her government was ruthlessly centralizing and authoritarian, seeking (as   121
Stuart Hall argues) "to impose a new regime of social discipline and leadership 'from above' in a society increasingly experienced as rudderless and out
of control."[20] In key respects, her professed antistatist stance acted as a cover
under which this new activist role for government could be developed, enabling the administration to pose as being on the side of "the people"
against an imaginary power bloc, a government fighting against "the state."

One example from *The Downing Street Years* embodies this rhetorical
two-step. In the aftermath of the riots of 1981, a position paper emerging
from the government's Policy Unit described its general philosophy as follows: "This Government came to power asserting that it is the exercise of
responsibility which teaches self-discipline. But in the early stages of life it
is the experience of authority, when exerted fairly and consistently by
adults, which teaches young people how to exercise responsibility themselves. We have to learn to take orders before we learn to give them." An
ideology of individual freedom, then, but only in the context of a paternalistic authoritarianism that insists that there are right and wrong lessons
that first need to be absorbed. What follows from this passage is a discussion of education reform, which starts out advocating an increase in "parent power" and ends by putting forward the case for a centrally imposed
national curriculum and standardized testing, on the basis that too many
children are deficient in their understanding of "our country and society,
and our history and culture" (278). Later, this case is put more forcefully,
with the blame extended to "the new 'child-centered' teaching techniques,
the emphasis on imaginative engagement rather than learning facts, and
the modern tendency to blur the lines of discrete subjects and incorporate
them in wider, less definable entities like 'humanities,'" by which point the
emphasis has irreversibly shifted from the pole of freedom to that of discipline. In the process, the power of parents is reduced to the ability to recognize a child's progress through the results of "a nationally recognized
and reliably monitored system of testing," with the charge of defining useful knowledge and the best methods for its transmission entirely arrogated
to the central government. "The state," Thatcher concludes, "could not
just ignore what children learned: they were, after all, its future citizens and
we had a duty to them" (590), at which point she uncannily seems to echo
that staunch advocate of the Victorian state (and inspector of schools),
Matthew Arnold.

What sounded at the outset like a variation on the earlier-twentieth-
century nostalgia for the Victorians is thus more complicated, as Thatcher

122 in practice reversed her stated preference for less government and gained only partial consent for a renegotiation of the obligations of government that have accumulated with the growth of the welfare state. If, as I have suggested, she made some headway in opposing the abstract universalism underpinning modern bureaucracy, finding some support for distinguishing among population groups who might claim a greater or lesser entitlement to state assistance, this success was not underwritten by the more evangelical moralism that she and others would identify in Victorian social policy. Indeed, in contrast to her American counterparts, she had surprisingly little time or use for the voluntary sector or religious groups, which might be thought to connect the two central planks of welfare policy by taking over some of the burdens of the state and (in doing so) interjecting a moral discourse that preaches the need for personal reform. In many ways the dissonant authoritarianism of Thatcherism arises from her insistence that this language should also apply to government. In Raphael Samuel's characterization, her "Victorian values" are Methodist at heart, "invoking the plebeian virtues of self-reliance and self-help rather than the more patrician ones of chivalry and *noblesse oblige*," which means that philanthropic charity was cast as simply another form of do-goodism: "The 'caring' professions," Samuel notes, "with their heartland in the Welfare State, and their outriders in the churches and charities, were particularly suspect, protecting their privileges and comforts while pretending only to be concerned with others."[21] As we shall see, they play a very different role for neoconservatives in the United States, who are far more serious about reducing the scope of government and, as a consequence, are inevitably concerned about what other institutions might take its place, though even here it has proven extraordinarily difficult to imagine exactly how and on what basis such a transfer might occur.

Demoralization Then and Now: Gertrude Himmelfarb's U-Curve

In the epilogue to *The De-Moralization of Society*, the text in which she most explicitly advocates for a Thatcherite agenda, American historian Gertrude Himmelfarb ends with a graphic image to illustrate the resemblance she sees between the contemporary moment and Britain in the early nineteenth century. Drawing on the work of sociologist Christie Davis, she suggests that we could plot specific statistical information to produce a "U-curve model of deviance," with high levels of criminality and illegitimacy before about 1840 and after 1960 bookending a low point around the turn of the century.[22] (In fact, Himmelfarb suggests—and Davis has

agreed—that it looks more like a "J-curve," with dramatic upturns in both   123
categories over recent decades).[23] From such an image it is clear that she
sees the Victorian period as superior to what preceded and followed it,
with its positive influence continuing far into the twentieth century. Unlike Thatcher's more general invocation of values that might be "perennial"
or hegemonic up until World War II, Himmelfarb seems really to mean
that we should return to the Victorians themselves in order to reverse this
apparent upturn of deviancy.

It is, of course, easy to argue with her selection of statistical categories
and to insist that other patterns (and perhaps *any* letter of the alphabet?)
could be produced by choosing different criteria. The contemporary moment would certainly fare better if we took literacy rates as the key differ-
ential, say, or life expectancy; and what about incidents of child abuse,
which Himmelfarb offers as an example of a crime that has been "defined
up" so that "the normal becomes deviant," implying not only that contemporary figures might be too high (because "over-reported") but also that it
was once considered acceptable (234–36)? We might also wonder about
her insistence on linking crime and illegitimacy, as "those two powerful
indexes of social pathology" (252), especially when it so neatly echoes
Thatcher's own gendered division between riotous young men and pregnant, unmarried young women. As Stefan Collini points out, it is questiona-
ble whether "illegitimacy" can mean the same thing at such disparate historical moments: if, as he notes, recent figures suggest that 77 percent of
unmarried British mothers were still cohabiting five years later, then "rates
of non-nuptial childbearing are of limited value in telling us about the
number of adults involved in child-rearing."[24] By the same token, as Himmelfarb herself concedes, the single-parent family was rare in Victorian
Britain because divorce was, which meant that the greater problem "was
not the absence of a father but the presence of one who was irregularly
employed and regularly drunk and abusive" (42). Already, the finite numbers and direct correspondences come to seem a lot less instructive and the
entire enterprise of "learning from history" more complicated than Himmelfarb allows. As David Bromwich cautions in his review of her book,
"our degree of disorder (the staggering rate of out-of-wedlock births, for
example: five times that of England in 1870) may indicate a difference of kind
from the Victorians. Quantitative change does at some point turn quali-
tative, and it is senseless to think of the inner city today as Dickensian."[25]

That particular thought is far from Himmelfarb's mind, however, as
she sets out to reverse a popular image of Victorian poverty that she sees

124   as partly drawn from reading Dickens or seeing his novels adapted on-
screen. Her controversial discussion of the Poor Law workhouse, to which
I shall return in a moment, forms a central component of a wide-ranging
revisionist effort to replace that image with a more benevolent one. Crucial here is a careful finessing of the work of Charles Booth, whose massive
study of *Life and Labour of the People in London* (1889) gave empirical weight to
turn-of-the-century understandings of the problems of urban poverty.
Breaking the population of London into eight classes, Booth's statistical
study revealed that 7.5 percent of Londoners were casual laborers, living a
hand-to-mouth existence, with 1.2 percent below them in the ranks of the
hardcore criminal. Himmelfarb rightly concludes from this statistic that
Booth "was refuting the image of a sodden, 'submerged' tenth of the population" (38), a charge first leveled by H. M. Hyndman of the Social De-
mocratic Federation, but this interpretation conveniently sidesteps Booth's
more damning revelation that around 31 percent lived below the poverty
line, a number that included those he designated as irregular wage earners.
Himmelfarb is, of course, more interested in poverty as an index of immorality than of economic destitution, which helps to explain her emphasis on the very bottom of Booth's categories, but she is also prepared to mas-
sage his numbers to get the desired result, arguing in a later footnote that
"his 'poverty' was clearly not that of the early- or mid-Victorian periods. A
better basis for comparison would be his class of the 'very poor,'" by means
of which his original 31 percent magically drops to 7.5 percent (137–38).

This statistical manipulation is consistent with Himmelfarb's wider
rewriting of the period, exemplifying an untroubled readiness to recontex-
tualize and rephrase the firsthand testimony of Victorians themselves to
suit a contemporary neoconservative political agenda.[26] Perhaps the most
glaring instance is her reference to popular theories of "degeneration" toward the end of the century, which would seem to indicate a generalized
perception among those actually living that conditions were deteriorating,
especially in the urban centers. For Himmelfarb the emergence of such a
theory is both ironic and counterintuitive, however, given her own understanding of rising economic and moral conditions at this time, and the explanation she offers is predictably torturous: "In view of all the evidence
to the contrary," she speculates, "it is not too fanciful to suppose that the
alarm about physical and moral deterioration was itself a reflection of the
rise in aims and expectations among the people as a whole and more especially among social commentators" (44). This statement is in many respects a mirror-image inversion of crude applications of the work of

Michel Foucault, which can find the evils of panoptic surveillance lurking 125
beneath the most innocuous instances of Enlightenment rationality; for
if, as Fredric Jameson famously insisted of the latter, it "would seem slowly
and inexorably to eliminate any possibility of the *negative* as such," then
something similar might be said of Himmelfarb's optimistic variation,
which can presumably convert any critical commentary into evidence of
social improvement.[27]

In her critical review of *The De-Moralization of Society*, Marilynne Robinson makes a similar point about its reliance on selective statistics to counteract a considerable body of firsthand evidence about Victorian social
conditions. Citing a passage in which an "illegitimacy ratio" of 4.5 percent
for East London is adduced to counteract another of the "many myths"
often "shared by many Victorians" (this time "the vision of the Victorian
city as a hell-hole of degradation and iniquity"), Robinson asks what evi-
dentiary status such apparent facts can have, when "[b]y a single statistic,
taken to the first decimal place, Victorians such as Dickens, Disraeli, and
Carlyle are proved wrong about the cities they lived in and wrote about."[28]
This is not the only place where the authority of Dickens comes into question, moreover, since the most controversial chapter of Himmelfarb's book
takes aim at that most reviled of nineteenth-century institutions, the Poor
Law workhouse, arguing that "[t]he Dickensian image of the poor law, which
associated relief with the workhouse and the workhouse with naked, starv-
ing children, drunken matrons, and sadistic overseers, was far from the reality even in the early part of the century, still less later" (140).[29] She pauses
repeatedly to insist that they were not entirely benevolent institutions, either, and hardly above criticism, but it is not always clear on what grounds
she would criticize them. At one point, for instance, she elaborates on
workhouse inhabitants' own grievances, concerning "the separation of the
family within the house, the segregation from the community, the loss of
liberty, and, above all, the stigma attached to the house" (134–35), but
these would not be her complaints; indeed, the chapter ends by *endorsing*
any approach to poverty that "would stigmatize and censure violations" of
her own core Victorian values of work, independence, responsibility, and
respectability (142).

Elsewhere, her key charge against the New Poor Law is that it was
grounded in a philosophy that was "excessively rationalistic, utilitarian,
[and] single-minded" (140) in applying a strictly material workhouse test
to all claimants alike, so that the right to welfare was reduced to a simple
question of economics. I shall return to this point later, but first I want to

126   explore the grounds of Himmelfarb's objection, especially as they relate to Margaret Thatcher's thinking about the responsibilities of the state and the character of individual subjects. The "workhouse test" insisted, against the prevailing practices of the early nineteenth century, that relief be provided only within the workhouse itself, and at a rate that would be less than the lowest wages outside, with the idea that the "able-bodied" would inevitably prefer the latter and only the truly needy would apply for aid. The thinking here is predicated on the larger moral distinction that would isolate the "deserving" from the "undeserving" poor, as those in the former category would inevitably prefer low-wage employment outside of the workhouse, but the problem for Himmelfarb is that the test is still too indiscriminate in its action because it takes material rather than moral conditions as its criteria for determining eligibility. Like Thatcher's, her philosophy of welfare always begins from the individual and her/his personal qualities or failings, as opposed to the state, which inevitably begins to anticipate a bureaucratic machine as soon as it tries to fix a universal baseline for determining fitness for relief, even allowing that actual levels would vary according to regional economic circumstances.

The situation was complicated because, as Himmelfarb acknowledges, a parallel system of charitable philanthropy coexisted with the New Poor Law, which meant that "[i]f the able-bodied managed to stay out of the workhouse, it was not only because they preferred their liberty at all costs but because there were alternative means of relief" (135). This presumably should undermine what she takes to be the unmitigated good of the workhouse system (that only those who really needed help would choose to go there), but such a charitable supplement is instead seen as helping to make good the moral deficiencies of state provision, being "motivated by a genuine conviction that poor relief, unlike charity, had a demoralizing effect upon the poor and a deleterious effect on the economy" (138). Since this is surely Himmelfarb's conviction as well—given her enthusiastic paraphrase of T. H. Green, to the effect that "the state has the duty as well as the right to promote morality" (152)—this would logically suggest either a redefinition of the state along Thatcherite lines, as more judgmental and intrusive in matters previously deemed "personal," or its withdrawal from the business of welfare provision entirely in favor of private charity, a force that Thatcher herself treated (as we have seen) with considerable suspicion.[30]

It is presumably testimony to the scale and complexity of comprehensive benefits provision that Himmelfarb and other neoconservatives have held back from proposing the full-scale abolition of the welfare state, even

as they criticize it for having "divorced welfare—no longer called 'relief'—   127
from moral sanctions and imperatives," in the process rendering it "difficult
to pass any moral judgments or impose any moral conditions upon the recipients of relief" (242). As was the case with Thatcher's statements on the
issue, it is hard to see how the problem might be redressed once we begin
from such a diagnosis. Speaking to Mark Gerson, Himmelfarb characterizes her position as "committed to the New Deal kind of welfare state—by
present terms, a very minimal welfare state," adding that "Social Security is
something we regard as a very good thing."[31] *The De-Moralization of Society*
also spells out the inadequacy of relying solely on private charity or a free
market economy, which "does not automatically produce the moral and
social goods that [conservatives] value" (246). As a result, perhaps the
most that could be proposed at the present time is the kind of compromise
position that Stephen Davies has outlined, in which mutual aid societies
administer welfare payments that are directly funded by government taxation—although such a proposal suggests an awkward and probably un-
workable interface between a universalist principle of financing and a selective distribution of revenues, and risks exacerbating the popular resistance
(noted by Joel Krieger) to paying for programs that only benefit others.[32]

If this discussion suggests that the horizon for even the most conservative positions in the welfare reform debates remains a commitment to
some form of centralized state funding, then it is not clear for what ultimate purpose Himmelfarb has undertaken her comparison of present-day
Anglo-America with its Victorian counterpart, or exactly what policy implications she intends for contemporary legislators. As David Bromwich
suggests, whatever hints her book contains emerge "less from its explicit
argument than from a certain shading of style and the ease of the past-and-
present structure," with Newt Gingrich for one appearing to think that its
suggestions were entirely self-evident—it simply "isn't that complicated,"
he concluded from reading the book, to "re-establish" values and moral
leadership.[33] This may well be true, but it does not in itself dictate a future
course for welfare policy, any more than does his or Himmelfarb's invoking of the goal of a minimalist state or their nostalgic revisiting of a time
"before the welfare state." Any such efforts to summarize the past with an
eye to present interests is, as I hope this book has argued, inevitably prone
to charges of oversimplification and bias, and may be preferable only to
an alternative that would ignore history entirely. With such cautions in
mind, though, I want to suggest in what follows that the conclusions that
Thatcher, Himmelfarb, and Gingrich prefer to draw from the welfare debates

128   of the nineteenth century are not supported by the historical record. On my reading, the broad direction of those debates (including the contributions of some of Himmelfarb's favorite commentators) actually points in the opposite direction, making a stronger case for professionalized bureaucrats than for charitable amateurs, and for universalist criteria for determining beneficiaries instead of the moral index of personal character.

Victorian Reformers and the Welfare of the State

In summarizing his objections to the Himmelfarb thesis, Stefan Collini suggests that it is more plausible "to characterize the political thought and policy-making of the century between, roughly, 1880 and 1980" as exhibiting "a sustained, if uneven, and often inconsistent, attempt to remedy the inadequacies of [an] individualist approach" to social policy that insists first and foremost on viewing the need for aid as a personalized moral failing.[34] The best recent study of the nineteenth-century state, Lauren Goodlad's *Victorian Literature and the Victorian State* (2003), traces out the shifting relations between two broad approaches to issues of poverty and welfare dating back to the New Poor Law of 1834: an idealist view that held to a basically prescriptive view of human character as subject to moral influence, and a materialist view that was based on "a descriptive view of character" and, as such, "implied a comparatively limited view of individual improvement" while holding greater hope for benefits on a mass scale through government intervention.[35] While seeming to disavow a simple model of unidirectional change from the former to the latter, in favor of a more complex genealogy that sees the two approaches as less polarized than they first appear, Goodlad's language nonetheless betrays an instinct that the larger historical shift is in favor of a statist approach, suggesting, for instance, that her aim is to explore "Britain's distinctly liberal *path to* modern governance" by adumbrating the ways in which "industrial Britain had *inevitably to discover* suitable rationalizing alternatives" to a traditional "liberal ideal of mutual relations between autonomous actors" (23–24; emphasis added). I would agree that only within such a framework does it make sense to talk about the persistence of an alternative to welfare based on individual morality, often rooted at the core of a seemingly value-neutral approach that might seem to dismiss such considerations as entirely irrelevant—although this is saying something very different from Himmelfarb's stress on a secularized religious impulse as constituting the Hegelian *Geist* of the Victorian period.[36]

One of the best-known Victorian advocates for a strong state was Matthew Arnold, who argued in *Culture and Anarchy* (1869) that it is one

force capable of transcending narrow class- and self-interest and of articulating our amalgamated "best" rather than our merely "ordinary" selves,
"controlling individual wills in the name of an interest wider than that of
individuals."[37] Rather surprisingly, he offers as an emblem of this potential
the figure of the sovereign prince, whom he imagines as "the expression of
the collective nation, and a sort of constituted witness to its best mind";
perhaps less surprising, given his career as an inspector of schools, is the
example he gives of how royal patronage functions in the German educational system, in which "[t]he Sovereign, as his position raises him above
many prejudices and littlenesses, and as he can always have at his disposal
the best advice, has evident advantages over private founders in well planning and directing a school" (79). By contrast, the British system, as Arnold
saw it, left education in the hands of religious and professional groups, with
the predictable result that the best self always gives way to the narrowly
defined interests of the ordinary self. As a result, "[t]he Licensed Victuallers
or the Commercial Travellers propose to make a school for their children,"
whereas it was clear to Arnold that—in contrast to the more universaliz-
ing national interest supposedly held by the state—"to have a sheer school
of Licensed Victuallers' children, or a sheer school of Commercial Travellers' children, and to bring them all up, not only at home but at school
too, in a kind of odour of licensed victualism or of bagmanism, is not a wise
training to give to these children" (80). The net result, he suggests, is a
kind of atheism, with "no such thing at all as a best self and a right reason
having claim to paramount authority," working in tandem with a "quietism"
that presumes that each of the ordinary selves represented through their
respective educational institutions should thereby be seen as "pretty equal
in value" (81).

Arnold's enthusiasm for a national curriculum, famously based in what
he saw as the self-evident claim of culture to represent "the best which has
been thought and said in the world" (5), follows from these premises, since
the state not only represents the sole body capable of transcending self-
interest but is also well placed as a result to prescribe a sound basis for edu-
cating the population as a whole. As Steven Marcus wryly observes, in
commenting on the relevance of *Culture and Anarchy* today, twentieth-
century experience has cast considerable doubt on Arnold's specific faith
in state-run education, while nonetheless confirming his general belief that
the state would be "an inescapable fact, and an ever-expanding one, in all
our lives."[38] I earlier noted that Margaret Thatcher's rhetorical slide from advocating "parent power" to a national curriculum and standardized testing

130 ironically placed her on the side of Arnold in educational debates, and it is now clear why they should seem like strange bedfellows. After all, it was something very like "parent power" that he set himself against, believing that it would simply replicate existing class interests and antagonisms; and he is clearly not a believer in the minimalist state, wanting instead to expand its reach and power, if necessary by using repressive measures to enforce its supposedly disinterested understanding of the collective will.

Reading Arnold offers little comfort, then, to conservative efforts to return to the individual as the focal point of social policy, especially as his view of character formation falls, in Goodlad's taxonomy, on the descriptive rather than prescriptive side. While it is clear that education represents its best hope for individual and collective improvement, *Culture and Anarchy* concludes on a cautionary note, proclaiming that "[w]e, indeed, pretend to educate no one, for we are still engaged in trying to educate ourselves" (141). Arnold's is, in many respects, a rigidly deterministic account that condenses class and character into nearly synonymous concepts: to be born into, and especially to be *educated by*, a class is thus to adopt its narrowly conceived worldview, with the best prospect seeming to be that one might come to represent its "virtuous mean" and not its "excess" (66). He allows for one exception, however, predictably enough to account for people like himself who claim to have broken with the orthodoxies of their respective classes and thus can begin to generalize a national interest in their place. This is the category of the "aliens," by which Arnold refers to "persons who are mainly led, not by their class spirit, but by a general *humane* spirit, by the love of human perfection" (73; emphasis in original). Since their number is "capable of being diminished or augmented," presumably by the influence of education, they might represent a source of leadership in potential conflict with Arnold's naïve faith in monarchy; yet this is precisely the scenario that he actively disavows, arguing that "men of culture are just the class of responsible beings in this community of ours who cannot properly, at present, be entrusted with power"—in part, we can assume, because they would be unlikely to be recognized and elected in a class society (29).

This last hesitation would seem to clear the way for the state as a default form of authority, embodying what Arnold elsewhere notoriously termed "force till right is ready."[39] In its vision of the cultured class as déclassé iconoclasts working on the perfection of self, *Culture and Anarchy* also forestalls what we might see as a parallel development to the state during the nineteenth century, the rise of a professionalized bureaucracy of experts, even if Arnold himself would represent one such figure in the field of education. In nineteenth-century debates over welfare this issue constituted one persistent fault line separating the advocates of charitable philanthropy by private, concerned citizens from those who favored the state's provision of services via the intermediary action of qualified social workers. When the Royal Commission on the Poor Laws, meeting between 1905 and 1909, famously produced no consensus for welfare reform, it seemed to reproduce this antagonism in the published opposition of a Majority Report—which favored the individual casework approach of the Charity Organisation Society (COS)—and a Minority Report supporting the Fabian Society's preference for centralized state provision. In another sense, however, as Lauren Goodlad makes clear, this was actually a narrower argument about whether state officials could adequately fulfill the pastoral obligations formerly associated with private and church-based philanthropy. To the extent that the COS saw the caseworker as "a bulwark against bureaucratic impersonality" (202–4), it would have been fighting a losing battle, one it had already partially conceded as it increasingly sought to professionalize its charity officers.[40]

The other key principle underwriting the COS approach, and one that makes it more attractive to a neoconservative like Gertrude Himmelfarb, was its insistence on upholding morality as a key criterion for deciding who should get charitable assistance, in line with the Society's opposition to the "indiscriminate" benefits offered by the state. Here, though, the recognition of widespread levels of poverty and unemployment during the 1870s and 1880s did most to undermine such a selective approach, especially given its need for face-to-face encounters with (and intimate personal knowledge of) those in need. If one possible compromise was to replicate that approach on a mass scale by credentialing an army of paid social workers, the need for centralized state action nonetheless required that the firsthand evidence amassed should initially be aggregated in order to provide a general accounting of the problem. The methods employed by Charles Booth in his study of the *Life and Labour of the People in London* are exemplary here, for his trained volunteers by necessity had to work by extrapolation to derive large-scale social patterns from limited empirical evidence. Booth described his procedure as resting on the principle that "the facts should be reduced to some common measure of validity by being passed, as it were, through a sieve which should make it possible not only to reject the false and hold back the improbable, but also to tone down exaggeration" by relying "first and chiefly on mere average and consensus

132   resulting from the great number and variety of my source of information."[41] The basis for the study's geographical breakdown of poverty, for instance, ultimately rested on the reports of sixty-six School Board visitors in East London, with Booth proceeding on the assumptions that there would be a consistent ratio of married men with and without children of school age in particular occupations and a proportionate number of older and younger children across the population of the capital as a whole.

In this sense, the sheer size of these studies—magnified street by street and borough by borough—militated against a moral reading of poverty, and it is understandable why Booth was increasingly drawn to the analysis of large-scale factors in the internal structure of the professions themselves as the key indicators of poverty, as well as to an impersonal bureaucracy as the best solution to social problems that resisted face-to-face solutions. It is true that he was extremely reluctant to abandon the moral principles underwriting the 1834 Poor Law, even as his research and testimony before the Royal Commission discussing its reform helped to bring about its decisive modification; like a good ameliorist, he believed in the category of character as a decisive factor in human development, and he shared some of the suspicions against indiscriminate almsgiving that drove the COS and other welfare reformers of the period. At such times, he can read like a typical Victorian moralist, working back from prior assumptions to empirical evidence; at others, though, he proceeded like a rigid statistician who refuses to privilege theory over facts and who suspected that his studies proliferated at such length due to his own failure to reach any definitive conclusions.[42]

Each of these tendencies is represented in the conclusion to Booth's final volume, with its opening invocation of "the dark side of the picture" in which lives are "cursed by drink, brutality, and vice, and loaded down with ignorance and poverty" that religion and government have been equally incapable of ameliorating. Booth outlines twin aims—both "to raise the general level of existence" and "to increase the proportion of those who know how to use aright the means they have"—before seeming to privilege "Individual Responsibility" as the key factor in improvement; but then the stress shifts away from the particular and toward the most generalized efforts of governmental administration, in support of which "facts are still needed." Somewhat defensively, and in the guise of the pure statistician, he closes by commenting that "I have sought, however imperfectly, to show what is being done to ameliorate its conditions, and have suggested some directions in which advance might be made; but this last was no part of the original design, which was, solely, to observe and chronicle the actual, 133 leaving remedies to others. To this attitude I would now revert. For the treatment of disease, it is first necessary to establish the facts of its character, extent and symptoms" (338–39). It seems here as if Booth is consciously backtracking from even the modest policy solutions he has proposed, while also acknowledging that the form of the inquiry itself has led him to propose them. In doing so, I would argue, he also undercut the emphases on moral character and personal responsibility with which he began. While still maintaining that lack of employment and personal habit were both contributing factors in the causation of poverty, Booth consistently endorsed governmental action at the expense of individual initiatives or religious efforts, suggesting that for the eradication of structural problems in society, "voluntary effort is almost useless, for unless the inquiries spring from genuine energy of administration grounded in goodwill, no benefit can result"; at best, he argued, voluntary associations might draw governmental attention to their existence (287–88).

This viewpoint makes him less useful than Himmelfarb might think as a witness in support of her own cause of reinjecting morality into modern welfare debates, and puts him closer instead to the mainstream of late-Victorian thinking about the individual and the state.[43] Goodlad, for instance, argues that the New Poor Law's efforts to codify a uniform "workhouse test" to determine eligibility for relief were already working in practice to undermine "the idea of character as an antimaterialist concept of human individuality" (83), in a process that only intensified as a result of the "sheer scale, pace, and multiplicity of civilized social relations" (29). The British state did not grow anywhere near as rapidly as that of France, which already had close to a million civil servants by mid-century, as compared to only 280,000 in Britain by the onset of World War I; instead, as Goodlad notes, the pastoral function so cherished by the COS was gradually transferred to government services.[44] As part of this shift, as I have suggested, an increasing professionalism simultaneously deemphasized the moral component of the pastoral relationship (even among charity caseworkers), thereby preparing the groundwork for a host of value-neutral and universalist measures that were instituted by the New Liberal governments of the early twentieth century and that formed the core of the modern welfare state.

In 1886, for instance, the Liberal (and later Unionist) politician Joseph Chamberlain set out a revised rationale for welfare relief, arguing that aid should be granted to the able-bodied during periods of deep recession in the form of "work which will not involve the stigma of pauperism," as was

134   the case for stone-breaking or oakum-picking under the earlier system.[45] In doing so, he placed the responsibility for unemployment with society rather than the individual, thereby charging the authorities with the task of understanding local and national economic trends; indeed, the 1905 Unemployed Workmen Act, which grew out of the Chamberlain Circular, specifically mandated that local distress committees "shall make themselves acquainted with the conditions of labor in their area" as a basis for judging applications for relief, with the understanding that unemployment was often beyond the control of the unemployed themselves.[46] The year 1895 saw a Royal Commission take up the question of national insurance, helping to produce two significant legislative programs that together undermined the old distinction between the "deserving" and "undeserving" poor: noncontributory old-age pensions, first introduced in the 1908 budget (but initially still limited to those earning below a certain income threshold and excluding "paupers") and the 1911 National Insurance Act, which for the first time provided what Goodlad terms "nonstigmatic support for the unemployed" in exchange for compulsory contributions (234). In education, a 1902 Act created a system of public secondary schools, with compulsory meals and medical inspection added in 1906–7.

As Harold Perkin has argued, a crucial element in converting such piecemeal reforms into a coherent welfare state came when a redistributive principle of taxation was introduced to supplement what is otherwise a "horizontal" exchange "from the young, healthy and employed to the same people when old, sick or jobless."[47] With graduated income tax and death duties, the New Liberal administrations of the first decade of the twentieth century secured a change that Perkin sees as implicit in the steady process of professionalizing government and welfare that extended back into the late-Victorian period. In defining this paradigm shift, he mentions "the divergence of the professional from the capitalist social ideal, [and] the separation of the professional view that the rights of persons and the welfare of the community came before the rights of property, from the capitalist view that free and unfettered competition between political and legal equals led to prosperity for all" (140). Even if it was driven by a perception of national economic decline, in competition with Germany, Japan, and the United States, this response amounted to a fundamental shift in the state's relations to capital and labor, with an increasing readiness to intervene and redirect market forces (through, for instance, the piloting of labor exchanges in 1908) and to destigmatize those who would suffer from its failures.

What also emerged was a reformulated conception of citizenship, in which abstract social rights dominate over class interests. In the words of L. T. Hobhouse, the holder of the first British chair in sociology and an influential New Liberal theorist, the role of the state (at least in theory) was "to secure conditions upon which its citizens are able to win by their own efforts all that is necessary to full civic efficiency. It is not for the State to feed, house, or clothe them. It is for the State to take care that the economic conditions are such that the normal man who is not defective in mind or body or will can by useful labour feed, house, and clothe himself and his family."[48] In another version of this revised social contract, William Beveridge suggested that each citizen be offered a "place in free industry," which in turn would be predicated on "full employment and average earnings up to a definite minimum," although elsewhere the more punitive moral language of the Poor Law reemerged when he argued that those who refuse this offer "are not citizens in fact and should not be so in right"—disenfranchisement being "in this view . . . part of the 'stigma' of pauperism."[49] At moments like this, it is clear that the New Liberalism never fully dispensed with the moralism of the Poor Law, as the stakes for refusing consent to its model of normative citizenship are raised significantly. It might equally be argued, however, that those stakes are sufficiently high as to effectively rule out any potential resistance to its vision of the respective responsibilities of the state and its citizens. At any rate, Beveridge's advocacy of the targeted disenfranchisement of such stubborn resistors is not one that was ever realized, as Britain belatedly moved toward universal suffrage after World War I.

The name of Beveridge is important here as the person most closely associated with the post-1945 Labour government's introduction of legislative measures—including (within its first year in office) the National Health Service, family allowance, and national insurance—that collectively represent the heart of the modern welfare state. Forty years earlier, he had been a key figure in the New Liberal administration, arguing for labor exchanges and unemployment insurance. He is also a product of the late-Victorian university settlement movement, having served from 1903 to 1905 as a subwarden at London's Toynbee Hall, an institution that encouraged face-to-face interaction between undergraduates (most notably those from Oxford) and the East End poor. As such, Toynbee Hall stands as a monument to the philanthropic approach to issues of social deprivation, finding a predictable champion in Gertrude Himmelfarb's revisionist work on Victorian welfare. Its founders, Arnold Toynbee and Samuel Barnett,

136   she argues, "believed that social legislation and government administration were no substitute for the kind of private, voluntary educational and cultural institution represented by Toynbee Hall," which operated on the assumption of "shared common values and aspirations, and thus a common citizenship" (158–59).

However, her account gives neither the entire picture of Toynbee Hall nor a suggestion of its lasting importance, which consisted as much in the training of an entire generation of politicians and social legislators who would oversee the development of the twentieth-century welfare state.[50] Toynbee himself argued that "[w]here people are unable to provide a thing for themselves, and that thing is of *primary social importance*, . . . the State should interfere and provide it for them,"[51] and we can view the history of the institution that bears his name as similarly moving away from a mainly individualist focus on personal responsibility and face-to-face contact, recognizing in its place the increasing priority that was granted to governmental action by Booth and growing sections of the Liberal Party. As Standish Meacham notes, while Barnett began his work in Whitechapel in full accord with the principles of the COS and continued to concentrate his own efforts locally, "he grew increasingly to believe that the problems of poverty and unemployment were not local problems, but ones demanding the attention and intervention of the state." Indeed, his insistence on ascribing "at least a portion of the misery in East London to environment rather than to individual moral failing alone" brought him into increasing conflict with the COS throughout the 1890s, as did his support for proposals for the centralized provision of health, education, and welfare relief—including old-age pensions and unemployment benefits. Beveridge later extended Barnett's move away from the strict localism of face-to-face connection, proposing to see "the welfare of the state as a whole . . . in a scientific way," while rejecting "the saving power of culture and mission and isolated good feeling" as entirely inadequate responses to large-scale social problems.[52]

In fact, it is telling to note how many of the architects of the British welfare state were themselves the products of an alternative tradition of private charity work that modern neoconservatives would like to see as supplanting or supplementing it. Another who shared Beveridge's growing dissatisfaction with the settlement house model was C. F. G. Masterman, who was a rising politician in Asquith's New Liberal government that came to power in 1908. Seven years earlier, while still living in the Albany Dwellings in Camberwell, which were connected with the Cambridge Univer-

sity Settlement, Masterman contributed to a collective New Liberal statement called *The Heart of the Empire* (1901), which hoped to capitalize on concerns about the disastrous Boer War campaign to focus attention on domestic poverty. The first essay, Masterman's "Realities at Home," delivers a
devastating critique of the university settlements, which it characterizes as
an idea whose time has passed, somewhere between "the Age of Slum-
ming" and "the Age of Philanthropy." "For my own part," he noted,

> I realise that the call has failed. The Universities and the cultured
> classes, as a whole, care little about the matter. The wave of en-
> thusiasm which created the modern settlement has ceased to ad-
> vance; the buildings remain and a few energetic toilers, and the
> memory of a great hope. . . . In all the London settlements, among
> over four million of toilers, there are not a hundred resident male
> workers; of these many will not stay for less than a year's residence.
> I cannot believe that this is the machinery destined to bridge the
> ever-widening gulf between class and class, and to initiate the new
> heavens and the new earth.[53]

The Heart of the Empire is thin on positive counterproposals, but the best in-
dication of what Masterman saw as taking the place of the settlement movement can be found in the political work he engaged in while in government:
working alongside Lloyd George and Winston Churchill in developing
model legislation for unemployment and health insurance programs.

The East London Labour Party politician George Lansbury cast a similar judgment on the ineffectiveness of the settlement movement, while at
the same time pointing to the unintended result of redirecting its participants' focus toward centralized solutions. Its main consequence, he noted
ironically, was "the filling up of the bureaucracy of government and administration with men and women who went to the East End full of enthusiasm and zeal for the welfare of the masses, and discovered the advancement of their own interests and the interests of the poor were best served
by leaving East London to stew in its own juice while they became members of parliament, cabinet ministers, civil servants . . ." (quoted in Perkin,
131). If this seems excessively cynical about the ultimate effects of their
work for the East End poor, it surely offers no support to Gertrude Himmelfarb's desire to revalue the settlement movement as a model for social
interactions between the classes that she sees as potentially superior to state
welfare because it was privately funded and based in face-to-face encounters,

138   thereby providing an opportunity for the more privileged to serve as moral examples for the less fortunate.

The redirection of that original (but short-lived) enthusiasm and energy into a longer-term project of shaping an inclusive, universal welfare system is consistent with a redefinition of the responsibilities of the state that dates back at least as far as Arnold's *Culture and Anarchy* and gains momentum with the appearance of large-scale sociological studies such as Booth's. In such a context, it is surely misleading to think of the Victorian period as one that was defined by a preference for a minimalist state, or to view present calls for a reduction in its obligations as consistent with a return to so-called Victorian values. Instead, it may be more accurate to rethink issues of periodization and forego such simple sloganeering in favor of a nuanced historical account that would show a developing rationale for—and willingness to support—the component elements of the modern welfare state, gathering momentum in the last third of the nineteenth century. Rather than taking 1945 as the key historical break (as Thatcher does), we might instead view it, as Gareth Stedman Jones has done, as "the last and most glorious flowering of late Victorian liberal philanthropy" and thus as "testif[ying] to a continuity of assumptions from the days of pre-1914 progressive liberal imperialism."[54] This would certainly help to explain Tony Blair's frequent invocations of Gladstone as his prime ministerial role model, as well as the supposed inspiration he has drawn from New Liberal theorists like Hobhouse and J. A. Hobson.[55]

For all of his faults, Blair understands that it is important, both in practice and rhetoric, for government in the twenty-first century to work with the legacies of the twentieth, instead of suggesting that progress can be accomplished on the basis of a revived Victorianism. As I have tried to argue, Britain in the nineteenth century was not only necessarily a complex phenomenon, and thus ill-suited to reductive formulae and summary, but also created the theoretical and practical conditions for the besieged modern state. Representing it as only the repository of positive moral values, or as the simple obverse and antidote to a perceived modern immorality, is to oversimplify history and to contradict much of the eyewitness testimony of the Victorians themselves. Most crucially, as I shall suggest in chapter 5, it misrepresents their understanding of the nature of society itself, as a network consisting of something more than just agglomerated individuals. Ultimately, it is this understanding that is threatened in the neoconservative discourse on welfare reform, and was underscored by a system that insisted on mutual responsibilities—indeed, one that was *systematic* to the extent

that it saw that individuals could not (and should not) be required to fend 139
for themselves or for others on a purely voluntary basis. As a "Victorian"
inheritance, this principle is one that seems worth defending, extending,
and—if necessary—reviving.

Other Victorians and the
Neo-Dickensian Novel

CHAPTER FIVE

Aside from her call for a return to "Victorian values," the other comment by Margaret Thatcher that was of most interest to cultural critics was her public statement that there was "no such thing as society." Instead, as she went on to insist in *The Downing Street Years,* "There are individual men and women, and there are families. And no government can do anything except through people, and people must look to themselves first. It's our duty to look after ourselves first and then to look after our neighbour."[1] This insight is linked in her memoirs, through a more general belief in personal as opposed to collective solutions, with her Victorian ancestors, even as it can sound very much like the Bloomsbury Group's oppositional, anti-Victorian championing of the sovereign individual—for, as I have tried to show, the nineteenth century has been viewed just as much as an age of collectivism as one of laissez-faire individualism. Put positively, the case can be made (as I suggested in chapter 4) that its legacy involves the recognition that large-scale social problems cannot be addressed at the level of the individual and instead require the action of the state; put negatively, it conjures the specter of a bureaucracy that inevitably operates against the interests of its citizens, as the oppressive machinery of government that troubled Carlyle, Arnold, and the Romantics long before modern-day neoconservatives.

Both implications can be found in Dickens, who perhaps stood in the 141 twentieth century as the most representative cultural emblem of the nineteenth. Alongside Thackeray, he was said to mean nothing to Leonard Woolf and the Bloomsbury circle, "or rather they stood for an era, a way of life, a system of morals against which we were in revolt."[2] E. M. Forster had more sympathy with the novelist's humanism yet still held him up (in 1927's *Aspects of the Novel*) as the master of the flat character, "no thicker than a gramophone record"; elsewhere, assessing developments in English prose between the wars, Forster suggested that Dickens saw the world in terms of "absolute good and evil," a view that was hard to sustain after Einstein and Freud.[3] By the time of David Lean's celebrated film adaptations of Dickens in the 1940s, as Raphael Samuel has noted, an image of "the Victorian as a time of oppression and fear" had been fixed in the popular imagination: thus, Miss Havisham in Lean's *Great Expectations* (1946) personified "a witch-like emblem of nineteenth-century claustrophobia, while the setting of *Oliver Twist* [1948] helped to fasten the epithet 'Dickensian' to slum housing." Appearing at what Samuel terms "the summit of some three decades of modernist revolt,"[4] these films acted in much the same way as contemporary heritage cinema to sum up the past and its distance from the present, only without the keynote of nostalgia that predominates in Merchant Ivory productions.

Dickens's reputation, if it ever needed it, has been fully rehabilitated in the intervening years, in part through a succession of stage, film, and television adaptations. Perhaps more surprising has been his growing influence on contemporary novelists, including Salman Rushdie, John Irving, Peter Carey, Sarah Waters, and Zadie Smith.[5] In a discussion of Smith's *White Teeth* (2000), for instance, James Wood identifies "the big, ambitious novel" as a new genre of fiction that traces its ancestry back to Dickens, whom he terms "the overwhelming influence on postwar fiction, especially postwar British fiction."[6] In spite of that last clause, Wood's examples are almost all Americans—such as Thomas Pynchon, Don DeLillo, and David Foster Wallace—but a similar development of the "neo-Dickensian" novel has been prophesized for British and Anglophone fiction at least since the success of *Midnight's Children* in 1981, after which (as Kazuo Ishiguro noted) "everyone was looking for other Rushdies."[7] With Rushdie or Zadie Smith, a recognizable stylistic inheritance from Dickens in terms of characterization, plot, narrative persona, and sheer scale is overlaid onto a postcolonial politics that seeks to foreground the repressed connections between Britain and its imperial possessions, and to rewrite the canonical British

142   novel so as to acknowledge its submerged colonial subtexts. I shall return
to this point later, in my discussion of Peter Carey's Australian rewriting of
Great Expectations in 1997's *Jack Maggs*. First, however, I want to consider
what it meant for fiction, in Britain and elsewhere, to be returning to Dickens as a stylistic model at roughly the same time that Thatcher was proclaiming that there was "no such thing as society"—for that model, in both
its original and "neo-Dickensian" varieties, is centrally concerned with
mapping the contours of social interaction and mutual interdependence,
in contrast to modernism's more solipsistic emphasis on "individual men
and women."

Midnight's Children offers the best illustration of the stakes that are involved in such a return to the Dickensian form, since Rushdie operates as
both a proponent and a commentator in that novel. As Timothy Brennan
has convincingly argued, Rushdie's status as a cosmopolitan intellectual reflecting on Indian independence from outside provides him with an ambivalent relationship to the nationalist project and its textual representation, in which he "proclaims his identity with a country whose artificiality
and exclusiveness have driven him into a kind of exile—a simultaneous
recognition of nationhood and an alienation from it."[8] Rushdie's narrator
Saleem speaks of a specifically Indian need, represented as a form of sick-
ness, "to encapsulate the whole of reality" through the search for a totaliz-
ing image, mythology, or allegory of the emerging nation itself. As a poly-
glot state forged from the legacies of imperial rule and partition, and with
still contested borders, however, India inevitably evades any such effort at
microcosmic encapsulation. The peepshow owner Lifafa Das, who tries to
actualize his advertised claims that his customers might "see the whole
world, come see everything," comes to recognize the folly of such an attempt, as his own "hyperbolic formula began, after a time, to prey upon his
mind; more and more picture postcards went into his peepshow as he tried,
desperately, to deliver what he promised, to put everything into his box."[9]

Of course, *Midnight's Children* itself needs to be seen as a similar attempt,
doomed to the same inevitable failure and yet insistent that no other rep-
resentational form would be adequate for the modern Indian novel. While
Saleem acknowledges, then, that he alone (as both the subject and narrator of his story) "give[s] meaning to it all," he is equally insistent that his
own "desperate need for meaning" is also India's, a symptom of what he famously terms a "national longing for form" (144, 190, 344). As I argue in
this chapter, the Dickensian template for fiction is similarly one to which
modern novelists have been drawn even as they recognize its shortcomings.

Since any literary form inevitably has limits, in terms both of what it can say   143
and what it can represent, we are dealing more with an attitude here, one
that affirms the need and ability of novels to delineate lines of intersection
and connection even at the risk of collapsing under the sheer weight of
material. It is in the sense, I think, that James Wood describes a particular
attitude toward storytelling in the "big, ambitious novel" that he glosses as
"the pursuit of vitality at all costs," in which "stories and sub-stories sprout
on every page, as these novels continually flourish their glamorous con-
gestion." At the same time that it draws from magic realism a pleasure in
caricature and coincidence, then, the neo-Dickensian novel feels endlessly
expansive, because what ultimately matters is the drawing of "an endless
web" of intertwining narrative lines and characters (41–42).

John Irving, who has explicitly acknowledged and explored his debt to
Dickens, has similarly described the model he inherited as marked by what
have struck many critics as "stylistic excesses," including sentimentality, exaggeration, "unlikely" plots, and "abundant" descriptions.[10] Recalling Wood's
image of an expanding web within which even the remotest of people and
events are shown to be connected, Irving's advice to a reader of Dickens
(and presumably of his own novels) is "very simply: just accept as a fact that
everyone of any emotional importance to you is related to everyone else
of any emotional importance to you; these relationships need not extend
to blood, of course, but the people who change your life emotionally—all
those people, from different places, from different times, spanning many
wholly unrelated coincidences—are nonetheless 'related'" (372). This approach, I would argue, is diametrically opposed to the Thatcherite emphasis on the private individual possessed with personal obligations, needs, and
abilities, and is much closer to what I have described as the late-Victorian
project of investigating the mutual responsibilities of classes of people for
each other, and of the state for its citizens. And yet the acknowledged un-
likeliness of the fictional connections—often between people of vastly
varying social classes and geographic locations, ranged widely across time
and space—also speaks to a constitutive effort that goes beyond the largely
descriptive ambitions of nineteenth-century sociology; as with Rushdie's
emphasis on Indian "longing" and the "urge" for totalization, this suggests
that novels might be able to force an understanding of social intercon-
nectedness into existence through a deliberate effort of will. In the process
we can see these fictions as helping to construct the sense of a society that
was being eroded by a conservative politics in the 1980s and 1990s, so that
those seemingly arbitrary lines of relation and causality come to stand in

144   for the frayed fabric of a community that might otherwise tend to think of itself in Thatcherite terms.

Theorizing the Neo-Dickensian Novel: Lukács and Bakhtin

In this chapter I want to think more about what that effort entails, especially as it involves a return to a mode of Victorian writing that was consciously demonized by literary modernism. In its place, as we have seen, Bloomsbury was quick to install a version of the sovereign individual, and with it a kind of stylistic constriction that is the mirror opposite of Dickensian expansion: hence, for instance, the emphasis on the monologic (and essentially private) "stream-of-consciousness" narrative in contrast to the polyglossia of Victorian and contemporary neo-Dickensian novelists.[11] In what remains a revealing study of the ideological underpinnings of literary modernism half a century after its first appearance, Georg Lukács's *The Meaning of Contemporary Realism* argues that its dominant figures and texts view the individual not (as is the case with realism) as a social animal but rather as "by nature solitary, asocial, unable to enter into relationships with other human beings."[12] Such a presupposition leads, according to Lukács, to a fundamentally descriptive naturalism that presents an image of the world as it is (or appears to be) yet allows for no possibility of dynamic change; to the extent that modernist texts present a coherent worldview, he suggests, it is one rooted in ontological angst and a perceived absence of meaning, thereby asserting "the unalterability of outward reality (even if this is reduced to a mere state of consciousness)" (36).

That last parenthetical phrase suggests that Lukács is working with a narrow notion of modernism, one largely defined by the technique of stream-of-consciousness fiction: indeed, he partially acknowledges this way of thinking when—in the course of a comparison of Franz Kafka and Thomas Mann—he cites Virginia Woolf as an "extreme example" of a more general tendency within modernism to equate "what is necessarily a subjective experience with reality as such, thus giving a distorted picture of reality as a whole" (51). But notwithstanding the reservation that a term such as "modernism" should be seen to encompass a much wider set of works and stylistic tendencies than its canonical representatives, his point remains a useful one: that the constriction that I have identified with Bloomsbury modernism, in contrast to (neo-)Dickensian expansion, is linked to a withdrawal from society into the privatized consciousness and, as a result, to a potential misreading of the social whole. "It is easy," Lukács comments in this context, "to understand that the experience of the contemporary capitalist world does produce, especially among intellectuals, *angst,* nausea, a sense of isolation, and despair. Indeed, a view of the world which *excluded* these emotions would prevent the present-day artist from depicting his [*sic*] world truthfully. The question is not: is *x* present in reality? But rather: does *x* represent the whole of reality?" (76; emphasis in original). With only minor corrections, most notably exchanging modernist despair for a fundamentalist belief in the benevolent power of capitalism, this might serve equally as a critique of Thatcherism, which similarly seeks to suppress the social and to project a particularized ideological perspective as a generalized truth about the world.

Lukács's analysis also helps make sense of what I take to be a countervailing tendency in contemporary fiction, one that moves in the opposite direction from the "big, ambitious" neo-Dickensian novel. In a passing discussion of Faulkner's *The Sound and the Fury,* he notes that a reductio ad absurdum of stream-of-consciousness technique can be found in cases where the privileged mind "is that of an abnormal subject or of an idiot" (26). It is arguable that one response to the politics of Thatcherism has been an intensification of such experiments with first-person narration, often projecting the thought processes and responses of marked social outcasts and victims: the unemployed and homeless, criminals, alcoholics and drug users, children, the abused. As representative examples, here are the openings of three recent winners of the British Booker Prize for fiction, each written in first person. Roddy Doyle's *Paddy Clark Ha Ha Ha* is told by a ten-year-old and was the prizewinner in 1993: "We were coming down our road. Kevin stopped at a gate and bashed it with his stick. It was Miss Quigley's gate; she was always looking out the window but she never did anything."[13] Next is James Kelman's alcoholic ex-con from 1994's *How Late It Was, How Late:* "Ye wake up in a corner and stay there hoping yer body will disappear, the thoughts smothering ye; these thoughts; but ye want to remember and face up to things, just something keeps ye from doing it, why ye no do it."[14] Lastly, 2000's *True History of the Kelly Gang* by Peter Carey, claiming to be the memoirs of the infamous Australian criminal: "I lost my own father at 12 yr. of age and know what it is to be raised on lies and silences my dear daughter you are presently too young to understand a word I write but this history is for you and will contain no single lie may I burn in Hell if I speak false."[15] The combined effect of such novels—with their paratactic sentences, repetitions, and nonstandard punctuation—is something very like that which Lukács traced in high modernism, where an overriding feeling of despair is matched with one of isolating anomie: "absolute primacy" is

146   granted to "the terminus a quo, the condition from which it is desired to escape," he insists, while "[a]ny movement towards a terminus ad quem is condemned to impotence" (36). The narrative momentum is back to a moment
of origin rather than forward in search of a better life, while the subjectivity that we find expressed is never collective but always idiosyncratically
and idiomatically unique.

Much of the contemporary fiction I am discussing here was explicitly
galvanized in opposition to Thatcherite politics, of course, most notably the
connected tendencies I discussed in chapter 4 to pathologize what it saw
as social failure and to withdraw welfare support from the weakest of society. It is surely no coincidence that so many of the texts that experiment with
first-person narratives have been written from the periphery of Britain, in
places where the effects of conservative policies were felt most sharply. In
this sense, we are dealing with a very different literary phenomenon from
Bloomsbury modernism, which originated (as we have seen) from within
the privileged classes themselves and articulated the nuanced ambivalence
of a fractional consciousness. Where Virginia Woolf and others are generally thought to have represented their own subjective feelings, with all the
suggestions of frankness and sincerity that first-person narration affords,
contemporary novelists as often presume to speak for those that have no
voice in modern life. While bearing such different political impulses in
mind, we can nonetheless highlight a formal convergence in modernist and
contemporary fiction, not only on the issue of first- versus third-person narrative but also in terms of *scale*: in each case, what we encounter is a conscious reduction of life to the viewpoint of the individual protagonist,
whose experience of the world necessarily stands in for the world itself.

The point I am making can be articulated equally well in terms of
Bakhtin's studies of the novel. For him, as for Lukács, fiction begins (or
at least should begin) "by presuming fundamentally differentiated social
groups, which exist in an intense and vital interaction with other social
groups."[16] In that sense, where poetry generally enacts the centripetal drive
of language, seeking to bring together the multiplicity of voices in society
under the dominance of a univocal master language, the novel is defined by
a countertendency, "historically shaped by the current of decentralizing,
centrifugal forces" (272–73). If we can recognize the Dickensian novel as
fully embodying that second polyglossic approach to language, in which
"the totality of the world of objects and ideas [is] depicted and expressed
in it, by means of the social diversity of speech types and by the differing
individual voices that flourish under such conditions," we can just as read-

ily view stream-of-consciousness technique in terms of the former tendency 147
toward centralization. On this account, what distinguishes Virginia Woolf's
first-person narratives from those of Roddy Doyle or James Kelman is a matter of how far spoken language also entails the formation of what Bakhtin
sees as a hierarchy of distinct sociolects, via "the incorporation of barbarians
and lower social strata into a unitary language of culture and truth" (271).
Where the first-person of Bloomsbury might register as speaking in a nor-
matively "high" sociolect, that employed in a novel like Kelman's demonstrates a resistance to its own incorporation through its use of a compacted
and sometimes impenetrable narrative voice.

Bakhtin suggests that the language of a literary text offers us a microcosmic snapshot of the state of interpersonal relations (including, most notably, the class struggle) prevailing within society, so that some dynamic of
domination and subordination would seem both inevitable and necessary
as a marker of where things might currently stand. The compression of linguistic variety implied by the use of a monologic subjective voice and perspective, however—regardless of how far that subject interacts with the
larger world—indicates a solipsistic withdrawal from society, in which it is
difficult to convey the kind of dynamic movement that Lukács demands,
because the first-person perspective is never really challenged by another
on anything approaching an equal footing. Ironically, then, one literary response to Thatcherism's attacks on the fabric of society—indeed, on the
very *idea* of society—paradoxically ends up mirroring its insistence that
"people must look to themselves first."

In focusing attention here on an alternative line of response, one that
looks back to a Dickensian model in order to defend and extend our understanding of communal bonds and social ties, I want to make clear that
I am not suggesting the simple revival or imitation of nineteenth-century
fictional forms, or the literary equivalent of the nostalgic heritage adaptations I discussed in chapter 3. In the following analysis of novels by Sarah
Waters, John Irving, and Peter Carey, I am mindful of the historical distance that separates them from Dickens, one that is partly conditioned by
twentieth-century retrospection and the assessments of the Victorian period I have discussed; in that sense, these works of rescription are closer to
the group of films (like *The French Lieutenant's Woman* and *The Governess*) with
which I ended chapter 3, in offering a metacritical commentary on the possibilities and limits of the fictional form they are adapting for modern uses.
In particular, they all seek to address—and *redress*—the key Victorian prohibitions on speaking about sexuality and imperialism, while simultaneously

148 working through and within the prevailing literary conventions and structures by which those silences were maintained.

Focusing on such topics also requires me, finally, to address what has
probably been the predominant image of the Victorian period (dating even
from before its official end) as an age characterized by hypocrisy—an assessment shared by such unlikely bedfellows as Margaret Thatcher, Leonard
Woolf, Lytton Strachey, and Gertrude Himmelfarb.[17] To view the nineteenth century as one that enacted either an outright repression of sex or
its sublimation has become a critical cliché, though not one that has been
immune to correction by historical scholarship, feminist and queer theory,
or popular journalism. Turning first to a landmark of academic revisionism, Steven Marcus's *The Other Victorians* (1966), I propose to investigate
the grounds of these critiques in order to situate one key strand of neo-
Dickensian fiction, which is its ability to move beyond its inherited form
in dealing with matters of sexuality and human reproduction. In doing so,
I will suggest that the target of these novels is not just the Victorians themselves (or a reconstructed image of them) but also the contemporary conservative discourse that seeks a return to silence and legal prohibition.

Other Victorians

In his study of Victorian pornography, Marcus suggests at least three ways
to understand the relationship between his "other Victorians" and the
larger social world. At the most simple level, they represent its repressed
underside, "a real, secret social life" that existed "amid and underneath the
world of Victorian England as we know it—and as it tended to represent
itself." In such a view, pornography allows us access to an experience that,
while surely known, did not constitute "part of the Victorians' official consciousness of themselves or of their society."[18] It might also function pro-
leptically, as a preview of aspects of a modern ("liberated") post-Victorian
subjectivity. Writing of a passage of introspective self-reflection in the
anonymous *My Secret Life*, for instance, in which the author questions why
seemingly "natural" homosexual or voyeuristic impulses should be considered deviant, Marcus writes that he "has evolved for himself out of his own
experiences, fantasies, and contemplations a point of view which—despite
the crudity and coarseness of his terminology—is a significant anticipation
of what is generally thought of as the modern, liberal, and liberated conception of sexual morality" (152).

Up to this point, Marcus is rehearsing what Foucault famously termed
"the repressive hypothesis," in which the Victorians function as a useful

scapegoat in narratives of personal and social liberation. As Foucault suggests in *The History of Sexuality*, if a man like the author of *My Secret Life* can view sex as having been "repressed, that is condemned to prohibition, nonexistence, and silence, then the mere fact that one is speaking about it has the appearance of a deliberate transgression. A person who holds forth in such language places himself to a certain extent outside the reach of power; he upsets established law; he somehow anticipates the coming freedom."[19] As a collective conversion narrative, structured around a tipping point that has been surprisingly difficult to specify, this is essentially the story that the twentieth century repeatedly told itself, in proclaiming its demonstrable superiority to its predecessor on the basis of its greater frankness and honesty about sexual matters, yet Foucault argues that it misrepresents both periods in its oversimplification. "Was there really a historical rupture between the age of repression and the critical analysis of repression," he asks, or do they instead represent stages in the continuous operation of power that works in part by putting sex "into discourse" (10–11)? The underground literature of pornography is, on this account, only one among a vast array of spoken and written discourses about sex (including, most notably, the legal, medical, and psychiatric) that can be dated from the nineteenth century.

For Foucault, then, the crucial object of analysis is not—as it was for Bloomsbury thinkers such as Strachey or his brother James, translator of Freud—a state-sanctioned silence about sex that finally erupts into language, but rather "the different ways of not saying such things, how those who can and those who cannot speak of them are distributed, which type of discourse is authorized, or which form of discretion is required in either case" (27). Marcus's study is useful for this project as well, since its account of the otherness of Victorian pornography identifies it with a specific form of silence operating within canonical realist novels of the period, most notably those of Dickens. Discussing a scene of rural rape in *My Secret Life*, for instance, in which an overseer of female field hands encourages them to take the author's money and trust that "the squire won't harm you," Marcus concludes: "*This* is the kind of thing, one wants to say, that it was all about; *this* is the kind of thing that the Victorian novelists could not but be aware of—even though their explicit dealings with it were very circumspect— that their work as a whole was directed against" (139; emphasis in original). He seems to mean that last word in two senses: both that novels took such attitudes as making the case for change (they were "against" such exploitative relations between rich and poor) and that they actively sought

150   to represent such relations differently (thereby working "against" a reality that could only find expression in an illicit genre like pornography).

In the second sense, Marcus suggests, reading underground works can contest and complicate our understanding of Victorian society by depicting what its successful novelists could not: thus, for instance, a scene from *My Secret Life* describing a teenage girl prostituting herself in order to supply food for her younger siblings, whom she leaves locked up at home, fills in a telling lacuna in Dickens's *Bleak House*, where younger children are similarly dependent on the labor of older sister Charley, who does washing; similarly, a dissolute military officer in the pornographic text helps explain *Dombey and Son's* Major Bagstock to Marcus, since its anonymous author could write plainly where Dickens was forced to use indirect ways "to communicate to the reader the intense, disturbed, and corrupted sexuality of the Major" (108–11). The consequences of such an implicit rewriting are not seen as entirely beneficial, however, as the larger cultural liberation narrative described by Foucault might presume. Seeking to introduce, within the established form of the Victorian novel, concrete details that it consciously excluded "could not be managed convincingly within the unmodified form itself," Marcus argues, with one possible effect being that the satirical intentions of a writer like Dickens tend to be blunted in the process (234).

We can equally miss what Marcus terms "certain positive values" that are "already inherent" in scenes of working-class life but only come to view as a result of the writer's "imaginative abstraction . . . and reconstruction" of them under the pressures of self-censorship (106). Pornography, he concludes, can readily "unmask society's official version of itself," yet it is unable to take "the next step of subversion: it cannot supply a vision that either transcends or transvalues what passes for current reality" (233). In this way, it begins to resemble the strategy of simple negation that I have described earlier in the cases of Bloomsbury's knee-jerk anti-Victorianism and Neil Kinnock's equally reflexive opposition to Thatcherism, where the end result is not a corrective revision of our understanding of the period so much as a positing of coexisting alternatives, just the kind of parallelism that the term "other" implies. At best, on Marcus's account, pornography fills in some gaps in the historical record, yet its status as underground literature can also have the paradoxical effect of confirming our dominant image of a society structured through a hypocritical suppression and sublimation of sex.

The more genuinely corrective effort that I see at work in the neo-Dickensian novels might be shown through a comparison with a text such as *Oliver Twist*, one that encapsulates much of what is commonly thought of as the "Dickensian" vision of Victorian society. If the impact of Dickens's 151 novel stemmed from its apparently frank depiction of urban poverty, contemporary readers might instead fault it for its reticence about what we know to be the real conditions of life in London, in the service of what now looks like a heavy-handed moralism. As Larry Wolff has persuasively argued, frankness and silence coincide in Dickens's 1841 preface, which claims, on the one hand, to have "banish[ed] from the lips of the lowest character I introduced, any expression that could by possibility offend" and, on the other, to have shown (by "unavoidable inference") "a very coarse and shocking circumstance . . . that Sikes is a thief, and Fagin a receiver of stolen goods; that the boys are pickpockets, and the girl is a prostitute."[20] Naming Nancy's profession in this way, however, does not entirely square with her role in the novel, throughout which (as Wolff points out) "the extent of her sexual immorality appears in her attachment to Sikes, which while hardly pleasant and perhaps illicit, is rather more romantic than mercenary" (235).

It is worth recalling at this point the dialogue from the modern plot of *The French Lieutenant's Woman* that I cited in chapter 3, in which two actors discover 80,000 prostitutes in London servicing two million clients per week and calculate that "outside of marriage, your Victorian gentleman could look forward to 2.4 fucks a week." Those statistics suggest that the Nancy that has come down to us, especially as interpreted in David Lean's film or Lionel Bart's 1968 adaptation *Oliver!* gives us a wholly inadequate picture of the period, in spite of Dickens's insistence (in a later preface) that he did not excise even "one scrap of curl-paper in the girl's dishevelled hair" to spare his reader's sensibilities.[21] Pinter's screenplay to Reisz's film underscores the reality that her clients would necessarily have included Victorian married gentlemen, and yet the effect of Dickens's novel is, as Franco Moretti shows in his *Atlas of the European Novel*, to split the city into two disconnected segments that separately contain the rich and poor, who as a result have little interaction of any kind. While not exactly Margaret Thatcher's celebration of the self-regulating individual, the society of *Oliver Twist* is thus made up of what Moretti terms "two half-Londons, that do not add up to a whole."[22] One clear intention of the neo-Dickensian novelists is to enable those halves to speak to each other, in a dialogue that foregrounds their sociolinguistic differences but also their repressed interdependence.

Sarah Waters, whom *Kirkus Reviews* has labeled "the lesbian Charles Dickens,"[23] represents this interdependence most effectively in the third of

152 her London novels, *Fingersmith* (2002), which immediately signals its debt by describing a staged performance of *Oliver Twist* on its very first pages. Waters's novel moves between a familiar "Dickensian" plot of underworld thieving and one set in a wealthy country estate, and yet it also connects its version of the slum environment of Sikes and Fagin far more effectively with the genteel world of Mr. Brownlow and the Maylies. Waters does this in part by positing a simple exchangeability between these locations and their inhabitants, so that a thief named "Gentleman," who is (wrongly) thought to have attended "a real gent's school" before gambling away the family fortune, can pose as a picture framer to gain access to the Gothic manor at Briar.[24] He is accompanied by a local "fingersmith" or thief who uses the alias of Susan Smith and masquerades as a maid for Briar's mistress, Maud Lilly, planning to exchange places with her and split her fortune with Gentleman. Crucially, the novel hinges on the resemblance between the illiterate South London thief and her wealthy mistress, who was herself supposed (also wrongly) to have been born in a madhouse then trained as a secretary to her bibliophile uncle at Briar. There is some existing physical likeness, since Sue is told that "we might be sisters" and confuses another of the servants when she first wears one of Maud's gowns, but the performance also requires her to acquire a softer skin and be better fed, so that Maud might as readily be believable as her servant (102).[25]

The mirroring does not stop there. Maud compares her uncle's labors over his books to the work of lunatics "at endless tasks—conveying sand from one leaking cup into another; counting the stitches in a fraying gown, or the motes in a sunbeam" (194); she, in turn, is referred to as "half a villain already" by Gentleman, even before he has explained to her his plans to double-cross Sue and split the profits with Maud (226). Ultimately, the interchangeability of Sue and Maud is given a literal meaning when we learn that the two have been switched at birth and the latter's gentility is revealed as merely learned behavior: "One baby becomes another," Gentleman tells her, meaning that "[y]our life was not the life you were meant to live, but Sue's" (335). The effect of Waters's rescripting of Dickens, who sought to draw social, geographical, and linguistic distinctions among characters that seem to inhabit even the different fictional modes of the sentimental and the comic, is thus to collapse the distances between them: the effect is as if the prostitute Nancy, the genteel Rose Maylie, the dissolute and diseased Monks, and the bourgeois Mr. Brownlow were all made to inhabit the same fictive space and (when called upon) to exchange places with each other.

Significantly, these exchanges are subtended—and indeed, enabled—
by a single fact revealed midway through the novel, that Maud's uncle is at
work on a monumental index of pornography. Modeled on the real-life
Henry Ashbee (to whom Steven Marcus devotes the second chapter of *The
Other Victorians*), Christopher Lilly comes to resemble a lunatic on account
of his monomaniacal dedication to the undertaking, and it is presumably
the semilegality of the work that prompts him to employ a man like "Gentleman" without fully checking into his credentials, or to neglect the task
of supervising the hiring of his niece's maid. In turn, the monotonous work
of reading, copying, and indexing pornography is what alerts Gentleman
to Maud's incipient criminality, and it enables her to construct a passable
imitation of lower-class speech. When still a girl, for instance, she is discovered watching a maid undress, and when asked what she is looking at,
she replies, "Your cunt"; on being questioned about where she learned such
words, she truthfully replies, "From my uncle" and has her mouth washed
with soap for her trouble (200–201). Waters's collapsing of the registers of
lower- and upper-class speech that a novel like *Oliver Twist* insists on keeping separate is also highlighted later when Sue is imprisoned in Maud's
place, during which her own language (especially the expression "For fuck's
sake!") serves only to confirm her warder's belief that hers is a case of a lady
"that thought herself a duchess's maid." The novel's ultimate irony is that
she really is the aristocrat that the nurses assume her to be, even if Sue is
equally correct in asserting that she "only got hands so white through being
maid to a lady" (410).

A form of linguistic polyvocality, as signified by the ability to speak
in at least two class registers or across the boundaries of polite and profane speech, characterizes most of the cast of *Fingersmith*. As a result, where
Christopher Lilly seeks to police the constituency for pornography, hoping by way of a pointing brass finger set in the floor of his library to mark
"the bounds of innocence" and keep it away from the likes of the illiterate
Sue (188), his efforts are doomed to failure. His illicit texts suffuse themselves throughout the novel and might be said (with criminality more generally) to constitute the very bonds of its society. This becomes apparent
when Maud takes over as narrator in the middle section of the novel, rere-
lating events that Sue has already described but from a position that literally knows what has gone on behind the closed doors of the study. In many
ways, her embedded narrative revision parallels Waters's of Dickens, re-
telling what we think we know with the benefit of a desublimated awareness of its sexualized subtexts.

154   In her earlier critical writing, Waters endorses a similar project of retroactive critical rereading, one that aims to recover both "the erotic imperatives of the period" when texts were produced (in this instance, Maude Meagher's 1930s historical novel, *The Green Scamander*) and "the strategies with which a visionary novelist might attempt to negotiate and challenge those imperatives."[26] Each of Waters's first three novels points to homosexual subtexts running through some of the classic genres of eighteenth- and nineteenth-century fiction (the picaresque in 1998's *Tipping the Velvet*, the sensation novel in 1999's *Affinity*) as well as some of their stock female characters—like the stage performer or the governess. To a greater and lesser extent, those genres are adaptable for the articulation of a modern lesbian subjectivity: it is, for example, readily expressible in the picaresque form of *Tipping the Velvet*, as well as in its concluding invocation of the late-Victorian "social problem" novel. *Affinity*, by way of contrast, respects the silences and indirections of the sensation novel and accordingly indicates same-sex desire only obliquely: as a "something" beyond words, at times sublimated into a purely spiritual "affinity" and at others the cause of an unspecified "disgrace."[27] In *Fingersmith* she turns the Dickensian crime novel inside out in a manner that is reminiscent of the claims that Steven Marcus makes for nineteenth-century erotica. When Sue and Maud first sleep together, for instance, the former recounts it as a necessary scene in the latter's sexual education, preparing her for marriage with Gentleman; with the benefit of hindsight, however, we later reprocess the scene as one predicated upon Sue's innocent gullibility, with Maud performing "how it is done in my uncle's books: two girls, one wise and one unknowing" (281).[28]

Waters's strategy here is different from the one that she deploys in either of her earlier novels. The effect is not quite (as with *Tipping the Velvet*) to minimize the distance separating historical and contemporary modes of homosexual experience and subjectivity, but neither does it reinforce that distance, as is the case with *Affinity*. We might, for instance, wish to value the greater frankness about sex that emerges from Maud's rewriting of the scene, with its implicit critique of the forms of sublimation that enable Sue to process it within the framework of the heterosexual marriage plot; at the same time, however, it might also be seen as short-circuiting a smug liberationist opposition between an enlightened present—one that might champion its own "lesbian Dickens"—and the supposed dark ages of the Victorian past, insisting on a continuum of same-sex desire as well as its function (then as well as now) as an element of heterosexual pornography. In many respects, Waters's fiction is not "about" lesbianism so much as its history of textual inscription and the cultural and generic blockages and evasions that have subtended it. If we choose to read *Fingersmith* as a reimagining of the Dickensian novel, we need at the same time to take into account what it has to say about the blind spots of Dickens as a Victorian novelist and the form in which he wrote, a form that has stood as one of the central inheritances of the period.

"Searching through Dickens"

Fingersmith's Sue has grown up in an East London house that combines the receipt and fencing of stolen goods with an orphanage, thereby fusing the twin locations of Oliver Twist's own early childhood. Yet if "there was not much that was brought to our house that was not moved out of it again, rather sharpish," Sue has to exempt herself from this general rule, as the "one thing that had somehow withstood the tremendous pull of that passage of poke" (11). In this she resembles another unwanted child, Homer Wells from John Irving's *Cider House Rules* (1985), who is equally the exception to the standard practice of the orphanage. The opening sentences of Irving's novel, where we learn that "two nurses were in charge of naming the new babies" at St. Cloud's, Maine,[29] seems designed to recall Dickens's description of Bumble's arbitrary arrangement for naming according to the letters of the alphabet, so that Oliver Twist follows Swubble into the world and narrowly avoids being named Unwin or Vilkins. In Irving's more benevolent institution, greater care is given with names, with Nurse Edna extemporizing variations on the name of St. Cloud's beloved Dr. Wilbur Larch (John Larch, John Wilbur, etc.) and Nurse Angela preferring natural formations and household pets (Fuzzy Stone, Snowy Meadows, Homer Wells). Already, we can see that *Cider House Rules* sets out to depict a kinder, gentler orphanage, a correction of Dickens that seems ironically confirmed when one set of adopted parents is forced to beat Homer in order to *make* him cry.

Irving might seem, in this sense, to be in sympathy with the efforts of Newt Gingrich and Gertrude Himmelfarb to promote orphanages as one element in plans for welfare reform, except that St. Cloud's is also a place where abortions are performed. Irving has downplayed the political implications of inserting what was one of the great polarizing issues of the 1980s into his otherwise nostalgic depiction of community formation in early-twentieth-century New England, suggesting in one interview that "It was a year before abortion entered the story, but it made perfect sense. In the early part of the century, what doctor would be most sympathetic to performing

156 abortions but a doctor who delivered unwanted babies, then cared for them in an orphanage?"[30] If this statement suggests that abortion's presence in the novel is somewhat accidental, however, Irving's writing makes clear his commitment to abortion rights and forestalls any potential recruitment of it to the conservative position that promotes adoption as part of an aggressively pro-life agenda. Instead, it asks (in the form of a rhetorical question posed by Larch), "For whom did some minds insist that babies, even clearly unwanted ones, *must* be brought, screaming, into the world?" (10).[31]

While overstating the novel's evenhandedness concerning the issue of abortion, Todd Davis and Kenneth Womack rightly point out that Larch's— and, by implication, the novel's—endorsement of a woman's right to choose arises out of "the pragmatics of physical circumstances as opposed to legalistic ideology," linking it in the process to Irving's consciously Dickensian humanism;[32] Larch himself looks back, from a time when abortion is illegal, to a more enlightened past in the mid-nineteenth century, when the law enshrined the "simple and (to Wilbur Larch) sensible" position that abortion be permitted until "the first, felt movement of the fetus" (47). In a revealing passage, he describes his professional identity in the following terms: "He was an obstetrician; he delivered babies into the world. His colleagues called this 'the Lord's work.' And he was an abortionist; he delivered mothers, too. His colleagues called this 'the Devil's work,' but it was *all* the Lord's work to Wilbur Larch" (67; emphasis in original).

As Davis and Womack argue, it is circumstances that dictate one course of action or the other, and not any abstract principle, yet there is also a sense in which experiencing those circumstances—in a novel where pregnancy or impending parenthood are issues for most of its younger protagonists— helps constitute the social bonds between characters that range across economic, social, and racial categories. Larch, for instance, initially performs abortions on two Boston women who stand at opposite ends of the social scale: a poor, thirteen-year-old Lithuanian girl who was raped by her father, and Missy Channing-Peabody, from a patrician family that he first hopes has invited him for a social visit.[33] Similarly, and despite his stated opposition to the practice, Homer Wells is faced with the pregnancy of his beloved Candy Kendall and also the African American apple-picker's daughter Rose Rose, who (like the Lithuanian girl) has been impregnated by her own father: circumstances argue for an abortion in the latter case, while in the former—in spite of the difficulty of Candy's prior relationship with Homer's best friend, Wally Worthington—they dictate that the child not only lives but grows up with three parents. The novel is thus far from

adopting a simplistic "pro-family" position, preferring instead to celebrate 157
the kind of provisional, improvised, and extended families that often emerge
at the end of Dickens's novels.

In this reading, I depart from the assessment made by Alison Booth, in
the course of an insightful discussion of the neoconservative revival of a
discourse of personal responsibility, that *Cider House Rules* "is based on a Victorian code of interdependence" yet "resolves into a more individualist self-
help that sustains an exclusive hierarchy." Underpinning her judgment is
an unacknowledged tension between the twin legacies of the nineteenth
century I highlighted in the last chapter, in which a celebration of the self-
reliant individual as valorized by a writer like Samuel Smiles exists side by
side with the more communitarian ethics that Booth herself identifies with
Victorian fiction, "the sort of microcosm that entails responsibility in a
Dickens or Eliot novel" (292). The desire to keep these two ways of thinking entirely distinct from each other leads Booth to reimagine them in
terms of a historical progression that moves inexorably "from the Victorian
vocational self-help, which was addressed as an exchange among men to
serve collective progress, into early-twentieth-century success literature
focused on personality and competition" (290).[34]

Irving's *Cider House Rules* is not simply a simulacrum of the Dickensian
novel, however, as Booth suggests in seeing its bildungsroman form as ne-
cessitating "a sort of dystopian exit from society and politics," but at the
same time a metacritical examination of its potential relevance in a contemporary world (289). Homer's whispering to himself of the famous first
line of Dickens's most autobiographical novel ("Whether I shall turn out to
be the hero of my own life . . .") finds its implicit answer in a culminating
act of service, for instance, when he decides to provide Rose Rose with an
abortion: "On his bedside table," we read, "between the reading lamp and
the telephone, was his battered copy of *David Copperfield*. Homer didn't
have to open the book to know how the story began" (562). Irving is certainly aware of the potentially anachronistic quality of Dickens's writing,
especially as it is typically packaged and promoted in contemporary culture. His *A Prayer for Owen Meany* (1989), for instance, includes a key scene
that is set against the backdrop of a ritualized and entirely ossified small-town
performance of *A Christmas Carol*, and it later finds its narrator, a teacher in
the Canadian high school system, bemoaning that "It's always *description*
that they miss; I swear, they think it's unimportant. They want dialogue,
they want action; but there's so much *writing* in the description."[35] This suggests one version of the Victorianist's challenge, when faced with students

158   more accustomed to modernist compression or to seeing nineteenth-century novels adapted to emphasize dialogue and visual action. Another is that exposure to a writer like Dickens often comes too early, with the result that—like the male orphans in *The Cider House Rules*, who have *Great Expectations* and *David Copperfield* read to them at bedtime—students are simply "too young for the Dickensian language" (26). The text is riddled with moments like this, as for instance when Homer's female counterpart Melony stumbles over the opening of *Little Dorrit*, "got lost, began again, got lost again" (224); or when she tries to read aloud from *Jane Eyre* (the female orphans' equivalent of the Dickens novels) for her fellow apple-pickers and has to pause to define particular words used in each successive sentence (319–20).

At the other end of the spectrum, however, Irving depicts an intense identification with the scenes, people, and language of the Victorian novel, in which his twentieth-century characters struggle to understand their own experience through and in terms of a fictional past. As the text makes clear, the choice of bedtime reading at St. Cloud's is no random act: as Larch notes in his journal, "What in hell else would you read to an orphan" except for novels that themselves feature orphaned protagonists (26)? The potential for immediate recognition is perhaps strongest in Melony, who "listened to *Jane Eyre* as if it were her life story being told to her" when she hears a passage like "I tired of the routine of eight years in one afternoon" (108–10). This can also take the form, though, of an inability to identify that results not (as with *Little Dorrit*) in simple frustration but instead in a significant insight into the larger world beyond St. Cloud's: Melony's nickname for Homer throughout the novel is "Sunshine," born out of her incredulous response to another passage in Brontë's novel concerning her "gleams of sunshine" at Gateshead Hall that provokes Melony to shout out, "Let her come here! Let her show *me* the gleams of sunshine!" (77; emphasis in original).

Orphans, Irving seems to suggest, need to compensate for the lack of knowledge of their place in the world, one that is typically derived from familial relationships, by looking instead to cultural forms. In such a project of subjective understanding, the novels of Victorian realism function better than the exotic films that Homer sees at a drive-in theater, replete with camels and bedouins: "His exposure to storytelling, through Charles Dickens and Charlotte Brontë, had ill prepared him," we read, "for characters who came from and traveled nowhere—or for stories that made no sense" (255).[36] Even his understanding of space is conditioned by his reading, so that he is surprised to see the size of England represented on a map because Dickens "had given him the impression of something much bigger" (344). Fiction is thus not simply the source of the Thatcherite lesson about becoming the hero of one's own drama, as Alison Booth suggests, or of a merely solipsistic self-knowledge, but also of an alternative impulse requiring us to situate ourselves in a larger social context and to recognize common interests and mutual responsibilities.

Reading not only tells Melony something about what her life is (and what it lacks) but also about Homer's, so that she can be said to be "searching through Dickens for specific characteristics she associated with Homer Wells," while he in turn can articulate his feelings for Wally Worthington only through adapting the language of David Copperfield's observation of Steerforth (that "He was a person of great power in my eyes"), with the result that he comes to understand the novel much better for having such a real-world experience for himself (219; 200). This kind of perfect identification between a text and its readers, which could presumably be multiplied and recalibrated for each of St. Cloud's orphans, represents a utopian project on the part of Dr. Larch, who felt that any boy like Homer "who has read *Great Expectations* and *David Copperfield* by himself, twice each—and had each word of both books read aloud to him, also twice—is more mentally prepared than most" for the outside world, despite his lack of a traditional family structure (27).

The reading process he illustrates can be thought of as an example of what Bakhtin termed the "intonational quotation marks" through which the novel incorporates and parodies other styles of speech and patterns of language—a kind of intertextual reference that is literalized every time Melony calls Homer "Sunshine." Such a practice foregrounds what both Bakhtin and Lukács view as an important trait of fiction, its capacity to represent various viewpoints or perspectives on the world and place them in conflict: as a result, as Bakhtin says of a passage from Pushkin's *Eugene Onegin*, its "hero is located in a zone of potential conversation with the author, in a zone of *dialogical contact.* . . . The image of another's language and outlook on the world, simultaneously represented *and* representing, is extremely typical of the novel" (44–45; emphasis in original). In the case of Irving's novel, we have what we could term a "Dickensian" outlook that is in simultaneous dialogue with its author's own contemporary views (including, most obviously, his support for abortion rights) and also with an early-twentieth-century reality that he has constructed, populated by heterogeneous characters with diverse life experiences and—as a result—with variable possibilities for identifying (and disidentifying) with those portrayed in *David*

160   *Copperfield.* As such, *The Cider House Rules* represents a New England society that is self-consciously "Victorian" in its foundations, yet also one that continues to debate its complex and often contradictory inheritance by distinguishing what remains of value from what no longer resonates. Given Dickens's own delight in linguistic parodies, especially those that expose calcified conventions and outmoded attitudes, this would seem to be an appropriate form of homage for a self-identified neo-Dickensian like Irving to perform.[37]

Writing Back

The Australian novelist Peter Carey's 1997 novel *Jack Maggs* is just as overt an homage to Dickens as Irving's *The Cider House Rules* and even more deliberately mimics the story of *Great Expectations'* Pip and Magwitch in its account of a long-deferred meeting in London between the returned convict Maggs and his protégé, Henry Phipps. The former's story begins, however, as a version of Oliver Twist's: an orphan, taken in by the criminal Silas Smith and the patriotically named Ma Brittan and apprenticed to burglary from an early age, on account of his ability to navigate down the chimneys of the wealthy. When he recounts this story, under mesmeric influence, to the novelist Tobias Oates (a double for Dickens, as we shall see), the writer imagines to himself that Maggs might be "a bastard son of noble parents" in planning his fictive "dark journey . . . inside the Criminal Mind" that he intends to follow up on the success of his Pickwickian *Captain Crumley*, "a comedy, a pantomime, broad strokes, great larks, a rowdy tale of old London."[38]

It is only later, after Jack has been set up by his adopted brother, separated from his beloved Sophina, and sentenced to transportation, that his story morphs from Oliver's into Magwitch's, in a very precise parody of *Great Expectations* that sees Henry Phipps give a pig's trotter to the shackled convict, who in response vows "that I would come back from my exile and take him from his orphanage, that I would spin him a cocoon of gold and jewels, that I would weave him a nest so strong that no one would ever hurt his goodness" (287). And yet, Henry's awareness of his benefactor's identity from the outset enables Carey to make a significant departure from the Dickensian blueprint, by insisting on his absolute unworthiness and ingratitude in the face of Jack's generosity: in this version, the debauched and decadent English "gentleman" conspires with his Oxford tutor "to gratify the needs of him who signed his letters 'Father,'" by sending to Australia a portrait of a handsome George IV and "labour[ing] together on the replies until young Henry finally found his voice" (353). If, as Mercy Larkin insists to him, Maggs's error has been to "prance round England trying to find someone who does not love you at all" while neglecting two sons born in Australia, the novel's ending sees him return to that country (with Mercy) to a successful life of prosperity, comfort, and respectability.

Carey has acknowledged the influence of Edward Said, who used *Great Expectations* as an initial starting point for his study of *Culture and Imperialism* (1993) in order to reconstruct "a vast history of speculation about and experience of Australia, a 'white' colony like Ireland, in which we can locate Magwitch and Dickens not as mere coincidental references in that history, but as participants in it, through the novel and through a much older and wider experience between England and its overseas territories." Whereas Dickens makes little effort to imagine the convict's life in New South Wales and takes for granted his desire to return to the imperial center, Said's analysis (and Carey's novel) makes clear that Magwitch "cannot be allowed a 'return' to metropolitan space, which, as Dickens's fiction testifies, is meticulously charted, spoken for, inhabited by a hierarchy of metropolitan personages."[39] As the leading novelist of London in the nineteenth century, of course, Dickens did more than most to advance its imaginative mapping; by making the city visible in its particular forms, he must share some of the responsibility for making it impossible for Magwitch/Maggs to successfully reenter and inhabit it.

Carey makes clear that Maggs's London is not only a fiction—consisting of "lovely English summers" in which he constructs for himself an idealized "picture of me and Henry puffing our pipes comfortably in the long evenings," even as he was "suffering the mosquitoes and the skin-rot" of Australia (317)—but also one that has been engendered partly through reading novels. The narrator describes how Jack, on being whipped as a convict in Australia, "would begin to build London in his mind . . . brick by brick as the horrid double-cat smote the air"; but the city he mentally reconstructs is not the slum landscape of his own youth but instead "a house in Kensington whose kind and beautiful interior he had entered by tumbling down a chimney." If this moment germinates the life he plans for Henry, it is also when he comes to recognize "that which he later knew was meant by authors when they wrote of England, and of Englishmen" (350). It initially might seem difficult to lay the blame on Dickens, whose representations of fashionable West End living uneasily coexisted (as we have seen) with more prosaic images of working-class London, but it is precisely this process of mystification that Carey depicts at work by incorporating

162   into the text of *Jack Maggs* a simulacrum of the author himself, engaged in
the very act of converting Jack's story into a "Dickensian" fiction.
The resemblances are so frequent as to leave no doubt about Carey's intentions: like Dickens, Tobias Oates "feared poverty" and "wrote passion-
ately about the poor," yet he also attended public executions and reported
on them "with a magistrate's detachment" (214); like the novelist's, his father has spent time in prison and continues to borrow money on the strength
of his son's reputation, causing Oates to publicly renounce him (193); his
investment in a sentimentalized vision of family life is clear, however, in
his proud possession of "a long dining table that could welcome his wife's
aunts and uncles," as well as "a splendid alcove in the parlour big enough to
accommodate a twelve-foot-high fir tree at Christmas" (42); finally, in an
echo of Dickens's intense erotic attachment to Mary Hogarth, Oates has
fallen out of love with his own wife and become romantically involved
with her sister. His writing also reflects a very Dickensian ability to convert London street life into comic and sentimental scenes: whether his raw
material is mined through mesmerism (as is the case with Maggs's own
story) or through keen observation and unceasing walks through the capital, it is rapidly transformed into sketches—with titles such as "Canary
Woman of Islington" or "An Altercation in High Holborn"—and accounted
for in a mental ledger according to which a face-off between two cab driv-
ers immediately suggests "two guineas to be made here. . . . Add his
sweeper boy (two guineas). Add his canary woman (two guineas)" (224).
Put positively, Oates is said to have "a great affection for Characters" (90);
less charitably, as his own cook tells Maggs, "He's looking at you like a
blessed butterfly he has to pin down on his board" (48).
The convict's appeal is, as this description suggests, as a rare specimen
of nature, and in this he embodies a key fascination of Australia itself, as a
supposed *terra nullis* to which the British exported its unwanted population
but of which they had little understanding. In his historical study *The Road
to Botany Bay*, Paul Carter argues that Australia was figured in the popular
imaginary as a place of exotic landscapes and natural life, yet as a result it
remained recalcitrant to linguistic description, strictly unrepresentable except through metaphorical comparison with the familiar.[40] Tobias Oates's
initial recognition of Maggs's history, as revealed under hypnosis, suggests
its exotic appeal, as he describes "[t]his Australian" as containing "pelicans
and parrots, fish and phantoms, things the Royal Botanist would give a sov
or two to hold in his unconscious mind" (97); his subsequent fictional re-
counting of the convict's life as one marked by a struggle to "walk once
more in England's green and pleasant land," unable to "bear the prospect of

never seeing [his] beloved motherland," in turn indicates his efforts to do- 163
mesticate that history for a British audience (252).[41]

This attitude is not, however, a national chauvinism that can be ascribed to fiction writers alone; Oates's celebration of the mother country,
after all, echoes the orphaned Maggs's own childhood loyalty to Ma Brittan, while his London employer Percy Buckle deploys an identical trope in
bemoaning his own sister's transportation and his shocked realization "that
Mother England would do such a thing with one of her own" (98). To the
extent that such a national and imperial ideology infects all of the London-
based characters in the novel, with the exception of Mercy Larkin, we can
understand its hold on Maggs's conscious mind: the effort it takes to maintain it can be glimpsed in the violence of his declaration to Buckle that "I
am a fucking *Englishman*, and I have English things to settle. I am not to
live my life with all that vermin" (140–41; emphasis in original), or his latter statement to Mercy, when the opportunity of returning to Australia first
presents itself, that "I am not of that race" (340). His mesmeric sessions
with Oates suggest otherwise, of course, and so does his language, which
seems to vacillate between Cockney and Australian slang. Others' attention to his low-class origins is first signaled by his use of a classically "Dickensian" underworld diction in asking, "Can a cove get a cup of something?"
(63), which indicates that he is not the footman he has pretended to be,
but that soon modulates as his speech is increasingly marked by the term
"mate" (frequently used by Londoners and Australians alike) and by words
like "da" (for father) or "pooka" (for a spirit he believes is infecting the
household), both of which suggest the Irish influence on Australian dialect.
The latter term, interestingly, is used at around the halfway point of the
novel, on the first occasion when the narrator—as opposed to a character
like Oates—refers to Maggs as "The Australian" (180). The trajectory of
the novel, in that sense, demands that he himself come to recognize a national identity that he has repressed but by which the reader has already
come to identify him.

That identity is, of course, one that has been formed through and
against others, most notably the British. As Carey has acknowledged, white
Australian subjectivity is contradictorily structured around a desire to dou-
bly differentiate itself: from a European colonial model on the one hand, and
from that represented by an indigenous population being erased by the concept of the country as *terra nullis* on the other. "The whole notion of who's
the victim" is thus, as he remarks, "complicated because you have the convicts in one sense—cruelly ripped from their own country and cast on the
moon—and yet, when you look at the early cases of the violence between

164   the races, the most likely perpetrators of the violence would be the convicts, the ex-convicts."[42] If violence against an aboriginal population is absent from *Jack Maggs*, just as much as it is from *Great Expectations*, it presumably helps underscore its protagonist's fierce need to identify himself as English, even to the point of distinguishing Australians as a race apart. Significantly, as his psychic investment in the empire unravels, and Maggs is finally forced to confront the reality of Henry Phipps (now aptly dressed in the uniform of a British solider), what replaces it is an equally mythical Australian hypermasculinity, one that is embodied in what Graeme Turner has termed "the holy trinity of men, sport, and beer."[43] After returning to New South Wales with Mercy, we read that they produce more children to add to Jack's neglected sons, at which point he sells the brickworks on which he has built his fortune, opens up a pub, and becomes president of the local cricket club.

One manifestation of Australian hypermasculinity is the sheer fecundity of Maggs, whose two previous children had been from different mothers; now, along with Mercy, he is said to preside over a "clannish" family that extends forward into "succeeding generations of Maggs who still live on those fertile river flats" (356). By contrast, English sexuality is invariably perverse and sterile in the novel: echoing the similar interface between orphans and abortions in *Cider House Rules*, Ma Brittan sells pills to women to force miscarriages, including the one that kills Oates's sister-in-law; that pregnancy is the result of a desire that is figured as sinful and incestuous in the novel; the decadent Henry Phipps is homosexual, at the center of a network of rent boys that includes Maggs's fellow footman Edward Constable, to whom he once refers as "Miss Molly Constable" (118); and while Percy Buckle sleeps with his servant, Mercy, he instructs her first to "[t]urn over my pretty one, and raise your sweet white bottom in the air" (128). This opposition between a sterile, debauched English sexuality and a ruggedly virile Australian masculinity that appeals equally to Constable and Mercy suggests a continuing investment in affirming Australia's superiority in competition—sporting as well as sexual—with its former colonial ruler. As Turner notes, the imperial past that links the two nations still poses difficulties for an Australian cultural studies that often finds itself wanting to assert a postcolonial identity while hoping to avoid falling into a reactionary national chauvinism; by the same token, he argues, efforts designed to deconstruct "'the national'—to install the 'international' or the 'European' or even the 'Asian'—must deal with a colonial history that categorically attributes such discourses to the regimes of the imperial Other."[44]

It is hard to decide how far *Jack Maggs*'s ending recapitulates or satirizes this dilemma. Its clearest success lies in its insights into the processes by which a figure such as Dickens might have written *Great Expectations*, with little knowledge of or interest in Magwitch's experience between his transportation and his return. If, as I began this chapter by asserting, one of the strengths of the Dickensian novel (especially in contrast to a high modernist alternative) lies in its ability to construct forms of communal belonging out of its heterogeneous cast of characters and dialects, Carey's novel shows the cost of such efforts, as some languages and subjectivities inevitably are relegated to second-class status; indeed, as the character of Maggs shows, such judgments are easily internalized, in the drive to identify with the larger collective. What Bakhtin refers to as the centripetal movement of language, in the direction of a hierarchical stratification aimed at "imposing specific limits to [heteroglossia], guaranteeing a certain maximum of mutual understanding and crystallizing into a real, although still relative unity" (270), is a crucial component of nationalism—and also of the classic nineteenth-century novel. By seeking to rewrite *Great Expectations* from the perspective of the bracketed Australian, Carey is simultaneously inside and outside of this process, opening it up to reveal another dynamic of domination and subordination that extends beyond the boundaries of the nation-state.

The legacies of imperialism dictate that former colonial countries will continue to be defined in part by Britain, as well as by the culture and mindset of empire. Carey has acknowledged, for instance, that texts such as *Jack Maggs* and *The True History of the Kelly Gang* participate in an Australian nationalism that "if it were America . . . would be sort of a nineteenth-century project," thereby signaling a cultural lag that is understandable in relatively new nations and identifying some of the continuing relevance of the Victorian novel for such projects.[45] To the extent that Australia, India, and other former colonies in the twentieth century have constructed myths of national origin, culture, and character through and against an imperial template, such nations inevitably share some elements of a recognizably "Victorian" social formation, in addition to consciously articulated differences. Throughout this book, I have been arguing the historical thesis that Britain has never fully escaped its past and arrived at a full-fledged moment of modernism, but we might also translate this argument into spatial terms: that the global nature of the empire that came into being in the nineteenth century means that the same must be said about large sections of the global population, who have continued to live and think in ways that are structured—both positively and negatively—by Victorian Britain.

Epilogue
Postcolonial Victorians

In responding to Edward Said's insistence that we rethink *Great Expectations* from an Australian perspective, seeing Victorian Britain and its colony as interdependent spaces, Carey's *Jack Maggs* opens up a final question for this study: to what extent is a label like "Victorian" applicable to the present or past subjects of colonial rule? If, after all, it seems improbable to imagine that all British citizens behaved in a comparable manner between 1837 and 1901, that improbability is only magnified when we extend it to the global citizens of an empire "on which the sun never set." By the same token, if it is absurd to imagine those Britons as suddenly behaving differently on 23 January 1901, how much more strange would it be to presume a mass transformation in distant territories such as Australia, India, and the Caribbean?

In his analysis of contemporary globalization, Arjun Appadurai usefully speaks of a mutual imbrication of temporal and spatial dimensions brought about by modernity, such that we might "simplify matters by imagining that the global is to space what the modern is to time. For many societies, modernity is an elsewhere, just as the global is a temporal wave that must be encountered in *their* present."[1] To the extent that we can consider, for the sake of argument, an earlier social formation that might be labeled "Victorianism," it (like modernity) would also be global in nature—at least as wide, in its geographic outreach, as it was long. To what extent, we might ask, was it also conceived as an "elsewhere" to colonial populations, because it emanated from a distant imperial center, and yet was also something that was experienced in a seemingly endless present? Indeed, can we recognize different aspects of a residual Victorianism in (post)colonial states and subjectivities? And if so, can any positives be drawn from such an inheritance?

One possible starting point here might involve thinking about whether the adjective "Victorian" works in connection with Britain's close ally and earliest former colony, the United States. The question has recently surfaced, as the United States has emerged from the Cold War as the unchallenged global superpower with a military, commercial, and cultural hegemony that recalls Victorian Britain's. Writing of the post-9/11 world, for instance, Robert Kaplan offers the United States "10 Rules for Managing the World," the last of which is to "speak Victorian, think pagan": in this formulation, Gladstonian liberalism's altruistic tones provide the rhetorical cover for a "pagan-Roman model of imperialism" emphasizing more narrowly nationalistic security concerns.[2] Meanwhile, in a more historicist (but equally polemical) vein, Gertrude Himmelfarb declares in her *One Nations, Two Cultures* that "Colonial and early republican America was "'Victorian' *avant la lettre*" and remained so throughout the nineteenth century.[3] Given her Thatcherite tendencies, already discussed in chapter 4, it is not surprising that Himmelfarb insists that the United States needs to reconnect to that earlier spirit of "Victorianism" and reject the counterculture(s) that she sees as having challenged it in the twentieth century, even as it is confusing—and somewhat counterintuitive—to see her castigating feminists as "New Victorians" in the postscript to *The De-Moralization of Society* (see 259–63).

A similar argument about the "Victorian" tendencies of American society is offered, from a very different political perspective, in James Morone's *Hellfire Nation*, which aims to read U.S. history through its attitudes toward sin. Morone traces a pattern of oscillation over the past century and a half between what he terms a "Victorian quest for virtue" (between 1870 and 1929, but then returning in the Reagan years) and a "Social Gospel" approach in the intervening years that sought more collective solutions to problems of poverty, unemployment, and hunger. His argument in some ways intersects with the one I outlined in chapter 4, most notably in backdating the growth of an interventionist state and linking it to a "Victorian" outlook, instead of to the New Deal thinking that followed: the conventional view of the United States as operating through "a weak, carefully limited government" makes little sense, Morone rightly suggests, when it has passed measures such as a national prohibition on liquor sales that

168 belong more to the repertoire of "the 'nanny state' that modern conservatives love to hate."[4]

And yet, it is not clear to me exactly what the epithet "Victorian" connotes or why it seems appropriate for Morone's argument. Its historical parameters (1870–1929) imply something other than a strictly chronological designation and something more like a moralistic way of seeing the world and the responsibilities of government. Its key representative would seem to be the antiobscenity crusader Anthony Comstock, who introduced an 1873 bill granting sweeping powers to the postal service (and more particularly himself) to seize, inspect, and prosecute vaguely defined obscene publications. But if Comstock represents an American "eminent Victorian" in Morone's eyes, he is also shown to have been a figure for public ridicule within the very period he comes to represent, mocked by *Life* magazine in the mid-1880s for opposing outdoor concerts on Sundays and "derided on almost every side" by the end of his career (240). Meanwhile, the counterwave of Social Gospel thinking is said to have been already visible by the early 1890s, when the Women's Christian Temperance Union's Frances Willard was disputing "the central pillar of Victorian moralizing—that social ills come from personal failings" (244).

It is hard to see even a minimal heuristic advantage to using the term "Victorian" in such a context. Its limits are just as clearly evident in an introductory overview by Daniel Walker Howe that opens a 1976 collection of essays titled *Victorian America*, in which he first narrows its point of reference to "a set of cultural motifs," shared mainly among white, Anglo-Saxon Protestants;[5] even so, "American Victorianism" is said to embody the attributes of "diversity and contradiction," as a "composite" within which "traditional, pre-modern patterns continued to exist alongside new ones and often interacted creatively with them" (14, 21). While Howe and Morone acknowledge the historical tensions within the period(s) they describe, both stubbornly hold on to the conviction that "Victorian" can function as a unitary descriptive term, even when a capacity for contradiction comes to emerge as an inherent and constitutive element. As I have been arguing, however, it is precisely the instability of the term that has allowed it to be articulated to a broad range of political, social, and cultural interests over the course of the past century.

If we shift focus from the United States to states and populations that have more recently gained their independence from Britain, we see a very different way of thinking about the legacies of the Victorians. Even the universalism that I highlight in chapter 4 as a positive inheritance from the

nineteenth century can be seen as instrumental in the implementation and   169
administration of empire, especially to the extent that it grounds a system
of welfare provision and an ethos of collective responsibility that is local-
ized in the state. As Uday Singh Mehta convincingly argues in *Liberalism
and Empire*, the "universality and politically inclusionary character" that is a
defining hallmark of the thinking of Victorian liberals such as Macaulay,
James, and John Stuart Mill seems to evaporate when we come to the political practices they advocate for the empire, which are "unmistakably
marked by the systematic and sustained political exclusion of various groups
and 'types' of people."[6] The tension rests, in many respects, on the same
paternalistic outlook that I discussed in chapter 4, which meant that New
Liberal thinking about the state was never able to fully abandon an earlier
strain of moralism whenever it set about defining a model of normative citizenship. Mehta is surely right that it is not sufficient to label this as a mere
contradiction within liberalism, in which an admirable universalist theory is
abandoned in a discriminatory praxis; instead, we must recognize that "behind the capacities ascribed to all human beings exists a thicker set of social credentials that constitute the real bases of political exclusion" (49). On
such a basis, he concludes, some forms of experience are simply invali-
dated and entire nations and cultures dismissed as ahistorical, effectively
occupying a black hole in time in a teleological schema that elevates a particular variant (Western subjectivity, liberal democracy, modernity) as a
universal goal.[7]

  The imperial way of thinking under discussion recalls Hegel's *Philosophy of History*, another text that treats spatial and temporal coordinates as in-
terchangeable. Whereas, for Hegel, Africa in particular represents a timeless
space outside of history, progress is at the same time conceived as a geographic movement westward: as "the first Historical People," the Persians
give way to the Phoenicians, then on through the Jews, Egyptians, Greeks,
and Romans, until eventually we reach the supposed pinnacle of civilization in Western liberal democracies.[8] This influential account presumes a
temporal lag, in which the states more distant from Europe are at the same
time relegated to an earlier historical phase of development, thereby neces-
sitating the kind of condescending paternalism that Mehta sees as offsetting the universalism at liberalism's core. Without wanting to endorse such
a theory, it is evident that we can identify a powerful twentieth-century
hangover in postcolonial states that have struggled, in ways that seem very
different from the British experience I have been documenting in this book,
to break free from the legacies of Victorian imperialism.

170   One fascinating instance has been documented by Jeremy Seabrook, in his analysis of homophobia in postimperial states. Examining the 1962 constitution for the newly independent Caribbean nations of Jamaica, Trinidad and Tobago, and Barbados, Seabrook points out that "its architects honoured their former rulers by preserving colonial values which would themselves be abolished in Britain within five years," including what he terms a "Victorian morality" that was embraced "enthusiastically by the black nationalist middle class." I shall return to the Caribbean in a moment, in taking up the example of the Trinidadian Marxist C. L. R. James, but first I want to note Seabrook's extension and complication of this idea of a Victorian holdover. Studying postcolonial laws concerning homosexuality in particular, he finds a kind of "off-the-peg penal code" in places such as India, Malaysia, Nigeria, and Uganda that share little in common besides their status as former British colonies. Ironically, these laws were, Seabrook argues, "often inspired by imperial anxieties about homosocial cultures among subordinate peoples," and yet they have lingered long past the official end of colonial rule. "The penitent imperialists have, by and large, revised their earlier repressive sexual attitudes," he concludes, but are still being "confronted by voices from the grave, the far from still tongues of our long-deceased predecessors."[9]

It seems worth asking, in such a context, whether it is possible to characterize the legacy of the Victorians for colonial populations as anything other than a simple and unmitigated negative. Can we identify equivalents for the relative benefits that I have attempted to highlight in this book, or analyze that inheritance as in some constitutive sense divided or self-contradictory? Two possible starting points for such a project suggest themselves to me, addressing (post)colonial attitudes toward British literature and sport. The idea that a canon of written texts plays a part in legitimating empire is a long-standing one, receiving its most notorious recommendation in Macaulay's 1835 "Minute on Indian Education," in which he declares that "I have never found one among [the Orientalists] who could deny that a single shelf of a good European library was worth the whole native literature of India and Arabia."[10] Whether for reasons of political expediency or a genuine desire for improvement, Indians themselves (as Macaulay sees it) recognize how superior to their native, vernacular culture is an imported British literary canon; to pretend otherwise, he concludes, means "withholding from them the learning for which they are craving, . . . forcing on them the mock-learning which they nauseate" (198).

The tone of condescension is hard to miss here, but it is useful to   171
contrast it with an account of what the Indian middle class actually *read* of
British literature, as has been provided by Priya Joshi in her study of the
English novel in India. In a remarkable account of Indian readers and their
reaction to the British novels that were exported, translated, and marketed
to them, Joshi provides a useful example of a reading practice that resisted
a straightforward absorption of imperial Victorian values and instead enthusiastically embraced the unfashionable sensational melodramas of nineteenth-
century authors like G. W. M. Reynolds and F. Marion Crawford. Whereas
such perceived "bad taste" in fiction has long been explained as the result
of publishers dumping unwanted texts abroad, Joshi takes seriously the
positive response of Indian readers (including her own) as an active assertion of a cultural preference. Citing a late-nineteenth-century translator of
Reynolds as approving his encouragement of "a strong feeling of hatred
against vice and social inequality" among his audience, she suggests that
such emotions might resonate not only with readers' understanding of contemporary Indian politics—debates over child marriage or priestly corrup-
tion, for instance—but also with their perceptions of "the inequities of the
colonial state."[11] The process first requires an openness to the ideological
self-representations of that state, and to the novel as its preferred cultural
vehicle, but then also an allegorical hermeneutic that is able to turn such
representations back on themselves; in doing so, as Joshi argues, Indian readers could use Victorian novels to articulate a critique of Victorian imperialism by stressing its failure to live up to its own rules and abstract ideals.

In a similar study of C. L. R. James and Liberian black nationalist
Alexander Crummell, Simon Gikandi coins the term "colonial Victorianism"
to designate this kind of "self-willed identification" with the metropolitan-
imperial center, especially as it continually highlights and reinscribes the
distance between colonial theories and practices.[12] James was born in
Trinidad in the year of Victoria's death, and refers to himself in his 1963
memoir *Beyond a Boundary* as "[a] British intellectual long before I was ten,"
already feeling "an alien in my own environment among my own people,
even my own family."[13] While his early thinking is said to be "still enclosed
within the mould of nineteenth-century intellectualism," and hence initially resistant to an anti-imperialist politics, that formative influence proves
decisive in prompting James's later development as a Marxist and black nationalist (113). He identifies his colonial inheritance in particular through
the novels of Dickens and Thackeray and the ideals of sportsmanship, to
which he was exposed by playing cricket, a game that Arjun Appadurai

172   argues "came closer than any other public form to distilling, constituting, and communicating the values of the Victorian upper classes in England to English gentlemen as part of their embodied practices, and to others as a means for apprehending the class codes of the period."[14] For James, cricket and literature are both central to a process of enculturation that he came to understand as insisting "that our masters, our curriculum, our code of morals, *everything* began from the basis that Britain was the source of all light and leading, and our business was to admire, wonder, imitate, learn; our criterion of success," he recognizes, "was to have succeeded in approaching that distant ideal—to attain it was, of course, impossible" (30; emphasis in original).

If that last sentence sounds satirical or hyperbolic, James is quick to acknowledge that he derived a real value from an education that—with its invocation of Thomas Arnold's Rugby and Thomas Hughes's *Tom Brown's Schooldays* (1857)—seems almost parodic of the English upper classes. Lessons about loyalty and honor, in particular, remained with him long after his conversion to revolutionary politics, as his expressed outrage at a 1950 match-rigging scandal in U.S. college basketball indicates: when discussing it with young comrades on the Left, James recalls a general bewilderment that "I, a colonial born and bred, a Marxist, declared enemy of British imperialism and all its ways and works," should articulate the values of "the old-school tie"—and he admits that "for some little while I was looking at myself a little strangely" (45). Another recollection, this time of how the Caribbean masses reacted to visiting English cricketers, suggests the depth of investment on the part of colonial subjects in a form of imperial ideology. West Indians, James recalls, "knew the code as it applied to sport, they expected us, the educated, the college boys, to maintain it; and if any English touring team or any member of it fell short they were merciless in their condemnation and shook their heads over it for years afterwards" (40). As this suggests, an identification with seemingly outmoded (and "alien") rules of conduct can inculcate an anti-imperialist politics just as much as a feeling of comparative inadequacy.

For Simon Gikandi, this example illustrates a complex relationship to colonial rule that enacts a reconfiguring of its central beliefs and priorities. An attitude like the one James describes only seems strange, Gikandi argues, "if we fail to recognize that Victorian ideas and categories had undergone significant, if not radical, transformations in the hands of the colonized themselves," whose goal "was to reformulate and rewrite Victorian ideas and institutions, not to discard them, to claim them as their own, not

to go beyond them." As the above example illustrates, one way to do this
is simply to take them at face value, expecting that the rulers live according to their own rules. In doing so, colonial subjects insist upon celebrating the abstract universalism at the heart of classical liberalism, especially
when it highlights the glaring discrepancies between theory and practice
noted by Uday Singh Mehta: "The desire for a liberated consciousness," as
Gikandi concludes, thus arises in part from an "awareness of the gap between their public investment in Victorian ideals and social practices (which
were a source of status and empowerment in colonial society) and their
very private disenchantment with the way such ideals had been corrupted
by racism and racialism" (163).

This way of thinking about Victorian values in terms of an idealized
code of conduct, designating a kind of horizon of abstract expectations for
the behavior of the individual or the nation, recalls a very similar emphasis in Lytton Strachey's *Eminent Victorians*. By demanding that imperial
Britain live up to its own standards, and yet knowing it will inevitably fail,
C. L. R. James's "colonial Victorianism" in essence submits the nineteenth
century to the same deconstructive critique as Strachey's, exposing in the
process the same fault lines in its understanding of the relationship between the public world and the private individual. The investment of a figure like James in these codified rules and ideals is, however, very different
from those of the Bloomsbury Group or Evelyn Waugh. In many respects,
he combines the latter's blind adherence with the cynicism of the former,
in a dialectic that constructs a forward-looking politics of colonial liberation and black self-determination on the terms of a decaying yet still active set of beliefs. In Raymond Williams's influential schema, they might
be designated simultaneously as "residual" in Britain and "dominant" in the
Caribbean, and as a result capable of a progressive articulation only in the
postcolonial space; otherwise, it would more closely resemble the recycled
kitsch that so delighted Waugh and his friends in the same period.[15]

To the extent that we can generalize about an abstract system of "Victorianism," its outline would be distinctly different even for contemporaries
such as James and Leonard Woolf, who might otherwise have a great deal
in common, and that difference inflects the larger question of how its relationship to modernity was conceptualized by metropolitan and colonial
intellectuals. As Gikandi proposes, "[w]e have become so used to associating Victorianism with traditional values that we have often forgotten how,
for the colonized in particular, Victorian ideas and practices heralded the
irruption of modernity onto the colonial sphere" (162). As I have tried to

174   argue, what blinds us to this irruption—and still obscures the progressive potential of key elements in nineteenth-century thought—is a continuing insistence on seeing the Victorians in terms that were established by self-defined modernists in their first moment of recoil. Doing so also commits us to a perpetuation of modernism's sense of itself as a negation of the past, an attitude that has already helped generate more than a century of denigrations and revivalist reversals. Each of these has tended to recycle the same clichés and characteristics; as if seen only through a rearview mirror of history, the Victorians have thus remained in a fixed relationship to the present, incapable either of being brought closer to us or of fading into the distance.

Notes

Introduction

1. *Observer* (2 January 2000), 24.
2. *Guardian* (31 December 1999), 19.
3. Quoted in Thomas, "Home of Time," 23.
4. Ibid., 38.
5. *The World in 2001* (London: The Economist Publications, 2000), 77.
6. Sweet, *Inventing the Victorians*, x, xxiii.
7. Masterman, *Heart of the Empire*, v.
8. Virginia Woolf, *Mr Bennett and Mrs Brown*, 4.
9. See Graves, *Goodbye to All That*, especially chapter 27; and Leonard Woolf, *Beginning Again*, 43.
10. Dangerfield, *Strange Death of Liberal England*, 315.
11. Collini, *English Pasts*, 115.
12. See Williams, *The Country and the City*, 9–12.
13. Thatcher, "The Good Old Days," quoted in Samuel, "Mrs. Thatcher's Return," 14.
14. Kinnock, quoted in Samuel, "Mrs. Thatcher's Return," 13.
15. Janet Wolff, *AngloModern*, 90.
16. Andrew Marr, "One Year On, Has Britain Changed?" *Guardian Weekly* 30 (August 1998), 13; illustration in *Guardian Weekly* 25 (May 1998), 19.
17. McGowan, "Modernity and Culture," 23.
18. See Morton, *A People's History of England*; Rowbotham, *Hidden from History*; and Duberman, Vicinus, and Chauncey, *Hidden from History*.
19. Marcus, *Other Victorians*, xix, 286.
20. Kucich and Sadoff, introduction to *Victorian Afterlife*, xv.
21. See Clayton, *Charles Dickens in Cyberspace*, 25.
22. Sweet, *Inventing the Victorians*, ix.
23. John McGowan identifies the origins of the phrase in John Stuart Mill's 1831 essay of the same name and comments that it exemplifies a curiously Victorian metacritical effort "to intervene in their society by explaining

176   the age to itself" ("Modernity and Culture," 3). James Chandler has pointed
      out that this drive to define the character of the time is both historically spe-
      cific and short-lived: "As early as 1831," he notes, the phrase "was being deni-
      grated as part of a fashionable cant of faction" (*England in 1819*, 81).

   24. *Saturday Review*, 29 December 1900.

   25. *St. James Gazette*, 23 January 1901, 5.

   26. *Reynolds Weekly Newspaper*, 27 January 1901, 1.

   27. *Saturday Review*, 26 January 1901, 100.

   28. *Pall Mall Gazette*, 30 December 1899, 1.

   29. *Reynolds Weekly Newspaper*, 27 January 1901, 1.

   30. *St. James Gazette*, 22 January 1901, 1.

   31. Lytton Strachey makes a similar point about Victoria's death, in language close to that of the *St. James Gazette*: "It appeared as if some monstrous
reversal of the course of nature was about to take place. The vast majority
of her subjects had never known a time when Queen Victoria had not been
reigning over them. She had become an indissoluble part of their whole
scheme of things, and that they were about to lose her appeared a scarcely
possible thought" (*Queen Victoria*, 245).

   32. Raymond Lamont-Brown notes *Punch*'s 1866 publication of a satirical
"Court Circular" reporting that "Mr John Brown walked on the slopes. / He
subsequently partook of a haggis," and also that the Pre-Raphaelites nick-
named Victoria "Empress Brown" (*John Brown*, xv–xvi). For a discussion of
the Madden film, see McKechnie, "Taking Liberties with the Monarch."

   33. Williams, "Bloomsbury Fraction," 156, 154, 167 (emphases in original).

   34. Fry, "The Ottoman and the Whatnot," 529.

   35. Graves and Hodge, *Long Week-End*, 278–79. As a consequence, they
argue, "The elaborateness of Victorian women's dress" could be copied
"without taking over the disadvantages in weight and constriction."

   36. Reporting on the latest wave of retro fashion, the Spring 2005 *New
York Times Style Magazine* tells how "'Brideshead Revisited' Is Revisited on the
Runways" (54), where the object of revival is not Waugh's novel or its own
pastiche of Victorianism but the look of the television adaptation of *Brideshead* in the 1980s.

   37. Green-Lewis, "At Home in the Nineteenth Century," 35.

   38. One fascinating strand of those debates, concerning photographs
that took their inspiration from passages of Victorian poetry, is discussed
at length in Groth, *Victorian Photography*.

   39. See Forster, "The Challenge of Our Time," in *Two Cheers for Democracy*,
55–56.

   40. Thatcher, *Downing Street Years*, 626.

Chapter One

1. Rosenbaum, *Victorian Bloomsbury*, 11, 21, 69, 88.
2. Virginia Woolf, "A Sketch of the Past," 127–31.
3. Kaplan and Simpson, *Seeing Double*, xii.
4. The attitude Woolf has in mind, with its obsessive attention to quantity of output, is exemplified by Bennett's preface to *The Old Wives' Tale* (1911), in which he boasts that "I calculated that it would be 200,000 words long (which it exactly proved to be), and I had a vague notion that no novel of such dimensions (except Richardson's) had ever been written before. So I counted the words in several famous Victorian novels, and discovered to my relief that the famous Victorian novels average 400,000 words apiece" (vii–viii).
5. The full list is as follows: *War and Peace, Vanity Fair, Tristram Shandy, Madame Bovary, Pride and Prejudice, The Mayor of Casterbridge,* and *Villette* (11).
6. Leonard Woolf, *Downhill All the Way*, 27.
7. See Brantlinger, "'Bloomsbury Fraction,'" 163.
8. Clive Bell offers a parallel theory of art in the concept of "significant form," without which "a work of art cannot exist" and which consists of "a combination of lines and colours, or of notes, or of words, in itself moving, i.e. moving without reference to the outside world" ("Roger Fry," in *Old Friends*, 72).
9. Leonard Woolf, *Growing*, 58. Hereafter cited within the text.
10. Leonard Woolf, *Sowing*, 151–52. Hereafter cited within the text.
11. See Althusser, "Ideology," 127–86.
12. Bell, "Lytton Strachey," in *Old Friends*, 31.
13. Ibid., 30.
14. "Roger Fry," in *Old Friends*, 80.
15. Leonard Woolf, *Beginning Again*, 36–37. Hereafter cited within the text.
16. Williams, "Bloomsbury Fraction," 163.
17. See Ehrenreich and Ehrenreich, "Professional-Managerial Class," 5–45.
18. Williams, "Bloomsbury Fraction," 155.
19. The challenge is repeated in almost pathological fashion in his short recollection "Bloomsbury"—a remarkable *six* times in the opening three pages alone. See Bell, "Bloomsbury," in *Old Friends*, 126–37.
20. See ibid., 130–31, and Leonard Woolf, *Beginning Again*, 22. The core group in each case consists of Lytton Strachey, Saxon Sydney-Turner, Leonard Woolf, Thoby Stephen, Clive Bell, Vanessa and Virginia Stephen (later Bell and Woolf, respectively), Duncan Grant, Roger Fry, and Maynard

178 Keynes, to whom Bell (but not Woolf) adds H. T. J. Norton, to whom Strachey's *Eminent Victorians* is dedicated. His periphery consists of Forster, Desmond and Molly MacCarthy (each of whom is also named by Woolf), and Gerald Shove (who is not).

21. See Williams, "Bloomsbury Fraction," 161.

22. Beyond homosexuality and matters of style, to which I return later, it is hard to specify the precise connection between Wilde and Strachey. Holroyd's biography of the latter provides some tantalizing hints, most of which seem veiled by a more general taboo concerning Wilde's name and reputation: Strachey seems to have modeled his dress and behavior at Cambridge on Wilde, "carrying on Oscar's business of challenging conventional morals" (*Lytton Strachey*, 102); he authored a petition in support of the sculptor Jacob Epstein, whose work on Wilde's tombstone was accused of indecency (258); and yet he was alarmed to have been sent Frank Harris's life of Wilde to review, with a note insisting the offer contained "no dark and sinister motive" (478).

23. Commenting on this trend in a critical consideration of Strachey's *Eminent Victorians*, Edmund Gosse notes in "The Agonies of the Victorian Age" (1918) that "Our younger contemporaries are slipping into the habit of approving of nothing from the moment that they are told that it is Victorian" (*Some Diversions*, 313).

24. Strachey, *Eminent Victorians*, vii. Hereafter cited within the text.

25. Holroyd, *Lytton Strachey*, 424.

26. Connolly and Wilson, quoted in ibid., 428, 424.

27. Gosse, *Some Diversions*, 318–19.

28. "Megatheria," 230.

29. Michael Holroyd lists twelve possible candidates—Henry Sidgwick, George Watts, Lord Hartington, Darwin, Mill, Carlyle, Benjamin Jowett, and Lord Dalhousie, in addition to the final four—and notes that those whom Strachey admired were "mostly scientists" (*Lytton Strachey*, 269).

30. See Knoepflmacher, "Subject of Biography," 2, 8.

31. The inherent tensions among these different selves have been discussed, in the case of Victoria, by Adrienne Munich in *Queen Victoria's Secrets* and by Laurie Langbauer in "Queen Victoria and Me."

32. See, for instance, the following on Nightingale: "her conception of God was certainly not orthodox. She felt towards Him as she might have felt towards a glorified sanitary engineer; and in some of her speculations she seems hardly to distinguish between the Deity and the Drains" (*Eminent Victorians*, 193).

33. Strachey's exposure to psychoanalysis was through his younger 179 brother James, who (along with his wife Alix) was analyzed by Freud in 1918, the year *Eminent Victorians* was published, and took over the role of English translators in 1921. Freud approved of Strachey's text, viewing it in toto as an attack on religion (Holroyd, *Lytton Strachey*, 405).

34. Spurr, "Camp Mandarin," 31–45. See also Sontag, "Notes on 'Camp.'"

35. Spurr, "Camp Mandarin," 31, quoting Anthony Kenny's "Evolution of a Primate" (1986).

36. See Ardis, *Modernism and Cultural Conflict*, chapter 2. A late example of this tendency to consider Wilde's influence mainly as a stylist is Max Beerbohm's 1943 Rede Lecture on Strachey, which traces a strong emphasis on "*manner* in literature" to the 1890s, even shading into linguistic preciosity, a fault of which he absolves Strachey on account of the good fortune of being a "merely growing boy" and not a young man in that decade (23–24). While Wilde is never named here, he seems to haunt Beerbohm's discussion of Strachey all the more for his absence; according to Holroyd's biography of Strachey, Beerbohm "felt that he was to Lytton what Oscar Wilde had been to him," an elder brother/mentor figure (479).

37. Dollimore, *Sexual Dissidence*, 308.

38. Ibid., 310.

39. A representative example might be Terry Eagleton's assessment that "Carnival, after all, is a *licensed* affair in every sense, a permissible rupture of hegemony, a contained popular blow-off as disturbing and relatively ineffectual as a revolutionary work of art" (*Walter Benjamin*, 148). The best discussion of these debates concerning the politics of carnival can be found in Stallybrass and White, *Politics and Poetics of Transgression*.

40. See Wilde, "Phrases and Philosophies for the Use of the Young."

41. Dollimore, *Sexual Dissidence*, 66.

Chapter Two

1. Forster, *Howards End*, 50.

2. Wright, *On Living in an Old Country*, 85; emphasis in original.

3. Light, *Forever England*, 10. As she suggests, the phrase "between the wars" acts as "a convenient and workable fiction," helping to give a tight focus to an analysis that may in fact need to be expanded to encompass larger concentric circles, covering 1914–56 or even "the 1890s to the present day" (18–19).

4. Forster, "The Challenge of Our Time," in *Two Cheers for Democracy*, 54. Hereafter cited within the text.

180   5. Trilling, *E. M. Forster*, 13.

6. Medalie, *E. M. Forster's Modernism*, 7.

7. Ibid.

8. Forster, *Howards End*, 100. Hereafter cited within the text.

9. I discuss these options for helping the poor, in the context of the London underclass, in *Capital Offenses*, chapters 4 and 5.

10. As a sign of how this also echoes a strain of Victorian thinking about the poor, compare Esther Summerson in Dickens's *Bleak House*: "I thought it best to be as useful as I could, and to render what services I could, to those immediately about me; and to try to let that circle of duty gradually and naturally expand itself" (154).

11. He later fills in the intermediate step for us, telling Helen that his parents, "who were dead, had been in trade; his sisters had married commercial travellers" (187).

12. Eagleton, *Exiles and Emigrés*, 58.

13. Hegglund, "Defending the Realm," 400.

14. Ibid., 402–3.

15. Ibid., 404; emphasis in original.

16. Marx, "Eighteenth Brumaire," 594.

17. Hewison, *Heritage Industry*, 59.

18. Waugh, *Decline and Fall*, 134. Hereafter cited within the text.

19. Gorra, "Through Comedy toward Catholicism," 205.

20. Eagleton, *Exiles and Emigrés*, 43–44.

21. Waugh, *A Handful of Dust*, 19. Hereafter cited within the text.

22. Gorra, "Through Comedy toward Catholicism," 217–18.

23. Waugh, "Come Inside" (1949), reprinted in *A Little Order*, 147–48, 149.

24. Gorra, "Through Comedy toward Catholicism," 213.

25. Waugh, *Brideshead Revisited*, 351. Hereafter cited within the text.

26. Eagleton, *Exiles and Emigrés*, 58.

27. This is not to suggest that blind adherence is absent from the novel: Charles's cousin Jasper tells him without explanation to "Always wear a tall hat on Sunday's during term" at Oxford (25; emphasis in original), for instance, while Lady Marchmain upholds a naïve and inexplicable belief in the restorative powers of hunting, as "something derived from centuries ago" (162). But mocking such faith in a reflex obedience to these ossified social rules and practices is no longer Waugh's prime purpose in the novel.

28. Eagleton, *Exiles and Emigrés*, 67.

29. Even the devout Catholic daughter Cordelia struggles with this recognition, telling Charles that on her last sight of it after her mother's fu-

neral, "suddenly, there wasn't any chapel there any more, just an oddly   181
decorated room" (220).

30. Comparable hints by Bridey's fiancée, Beryl Muspratt, about "the
way in which establishments of similar size had been managed at various
Government Houses she had visited," only work to confirm her status as
a middle-class *arriviste* and thus as socially ineligible to marry into the family (323).

31. Rothstein, "*Brideshead Revisited*," 327.

32. Waugh, quoted in Hewison, *Heritage Industry*, 64.

33. Williams, *The Country and the City*, 9–12.

34. Waugh, "Come Inside," in *A Little Order*, 148.

35. Humphrey Carpenter, for instance, cites the description of Sebastian's room but claims that "Waugh is recalling Acton's collection of Victoriana and other curios" (*Brideshead Generation*, 72).

36. Acton, *Memoirs of an Aesthete*, 119. Hereafter cited within the text.

37. Bracewell, *England Is Mine*, 23.

38. Waugh, quoted in Carpenter, *Brideshead Generation*, 39.

39. Ibid. For more on Auden's very different rebellion against the orthodoxies of the past, see Hynes, *Auden Generation*, chapter 1.

40. Waugh, "Let Us Return to the Nineties, but Not to Oscar Wilde"
(1930), reprinted in *A Little Order*, 19–20. Hereafter cited within the text.

41. Harold Acton, for instance, recalls both as having "preferred certain
circuses or music-hall turns—what I called the illegitimate stage—to the
'legitimate stage'" (*Memoirs*, 155).

42. Waugh, "A Call to the Orders" (1938), in *A Little Order*, 62–63.

43. Waugh, "The Philistine Age of English Decoration" (1938), in *A Little Order*, 65, 67; emphasis in original.

44. Acton, *Memoirs of an Aesthete, 1939–1969*, 226. This is the second volume of Acton's memoirs, originally published as *More Memoirs of an Aesthete*.
I cite this hereafter within the text as volume 2, to avoid confusion with the
first volume, published under the same title. On Waugh's anti-Americanism,
Acton later comments that it was "the only pose I considered unworthy of
him" (2:318).

45. Carpenter, *Brideshead Generation*, 66–67.

46. See Muggeridge, *Thirties*, 1971.

47. Carpenter, *Brideshead Generation*, 103–4.

48. Ibid., 212. At this stage of his life, as Anthony Burton notes, Betjeman's chief opponent was Nicholas Pevsner, who is typically seen as the
champion of architectural modernism, though prepared to trace its roots

182   back to the Crystal Palace and the arts and crafts movement. In another historical reversal, in 1963 the Victorian Society elected its second chair: as Burton notes, "Betjeman may well have expected such an honour; it was one of life's ironies that it went to Pevsner" ("Revival of Interest in Victorian Decorative Art," 130).

49. Carpenter, *Brideshead Generation*, 57.

50. Waugh's "The Philistine Age of English Decoration" cites a vague definition of the Whatnot as "a piece of furniture which serves occasional or incidental use and belongs indifferently to the dining-room, drawing-room, or parlour" (*A Little Order*, 68).

51. Fry, "The Ottoman and the Whatnot," 529–30. Hereafter cited within the text.

52. Samuel, *Theatres of Memory*, 51. Hereafter cited within the text.

Chapter Three

1. Golub, "Spies," 140.

2. Wollen, quoted in Higson, *English Heritage, English Cinema*, 71. Hereafter cited within the text.

3. Hewison, *Heritage Industry*, 73.

4. In his celebrated essay "Dickens, Griffith, and the Film Today," Eisenstein discusses how Griffith developed many important film techniques (including his use of close-ups and crosscutting between two lines of parallel action, occurring in different locations) from a reading of Dickens's novels. The passage in *A Tale of Two Cities* opens as follows: "Six tumbrils roll along the streets. Change these back again to what they were, thou powerful enchanter, Time, and they shall be seen to be the carriages of absolute monarchs" (385). "I must be excused," Eisenstein comments, "in leafing through Dickens, for having found in him even—a 'dissolve'" (reprinted in *Film Form*, 213).

5. During the dinner with Rex in Paris, for instance, "Charles feels such vulgar superiority to the ambitious Rex, who is, after all, paying for the meal, and congratulates himself so warmly on knowing that caviar shouldn't be eaten with onion or that brandy should not be taken in large balloon glasses, that I was tempted to write in a swift hack on the shins from Rex under the table" (Mortimer, "Adapting Waugh's *Brideshead*," 2:27).

6. Golub, "Spies," 151–52. Mortimer seems to concur, noting that he only came to use the voice-over technique after working for some time on the script, and only on the basis that "there is some conflict between the voice and the picture" ("Adapting"); among the film texts he cites as influ-

encing this decision is Truffaut's *Jules et Jim* (1962), a very different experiment with unreliable narration from the French New Wave.

7. The Companion Guide to the *Brideshead Revisited* DVD includes a section titled "Filming Locations" that describes in detail not only the series' use of Castle Howard but also locations in Oxford and Venice, as well as key substitutions it makes—Marchmain House is "played" by Tatton Park in Cheshire, for instance, and Malta stands in for Morocco. In a noticeable commitment to authenticity, "[t]he ocean liner deck scenes were shot in the Atlantic on the QE2 during a real storm" (16–17).

8. See Golub, "Spies," 146.

9. Director Charles Sturridge makes this same point in his notes on "The Making of *Brideshead*," contained in the Companion Guide to the DVD, describing Castle Howard as "in some ways the leading character of the story" (5–6).

10. As Fred Inglis approvingly notes, we get the "dutifully brochure-illustrating moments: an ominous shot of Sebastian drinking wine too eagerly at a fountain-side; coffee at Florian's; the gorgeous glass, mirrors and chandeliers in the Palazzo Pisani Moretta; the dazzling white facade of San Moise against the night sky"; and so on (*"Brideshead Revisited* Revisited," 191–92).

11. Orwell, *Coming Up for Air,* 257.

12. Stewart, "Film's Victorian Retrofit," 76–77.

13. Green-Lewis, "At Home in the Nineteenth Century," 37–39.

14. Fox Talbot, "Pencil of Nature," 75. Louis Daguerre used a similar metaphor to describe his even earlier invention of the daguerreotype, calling it "a chemical and physical process which gives nature the ability to reproduce itself" (quoted in Tagg, *Burden of Representation,* 41).

15. For an account of these larger debates concerning the status of photography, see Green-Lewis, *Framing the Victorians,* chapter 2.

16. For a fascinating discussion of Fox Talbot's emphasis on the domestic space, see McCusker, "Silver Spoons and Crinoline."

17. See Armstrong, *Fiction in the Age of Photography,* 187–88.

18. Roland Barthes suggests that "this-has-been" is the fundamental statement of any photograph: "In Photography, the presence of the thing (at a certain past moment) is never metaphoric; and in the case of animated beings, their life as well, except in the case of photographing corpses, and even so: if the photograph then becomes horrible, it is because it certifies, so to speak, that the corpse is alive, as *corpse*: it is the living image of a dead thing" (*Camera Lucida,* 78–79; emphasis in original).

19. Fox Talbot, "Pencil of Nature," 89.

184   20. Schaaf, "Notes on the Photographs," 107.

21. Fox Talbot, "Some Account of the Art of Photogenic Drawing" (March 1839), quoted in Green-Lewis, *Framing the Victorians*, 63; emphasis in original.

22. Tagg, *Burden of Representation*, 35.

23. See Bazin, "The Ontology of the Photographic Image," in *What Is Cinema?* 12–13.

24. Bazin, "The Evolution of the Language of Cinema," in *What Is Cinema?* 24. Hereafter cited within the text.

25. Armstrong, *Fiction in the Age of Photography*, 5.

26. Ibid., 11.

27. Green-Lewis, "At Home in the Nineteenth Century," 35.

28. Kracauer's is an early version of this split, which distinguishes between the "two main tendencies" of film as personified by the Lumières and Méliès and traces their roots back to what he terms the "realistic and formative" schools of nineteenth-century photography. See Kracauer, *Theory of Film*, 30–37.

29. Cohen, *Film and Fiction*, 39–40. Hereafter cited within the text.

30. John Berger and his collaborators make a similar point in *Ways of Seeing*: "The camera isolated fragmentary appearances and in so doing destroyed the idea that images were timeless. . . . What you saw depended upon where you were when. What you saw was relative to your position in time and space. It was no longer possible to imagine everything converging on the human eye as on the vanishing point of infinity." They also make the same comparison with developments in painting, noting that "For the Impressionists . . . the visible, in constant flux, became fugitive. For the Cubists, the visible was no longer what confronted the single eye, but the totality of possible views taken from points all round the object (or person) being depicted" (18).

31. Cohen has in mind here the famous experiment by Soviet director Lev Kuleshov, in which he edited the same image of an actor's face with unconnected images (of which various lists now exist: typically they include a bowl of soup, a corpse, and a child). When the film was screened, according to Kuleshov, the audience automatically read the same image of the actor, in retrospect, as signifying whatever emotion was summoned by what followed: hunger, grief, affection, and so on.

32. Newhall, *History of Photography*, 74.

33. Oscar Gustave Rejlander, "Desultory Reflections on Photography and Art" (1866), quoted in Green-Lewis, *Framing the Victorians*, 60.

34. Rejlander, "An Apology for Art-Photography" (1863); accessed June   185
2004 at http://albumen.stanford.edu/library/c19/rejlander.html.

35. Sir William J. Newton, "Upon Photography in an Artistic View, and
Its Relation to the Arts" (1853), quoted in Green-Lewis, *Framing the Victorians*, 56; emphasis in original.

36. Quoted in Newhall, *History of Photography*, 76. Robinson provoked
controversy with his 1858 photograph "Fading Away," which purported to
represent a young woman on the verge of dying; in fact, it was a combination print made up of five negatives and featured (Robinson admitted) "a
fine healthy girl of about fourteen," posed "to see how near death she could
be made to look" (ibid.).

37. Eisenstein, "The Cinematographic Principle and the Ideogram"
(1929), in *Film Form*, 30; emphasis in original. This is the ground of his opposition to the principle embodied in the Kuleshov effect, that meaning is
a process of retroactive connection but in essence the simple addition of
two consecutive shots—what he refers to in this essay as seeing shots as
"bricks" to be organized into "chains" (37).

38. Stephen's famous "muddle" is set out in conversation with Bounderby, to whom he goes to inquire about the possibilities of a divorce. Facing laws that would punish him for marrying or living with Rachael while
his wife lives and for leaving or hurting the latter, "Mine's a grievous case,"
Stephen concludes, "an I want—if yo will be so good—t'know the law that
helps me" (Dickens, *Hard Times*, 112–13).

39. Fowles, *French Lieutenant's Woman*, 16. Hereafter cited within the text.

40. "In spite of Hegel," the novel comments, "the Victorians were not a
dialectically minded age; they did not think naturally in opposites, of positives and negatives as aspects of the same whole. Paradoxes troubled rather
than pleased them" (197). Elsewhere, it describes the period as organized
around a "fatal dichotomy . . . which led them to see the 'soul' as more real
than the body" (288).

41. There are, in fact, three endings, since the text had earlier imagined
Charles returning to his fiancée, Ernestina, before explicitly declaring it "a
thoroughly conventional ending" and only what Charles had himself imagined, just as "today we incline more to put ourselves into a film" in order to
imagine our possible futures (266).

42. Gale, "Harold Pinter's *The French Lieutenant's Woman*," in *Films of Harold
Pinter*, 74.

43. See Foucault, *History of Sexuality*, volume 1, chapter 1.

44. Knapp, "Transformation of a Pinter Screenplay," 58; emphasis in original.

186
45. See Thomas, "Specters of the Novel," 301–3.

46. Ibid., 304; Stewart, "Film's Victorian Retrofit," 88–89. Dracula directly echoes the promoter's words, in asking Mina for directions to the cinematograph, stating that "I understand it is a wonder of the civilized world."

47. For a fascinating discussion of this story and what it says about our relationship to early film audiences, see Gunning, "Aesthetic of Astonishment."

48. See ibid. (among others) for accounts of the "cinema of attractions."

49. Thomas, "Specters of the Novel," 304.

50. This conversation about Carfax Abbey, which Jonathan records in his diary, opens the novel, with Jonathan telling Dracula that "I had not the key of the door leading to it from the house, but I have taken with my Kodak views of it from various points." Stoker, Dracula, 35. Hereafter cited within the text.

51. The film includes speeded-up sequences shot from the vampire's point of view, filmed through a pixelation process that edits out random frames, making him appear to move unevenly through space.

52. Stewart, "Film's Victorian Retrofit," 88.

53. Felber, "Capturing the Shadows of Ghosts," 35.

54. Janet Wolff, AngloModern, 90.

Chapter Four

1. Hall, Hard Road to Renewal, 2; Light, Forever England, 10.

2. See Hadley, "Past Is a Foreign Country."

3. Hall, Hard Road to Renewal, 86; emphasis in original.

4. Waugh, "Commentary for The Private Man," reprinted in A Little Order, 141. The essay ends with one of Waugh's most forceful (and reactionary) political statements, arguing that "The proper structure of a healthy state is pyramidical. The organic life of society should be a continuous process of evolving an aristocracy," although not a hereditary one. "[B]y and large," he continues, "the most valuable possession of any nation is an accepted system of classes, each of which has its proper function and dignity. . . . In general a man is best fitted to the tasks he has seen his father perform" (143–44).

5. Thatcher, Downing Street Years, 5–6. The term "Butskellite" refers back to a postwar period when near-identical policies were endorsed by the leadership of the Conservatives (R. A. Butler) and Labour (Hugh Gaitskell).

6. "Gingrich Looks to Victorian Age," A19.

7. Gingrich, "What Good Is Government and Can We Make It Better?" 20.

8. Samuel, "Mrs. Thatcher's Return," 12. Thatcher noted in her autobiography that she originally used the phrase "Victorian virtues," but (unlike

Gertrude Himmelfarb, as we shall see) she does not appear troubled by the 187
slippage: "I never felt uneasy about praising 'Victorian values' or—the
phrase I originally used—'Victorian virtues,' not least because they were by
no means just Victorian" (*Downing Street Years*, 627).

9. Kinnock and Thatcher both quoted in Samuel, "Mrs. Thatcher's Return," 13–14.

10. Walvin, *Victorian Values*, 163.

11. Clarke, *Question of Leadership*, 314–15; Krieger, *Reagan, Thatcher*, 63; Samuel, "Mrs. Thatcher's Return," 28.

12. Hall, *Hard Road to Renewal*, 164.

13. Samuel, "Mrs. Thatcher's Return," 10–11, 22–23. Stefan Collini concurs on this last point, asking, "What does thrift really mean, what can it mean, for a generation scarred by the corrosive effects of high inflation and bombarded with invitations to take advantage of a variety of loans and deferred payments? An 'enterprise culture' is not only one where it may be economically rational to be in debt, but one where it is actually sanctioned by the implications of the official rhetoric." See his "Victorian Values: From the Clapham Sect to the Clapham Omnibus," in *English Pasts*, 105.

14. Samuel, "Mrs. Thatcher's Return," 14, 22.

15. Thatcher, *Downing Street Years*, 367. Hereafter cited within the text.

16. Hadley, "Past Is a Foreign Country," 24.

17. See Krieger, *Reagan, Thatcher*, 88–89.

18. Clarke, *Question of Leadership*, 308.

19. See, for instance, Blair's conception of responsibility in his 1998 description of a "Third Way" in politics: "For too long, the demand for rights from the state was separated from the duties of citizenship and the imperative for mutual responsibility on the part of individuals and institutions. Unemployment benefits were often paid without strong reciprocal obligations; children were unsupported by absent parents." Blair, "The Third Way: New Politics for the New Century," reprinted in Chadwick and Heffernan, *New Labour Reader*, 30. In their introduction, the editors summarize New Labour as "believ[ing] in redistribution, but only for poverty alleviation, not for the purposes of broader social equality" (9), suggesting that it is responsive to the shifting attitudes outlined in the survey cited by Krieger.

20. Hall, *Hard Road to Renewal*, 84.

21. Samuel, "Mrs. Thatcher's Return," 20, 26.

22. Himmelfarb, *De-moralization of Society*, 234. Hereafter cited within the text.

23. See Davis, "What Made Them Moral?" 63.

24. See Collini, "Speaking with Authority: The Historian as Social Critic," in *English Pasts*, 89.

25. Bromwich, "Victoria's Secret," 32.

26. In *Capital Offenses* I suggest something similar about Himmelfarb's critique of Henry Mayhew, in which she is forced to conjure an imaginary "critical reader" to counteract the inconvenient testimony of his actual ones (105–6).

27. See Jameson, *Political Unconscious*, 91; emphasis in original. The classic example of the positive spin I am discussing here is that of rising crime statistics, which can always be reinterpreted as pointing to greater police efficiency and a rising public confidence to report crimes.

28. Robinson, "Modern Victorians," 77; the relevant passage is from Himmelfarb, *De-moralization*, 254–55.

29. In an related op-ed for the *New York Times*, Himmelfarb goes further, suggesting that while "Victorian England was not nearly as 'Dickensian' as Dickens's novels would have us believe," even the novelist was far from embodying the spirit of Dickensianism, having quite confusingly been "an enthusiastic advocate of the institutions he satirized in his novels"! See Himmelfarb, "Victorians Get a Bad Rap," A15:3.

30. Indeed, this would seem to be the logic of her endorsement of a statement by Gingrich, in the context of the debates on welfare reform, "that charity would step in to help unwed mothers who would no longer receive relief." See ibid.

31. See Gerson, *Neoconservative Vision*, 243–44.

32. See Davies, "Beveridge Revisited," and Krieger, *Reagan, Thatcher*, 88–89.

33. Bromwich, "Victoria's Secret," 31; "Gingrich Looks to Victorian Age."

34. Collini, "Speaking with Authority," 92 (see note 24).

35. Goodlad, *Victorian Literature and the Victorian State*, 24–25. Hereafter cited within the text.

36. See *De-moralization*, 146–47, where Himmelfarb adapts the phrase from Beatrice Webb as an umbrella term under which she can include such disparate efforts as a Fabian socialist belief in rational economic planning, "systematic" sociological investigations into the causes of poverty, the organized distribution of charity, and the educational efforts of the University Settlement movement. As I hope to make clear, I would instead view these examples as representing two distinct and largely incompatible approaches that prioritize either aggregated collectives or atomized individuals as the object of their respective inquiries.

37. Arnold, *Culture and Anarchy*, 50–51. Hereafter cited within the text.

38. See Marcus, "*Culture and Anarchy* Today," in Arnold, *Culture and Anarchy*, 179. This is one of four present-day commentaries that are appended to Arnold's text, and it is interesting to note that they do not break down along political lines: among more liberal commentators, Marcus sees considerably more use in Arnold than Gerald Graff, who views *Culture and Anarchy* as a precursor text to the modern culture wars, sharing many of the present problems of seeking to legislate a "common culture"; on the right, Samuel Lipman's generally positive assessment of Arnold's continuing relevance, in part as a redress to contemporary popular culture, is balanced by Maurice Cowling's concerns over the ways in which religion is superseded by culture.

39. Arnold, "Function of Criticism at the Present Time," 730.

40. See Perkin, *Rise of Professional Society*, 124.

41. Quoted in Fried and Elman, *Charles Booth's London*, 284–85. Hereafter cited within the text.

42. I extend these thoughts, in the context of Booth's relation to the various strands of early British sociology, in "Victorian Continuities."

43. On my reading, Booth is actually more of a collectivist than a comparable figure such as Henry Mayhew, who seems in many ways to be a more likely hero for modern conservatives. As David Englander and Rosemary O'Day note in their introduction to *Retrieved Riches*, a spirit of political partisanship underwrites Himmelfarb's consistent attacks on Mayhew, who "might reasonably have been included as a fair specimen of the compassionate middle classes" to which she looks; however, he "receives a battering less, one suspects, because of what he wrote and more because of the way in which he has been taken up and lionized by those whose politics Himmelfarb abhors" (32), especially E. P. Thompson.

44. Goodlad's *Victorian Literature and the Victorian State* is, in some respects, a history of the stages of that transfer, working on the presupposition that "Political Economy was often understood in decidedly Christian and Evangelical terms," at the same time that "those who were most invested in the liberal ideal of self-reliant individuals and communities often spearheaded innovations that later became associated with the bureaucratic state" (36). Among a series of hybridized or transitional enterprises, Goodlad lists James Kay-Shuttleworth's "blend of the scientific and personal" (93), an "unmistakably British hybrid of voluntarism and professionalism" during Dickens's day (109), and the "professionalized and quasi-collective paternalism" of the COS (203).

190   45. Quoted in Rose, *English Poor Law*, 259.

46. Ibid., 261–62. These developments are discussed in Fraser, *Evolution of the British Welfare State*, chapter 7.

47. Perkin, *Rise of Professional Society*, 168–69. Hereafter cited within the text.

48. L. T. Hobhouse, *Liberalism* (1911), quoted in Collini, *Liberalism and Sociology* 137. As Stuart Hall has commented, this is in essence a negative conception of rights, seeking "to compensate those who visibly suffered gross privation on account of their being unable, for whatever reason, to participate fully in market relations." See Stuart Hall and Bill Schwartz, "State and Society, 1880–1930," in *Hard Road to Renewal*, 111.

49. Beveridge, "The Problem of the Unemployed" (1907) and "Unemployment in London" (1905), both quoted in Meacham, *Toynbee Hall and Social Reform*, 149–50.

50. Besides Beveridge and Clement Atlee (the Labour prime minister elected in 1945), the list would include people such as Hubert Llewellyn Smith, first head of the Labour Department at the Board of Trade; E. J. Urwick, director of the London School of Sociology (later the LSE); and Cyril Jackson, who served on the London County Council and advocated child welfare legislation.

51. Meacham, *Toynbee Hall and Social Reform*, 17, quoting Toynbee's lecture "Are Radicals Socialists?" (emphasis in original).

52. See ibid., 69–71 (on Barnett) and 137 (on Beveridge).

53. C. F. G. Masterman, *Heart of the Empire*, 35.

54. Stedman Jones, "Why Is the Labour Party in a Mess?" 246.

55. See, for instance, Chadwick and Heffernan's introduction to *The New Labour Reader*, 15.

Chapter Five

1. Margaret Thatcher, *The Downing Street Years*, 626.

2. See Leonard Woolf, *Sowing*, 165.

3. Forster, *Aspects of the Novel*, 109, and "English Prose Between 1918 and 1939," in *Two Cheers for Democracy*, 269. Virginia Woolf shared Forster's assessment, noting of Dickens's characters that they were "caricatures," "very simple" yet also "immensely alive." See her "A Sketch of the Past," 73.

4. Samuel, *Theatres of Memory*, 402.

5. For more on the influence of Dickens on contemporary literature, see Clayton, *Charles Dickens in Cyberspace*, especially chapter 6.

6. Wood, "Human, All Too Human," 41–45. Hereafter cited within the text.

7. Quoted in O'Brien, "Serving a New World Order," 798.

8. Brennan, "National Longing for Form," 63.

9. Rushdie, *Midnight's Children*, 81–82. Hereafter cited within the text.

10. Irving, "King of the Novel," 358, 359. Hereafter cited within the text.

11. As chapter 1 makes clear, Bloomsbury critiques also routinely focused on issues of *scale*: consider, in this context, Virginia Woolf's imagining of "a three-volume novel" about Mrs. Brown's son, or Strachey's of "those two fat volumes" by which the Victorians commemorated the dead in biographical form. As I shall argue, the crash diet they forced upon the modern novel has an impact on its ability to represent the social whole.

12. Lukács, *Meaning of Contemporary Realism*, 19–20. Hereafter cited within the text.

13. Doyle, *Paddy Clarke Ha Ha Ha*, 1.

14. Kelman, *How Late It Was, How Late*, 1.

15. Carey, *True History of the Kelly Gang*, 7. Other recent prizewinning novels that similarly use variations on stream-of-consciousness narration include Irvine Welsh's *Trainspotting* (1993), Alan Warner's *Morvern Callar* (1995), Roddy Doyle's *The Woman Who Walked into Doors* (1996), Patrick MacCabe's *The Butcher Boy* (1992), and Mark Haddon's *The Curious Incident of the Dog in the Night* (2003).

16. Bakhtin, *Dialogic Imagination*, 368. Hereafter cited within the text.

17. Interestingly, the issue of hypocrisy represents a rare fault line among conservative advocates of Victorian values. As Himmelfarb reports, Thatcher is said to have wanted to restore all such values "with the exception of hypocrisy," whereas her own *De-moralization of Society* presents an ingenious defense of that characteristic, arguing that it was admirable that "[t]he Victorians thought it no small virtue to maintain the appearance, the manners, of good conduct even while violating some moral principle" (22–23).

18. Marcus, *Other Victorians*, 102. Hereafter cited within the text.

19. Foucault, *History of Sexuality*, 6. Hereafter cited within the text.

20. Dickens, 1841 preface, quoted in Larry Wolff, "'Boys are Pickpockets,'" 227–28. As Wolff points out, even the frankness of the final declaration can be read as evasive, seeming to rule out not just that Nancy, too, is a thief but also the possibility that the boys might be prostitutes. Wolff hereafter cited within the text.

21. Dickens, 1850 preface to *Oliver Twist*, 33.

22. Moretti, *Atlas of the European Novel*, 86. I discuss the spatial geography of the novel in greater depth in *Capital Offenses*, chapter 2.

192   23. Quoted in "Our Own Dickens," 62.

24. Waters, *Fingersmith*, 21. Hereafter cited within the text.

25. "How well you look," Maud comments during a similar scene when Sue wears her clothes. "The colour sets off your eyes and hair. I knew it would. Now you are quite the beauty—aren't you? And I am plain—don't you think?" (165).

26. Waters, "Wolfskins and Togas," 188.

27. See in particular the following: "As to that larger power that [Selina] was talking of now—her rareness—well, I have felt a little of that, haven't I? I cannot dismiss it, I know that it is *something*. But there is still a mystery to her, a shadow in the design, a gap" (Waters, *Affinity*, 168; emphasis in original). Protagonist Margaret Prior (who is narrating this passage) makes clear from her own private writing that she has had a past experience with her sister-in-law, Helen, with her bed still being "haunted, by our old kisses," and yet she can only vaguely articulate a need for "liberty," so that when asked "to do what?" she "could not answer" (204).

28. In this sense the novel inverts Victorian stereotypes of the knowing thief and the innocence of gentility, so much in evidence in a novel like *Oliver Twist* as the basis for showing the idiosyncrasy of characters like Oliver or Nancy, who remain relatively unmarked by knowledge that they should inevitably acquire from their social environment. As Maud says of the deceived Sue, "She looks so taken with this—so *taken in*, by her own fiction—so innocent, not sly" (243; emphasis in original).

29. Irving, *Cider House Rules*, 1. Hereafter cited within the text.

30. Quoted in Davis and Womack, "Saints, Sinners, and the Dickensian Novel," 303.

31. In another interview, Irving has asserted that "There is no Right to Life position represented in *Cider House*, everything in the story happens because this procedure is illegal, and here's what it's like. It's an historical statement. . . . I don't think we want to go back there" (quoted in Booth, "Neo-Victorian Self-Help, ," 294; hereafter cited within the text).

32. Davis and Womack, "Saints, Sinners, and the Dickensian Novel," 305.

33. The connection between the two scenes is cemented when, on arriving at the Channing-Peabody home, Larch discovers he still has in his pocket the underwear of another woman he had witnessed having a back-alley abortion before he decides to help the Lithuanian girl (62).

34. The historical distinction she makes here underpins Booth's insistence that Irving's novel and the 1999 film adaptation by Lasse Hallström, centered more exclusively on Homer Wells, in effect instantiate two dif-

ferent modes of social thinking, with the novel harking back to a Victorian 193
self-help ethos and the film mimicking the later variant (290).

35. Irving, *A Prayer for Owen Meany*, 522; emphasis in original.

36. Interestingly, and perhaps appropriately given its own status as a cinematic adaptation, Hallström's film substitutes the repeated viewing of *King Kong* for the novel's reading aloud of Dickens and Brontë.

37. While such forms of intertextual dialogism seem especially apt for an author like Dickens, however, they are not limited to realist novels; indeed, as Michael Cunningham's *The Hours* (1998) demonstrates, similar forms of "dialogical contact" can be made with a text like Woolf's *Mrs. Dalloway*, even though the original novel represents an opposing tendency toward linguistic centralization and monology.

38. Carey, *Jack Maggs*, 224, 194–95. Hereafter cited within the text.

39. Said, *Culture and Imperialism*, xv–xvi. Carey mentions the influence of Said's work in Moss, "Car-Talk," 92.

40. See Carter, *Road to Botany Bay*, chapter 1.

41. As Kathleen J. Renk has argued, this inability to recognize Maggs as an Australian, and instead to assimilate him to a vision of the loyal working-class Briton, is another parallel between Oates and Dickens: "The great apologist for the underclass," she notes, "had little sympathy for the plight of the colonials" in places such as Jamaica's Morant Bay. See Renk, "Rewriting the Empire of the Imagination," 62–63.

42. Quoted in Moss, "Car-Talk," 91.

43. See Turner, "'It Works for Me,'" 645.

44. Ibid.

45. See O'Reilly, "Voice of the Teller," 164.

Epilogue

1. Appadurai, *Modernity at Large*, 9; emphasis in original.

2. Kaplan, "Supremacy by Stealth," 83.

3. Himmelfarb, *One Nation, Two Cultures*, 7.

4. Morone, *Hellfire Nation*, 282. Hereafter cited within the text.

5. Howe, *Victorian America*, 13. Hereafter cited within the text.

6. Mehta, *Liberalism and Empire*, 46. Hereafter cited within the text.

7. See Mehta's conclusion to *Liberalism and Empire* (on "Experience and Unfamiliarity") and Dipesh Chakrabarty's *Provincializing Europe* for useful discussions of the implications of such a presupposition.

8. Hegel, *Philosophy of History*, 173.

9. Seabrook, "It's Not Natural."

194   10. Macaulay, "Minute on Indian Education," 196. Hereafter cited within the text.

11. Joshi, *In Another Country*, 81–82.

12. Simon Gikandi, "Embarrassment of Victorianism," 162. Hereafter cited within the text.

13. James, *Beyond a Boundary*, 18. Hereafter cited within the text.

14. Appadurai, *Modernity at Large*, 91.

15. See Williams, *Marxism and Literature*, 121–27.

Works Cited

Acton, Harold. *Memoirs of an Aesthete*. London: Methuen, 1948.

———. *Memoirs of an Aesthete, 1939–1969*. New York: Viking Press, 1970.

Althusser, Louis. "Ideology and Ideological State Apparatuses (Notes Towards an Investigation)." In *Lenin and Philosophy*, translated by Ben Brewster, 127–86. New York: Monthly Review Press, 1971.

Appadurai, Arjun. *Modernity at Large: Cultural Dimensions of Globalization*. Minneapolis: University of Minnesota Press, 1996.

Ardis, Ann L. *Modernism and Cultural Conflict, 1880–1922*. Cambridge: Cambridge University Press, 2002.

Armstrong, Nancy. *Fiction in the Age of Photography: The Legacy of British Realism*. Cambridge, MA: Harvard University Press, 1999.

Arnold, Matthew. *Culture and Anarchy*. 1869. New Haven: Yale University Press, 1994.

———. "The Function of Criticism at the Present Time." 1864. In Mermin and Tucker, *Victorian Literature*, 727–39.

Bakhtin, M. M. *The Dialogic Imagination*. Translated by Caryl Emerson and Michael Holquist. Austin: University of Texas Press, 1981.

Barthes, Roland. *Camera Lucida: Reflections on Photography*. Translated by Richard Howard. New York: Hill and Wang, 1982.

Bazin, André. *What Is Cinema?* Translated by Hugh Gray. Berkeley: University of California Press, 1967.

Beerbohm, Max. *Lytton Strachey*. Cambridge: Cambridge University Press, 1943.

Bell, Clive. *Old Friends: Personal Recollections*. Chicago: University of Chicago Press, 1973.

Bennett, Arnold. *The Old Wives' Tale*. Garden City, NJ: Doubleday, 1928.

Berger, John. *Ways of Seeing*. London: Penguin, 1972.

Booth, Alison. "Neo-Victorian Self-Help, or Cider House Rules." *American Literary History* 14, no. 2 (Summer 2002): 284–310.

Bracewell, Michael. *England Is Mine: Pop Life in Albion from Wilde to Goldie*. London: HarperCollins, 1997.

196   Brantlinger, Patrick. "'The Bloomsbury Fraction' versus War and Empire."
      In Kaplan and Simpson, *Seeing Double*, 149–67.
      Brennan, Timothy. "The National Longing for Form." In *Nation and Narra-
      tion*, edited by Homi Bhabha, 44–70. London: Routledge, 1990.
      Bromwich, David. "Victoria's Secret" (review of Himmelfarb, *The De-
      moralization of Society*). *New Republic*, 15 May 1995, 28–32.
      Burton, Anthony. "The Revival of Interest in Victorian Decorative Art and
      the Victoria and Albert Museum." In *The Victorians since 1901: Histories,
      Representations and Revisions*, edited by Miles Taylor and Michael Wolff,
      121–37. Manchester: Manchester University Press, 2004.
      Carey, Peter. *Jack Maggs*. New York: Vintage, 1999.
      ———. *The True History of the Kelly Gang*. New York: Vintage, 2000.
      Carpenter, Humphrey. *The Brideshead Generation: Evelyn Waugh and His Friends.*
      Boston: Peter Davison, 1990.
      Carter, Paul. *The Road to Botany Bay: An Essay in Spatial History.* London:
      Faber and Faber, 1987.
      Chadwick, Andrew, and Richard Heffernan, eds. *The New Labour Reader.*
      London: Polity Press, 2003.
      Chakrabarty, Dipesh. *Provincializing Europe: Postcolonial Thought and Historical
      Difference.* Princeton, NJ: Princeton University Press, 2000.
      Chandler, James. *England in 1819: The Politics of Literary Culture and the Case of
      Romantic Historicism.* Chicago: University of Chicago Press, 1998.
      Clarke, Peter. *A Question of Leadership: Gladstone to Thatcher.* London: Hamish
      Hamilton, 1991.
      Clayton, Jay. *Charles Dickens in Cyberspace: The Afterlife of the Nineteenth Century
      in Postmodern Culture.* Oxford: Oxford University Press, 2003.
      Cohen, Keith. *Film and Fiction: The Dynamics of Exchange.* New Haven: Yale
      University Press, 1979.
      Collini, Stefan. *English Pasts: Essays in History and Culture.* Cambridge: Cam-
      bridge University Press, 1999.
      ———. *Liberalism and Sociology: L. T. Hobhouse and Political Argument in England,
      1880–1914.* Cambridge: Cambridge University Press, 1979.
      Dangerfield, George. *The Strange Death of Liberal England.* Stanford, CA: Stan-
      ford University Press, 1997.
      Davies, Stephen. "Beveridge Revisited: Foundations for Tomorrow's Wel-
      fare." In *Politics of Thatcherism: Thoughts of a London Thinktank*, edited by
      Richard Haas and Oliver Knox, 123–59. Lanham, MD: University Press
      of America, 1991.
      Davis, Christie. "What Made Them Moral?" (review of Himmelfarb, *The
      De-moralization of Society*). *National Review*, 3 April 1995, 63.

Davis, Todd F., and Kenneth Womack. "Saints, Sinners, and the Dicken-   197
sian Novel: The Ethics of Storytelling in John Irving's *The Cider House
Rules.*" *Style* 32, no. 2 (Summer 1998): 298–316.

Dickens, Charles. *Bleak House.* 1852–53. Harmondsworth: Penguin, 1971.

———. *Hard Times.* 1854. Harmondsworth: Penguin, 1969.

———. *Oliver Twist.* 1838. Harmondsworth: Penguin, 1985.

———. *A Tale of Two Cities.* 1859. London: Penguin, 2000.

Dollimore, Jonathan. *Sexual Dissidence: Augustine to Wilde, Freud to Foucault.*
Oxford: Clarendon Press, 1991.

Doyle, Roddy. *Paddy Clarke Ha Ha Ha.* London: Penguin, 1993.

Duberman, Martin, Martha Vicinus, and George Chauncey, eds. *Hidden from
History: Reclaiming the Gay and Lesbian Past.* New York: Penguin, 1989.

Eagleton, Terry. *Exiles and Emigrés: Studies in Modern Literature.* New York:
Schocken Books, 1970.

———. *Walter Benjamin: Towards a Revolutionary Criticism.* London: Verso,
1981.

Ehrenreich, Barbara, and John Ehrenreich. "The Professional-Managerial
Class." In *Between Labor and Capital,* edited by Pat Walker, 5–45. Boston:
South End Press, 1979.

Eisenstein, Sergei. *Film Form: Essays in Film Theory.* Translated by Jay Leyda.
New York: Harcourt, 1949.

Englander, David, and Rosemary O'Day, eds. *Retrieved Riches: Social Investigation in Britain, 1840–1914.* Aldershot, UK: Scolar Press, 1995.

Felber, Lynette. "Capturing the Shadows of Ghosts: Mixed Media and the
Female Gaze in *The Women on the Roof* and *The Governess.*" *Film Quarterly* 54,
no. 4 (2001): 27–37.

Forster, E. M. *Aspects of the Novel.* New York: Harcourt, Brace, 1927.

———. *Howards End.* New York: Signet, 1992.

———. *Two Cheers for Democracy.* London: Edward Arnold, 1972.

Foucault, Michel. *The History of Sexuality.* Vol. 1, *An Introduction.* Translated
by Robert Hurley. New York: Vintage, 1990.

Fowles, John. *The French Lieutenant's Woman.* New York: Signet Books, 1969.

Fox Talbot, Henry. "The Pencil of Nature." 1844. Reprinted in *Henry Fox
Talbot: Selected Texts and Bibliography,* edited by Mike Weaver, 75. Boston:
G. K. Hall and Co., 1993.

Fraser, Derek. *The Evolution of the British Welfare State: A History of Social Policy
since the Industrial Revolution.* New York: Barnes and Noble, 1973.

Fried, Albert, and Richard M. Elman, eds. *Charles Booth's London: A Portrait of
the Poor at the Turn of the Century, Drawn from His "Life and Labour of the People
in London."* New York: Pantheon, 1968.

198   Fry, Roger. "The Ottoman and the Whatnot." *Athenaeum*, 27 June 1919, 529–30.

Gale, Steven H., ed. *The Films of Harold Pinter*. Albany: SUNY Press, 2001.

Gerson, Mark. *The Neoconservative Vision: From the Cold War to the Culture Wars*. Lanham, MD: Madison Books, 1996.

Gikandi, Simon. "The Embarrassment of Victorianism: Colonial Subjects and the Lure of Englishness." In Kucich and Sadoff, *Victorian Afterlife*, 157–85.

Gingrich, Newt. "What Good Is Government and Can We Make It Better?" *Newsweek*, 10 April 1995, 20.

"Gingrich Looks to Victorian Age to Cure Today's Social Failings." *New York Times*, 14 March 1995, A19.

Golub, Spencer. "Spies in the House of Quality: The American Reception of *Brideshead Revisited*." In *Novel Images: Literature in Performance*, edited by Peter Reynolds, 139–56. London: Routledge, 1993.

Goodlad, Lauren M. E. *Victorian Literature and the Victorian State: Character and Governance in a Liberal Society*. Baltimore: Johns Hopkins University Press, 2003.

Gorra, Michael. "Through Comedy toward Catholicism: A Reading of Evelyn Waugh's Early Novels." *Contemporary Literature* 29, no. 2 (1988): 201–20.

Gosse, Edmund. *Some Diversions of a Man of Letters*. Freeport, NY: Books for Libraries Press, 1971.

Graves, Robert. *Goodbye to All That*. New York: Doubleday, 1957.

Graves, Robert, and Alan Hodge. *The Long Week-End: A Social History of Great Britain, 1919–1939*. New York: W. W. Norton, 1963.

Green-Lewis, Jennifer. *Framing the Victorians: Photography and the Culture of Realism*. Ithaca, NY: Cornell University Press, 1996.

———. "At Home in the Nineteenth Century: Photography, Nostalgia, and the Will to Authenticity." In Kucich and Sadoff, *Victorian Afterlife*, 29–48.

Groth, Helen. *Victorian Photography and Literary Nostalgia*. Cambridge: Cambridge University Press, 2003.

Gunning, Tom. "An Aesthetic of Astonishment: Early Film and the (In)Credulous Spectator." In *Viewing Positions: Ways of Seeing Film*, edited by Linda Williams, 114–33. New Brunswick: Rutgers University Press, 1995.

Hadley, Elaine. "The Past Is a Foreign Country: The Neo-Conservative Romance with Victorian Liberalism." *Yale Journal of Criticism* 10, no. 1 (1997): 7–38.

Hall, Stuart. *The Hard Road to Renewal: Thatcherism and the Crisis of the Left*. London: Verso, 1988.

Hegel, G. W. F. *The Philosophy of History.* Translated by J. Sibree. New York: 199
Dover, 1956.

Hegglund, Jon. "Defending the Realm: Domestic Space and Mass Cultural
Contamination in *Howards End* and *An Englishman's Home.*" *ELT* 40, no. 4
(1997): 398–421.

Hewison, Robert. *The Heritage Industry: Britain in a Climate of Decline.* London:
Methuen, 1987.

Higson, Andrew. *English Heritage, English Cinema: Costume Drama since 1980.*
Oxford: Oxford University Press, 2003.

Himmelfarb, Gertrude. *The De-moralization of Society: From Victorian Virtues to
Modern Values.* New York: Vintage, 1994.

———. *One Nation, Two Cultures.* New York: Alfred A. Knopf, 1999.

———. "The Victorians Get a Bad Rap." *New York Times*, 9 January 1995,
A15:3.

Holroyd, Michael. *Lytton Strachey.* London: Chatto and Windus, 1994.

Howe, Daniel Walker, ed. *Victorian America.* Philadelphia: University of
Pennsylvania Press, 1976.

Hynes, Samuel. *The Auden Generation: Literature and Politics in England in the
1930s.* London: Bodley Head, 1976.

Inglis, Fred. "*Brideshead Revisited* Revisited: Waugh to the Knife." In *The Classic Novel: From Page to Screen*, edited by Robert Giddings and Erica Sheen,
176–96. Manchester: Manchester University Press, 2000.

Irving, John. *The Cider House Rules.* New York: Ballantine, 1993.

———. "The King of the Novel." In *Trying to Save Piggy Sneed*, 349–79.
New York: Arcade, 1996.

———. *A Prayer for Owen Meany.* New York: Ballantine, 1989.

James, C. L. R. *Beyond a Boundary.* 1963. Durham, NC: Duke University
Press, 1993.

Jameson, Fredric. *The Political Unconscious: Narrative as a Socially Symbolic Act.*
Ithaca, NY: Cornell University Press, 1981.

Joshi, Priya. *In Another Country: Colonialism, Culture, and the English Novel in India.*
New York: Columbia University Press, 2002.

Joyce, Simon. *Capital Offenses: Geographies of Class and Crime in Victorian London.*
Charlottesville: University of Virginia Press, 2003.

———. "Victorian Continuities: Early British Sociology and the Welfare of
the State." In Amanda Anderson and Joseph Valente, eds., *Disciplinarity at
the Fin de Siècle*, 261–80. Princeton, NJ: Princeton University Press, 2002.

Kaplan, Carola M., and Anne B. Simpson. *Seeing Double: Revisioning Edwardian and Modernist Literature.* New York: St. Martin's Press, 1996.

200 Kaplan, Robert. "Supremacy by Stealth: 10 Rules for Managing the World." *Atlantic Monthly* (July–August 2003): 75–83.

Kelman, James. *How Late It Was, How Late.* New York: Delta, 1994.

Knapp, Shoshona. "The Transformation of a Pinter Screenplay: Freedom and Calculators in *The French Lieutenant's Woman.*" *Modern Drama* 28, no. 1 (1985): 55–70.

Knoepflmacher, U. C. "The Subject of Biography: The Victorianism of *Eminent Victorians.*" *Victorians Institute Journal* 18 (1990): 1–14.

Kracauer, Siegfried. *Theory of Film: The Redemption of Physical Reality.* New York: Oxford University Press, 1960.

Krieger, Joel. *Reagan, Thatcher, and the Politics of Decline.* New York: Oxford University Press, 1986.

Kucich, John, and Dianne F. Sadoff, eds. *Victorian Afterlife: Postmodern Culture Rewrites the Nineteenth Century.* Minneapolis: University of Minnesota Press, 2000.

Lamont-Brown, Raymond. *John Brown: Queen Victoria's Highland Servant.* Stroud, UK: Sutton, 2000.

Langbauer, Laurie. "Queen Victoria and Me." In Kucich and Sadoff, *Victorian Afterlife,* 211–33.

Light, Alison. *Forever England: Femininity, Literature and Conservatism Between the Wars.* London: Routledge, 1991.

Lukács, Georg. *The Meaning of Contemporary Realism.* Translated by John and Necke Mander. London: Merlin Press, 1963.

Macaulay, Thomas Babington. "Minute on Indian Education." In Mermin and Tucker, *Victorian Literature,* 196–98.

Marcus, Steven. *The Other Victorians: A Study of Sexuality and Pornography in Mid-Nineteenth Century England.* New York: Bantam Books, 1967.

Marx, Karl. "The Eighteenth Brumaire of Louis Bonaparte." 1852. In *The Marx-Engels Reader,* edited by Robert Tucker, 594–617. New York: W. W. Norton, 1978.

Masterman, C. F. G. *The Heart of the Empire: Discussions of the Problems of Modern City Life in England.* 1901. Brighton, UK: Harvester Press, 1973.

McCusker, Carol. "Silver Spoons and Crinoline: Domesticity and the 'Feminine' in the Photographs of William Henry Fox Talbot." In *First Photographs: William Henry Fox Talbot and the Birth of Photography,* edited by Michael Gray, Arthur Ollman, and Carol McCusker, 17–22. New York: PowerHouse Books, 2002.

McGowan, John. "Modernity and Culture, the Victorians and Cultural Studies." In Kucich and Sadoff, *Victorian Afterlife,* 3–28.

McKechnie, Kara. "Taking Liberties with the Monarch: The Royal Bio-Pic   201
in the 1990s." In *British Historical Cinema*, edited by Claire Monk and Amy
Sargeant, 217–36. London: Routledge, 2002.

Meacham, Standish. *Toynbee Hall and Social Reform, 1880–1914: The Search for
Community*. New Haven: Yale University Press, 1987.

Medalie, David. *E. M. Forster's Modernism*. New York: Palgrave, 2002.

"Megatheria." *Times Literary Supplement*, 16 May 1918, 230.

Mehta, Uday Singh. *Liberalism and Empire: A Study in Nineteenth-Century British
Liberal Thought*. Chicago: University of Chicago Press, 1999.

Mermin, Dorothy, and Herbert F. Tucker, eds. *Victorian Literature, 1800–1900*.
Fort Worth: Harcourt College Publishers, 2002.

Moretti, Franco. *Atlas of the European Novel, 1800–1900*. London: Verso,
1998.

Morone, James. *Hellfire Nation: The Politics of Sin in American History*. New Haven,
CT: Yale University Press, 2003.

Mortimer, John. "Adapting Waugh's *Brideshead*: Nostalgia Revisited." *New
York Times*, 17 January 1982, 2:27.

Morton, A. L. *A People's History of England*. London: Gollancz, 1938.

Moss, Laura. "Car-Talk: Interview with Peter Carey." *ARIEL: A Review of International English Literature* 22, no. 4 (October 2001): 88–102.

Muggeridge, Malcolm. *The Thirties: 1930–1940 in Great Britain*. London: Hamish
Hamilton, 1940.

Munich, Adrienne. *Queen Victoria's Secrets*. New York: Columbia University
Press, 1996.

Newhall, Beaumont. *The History of Photography from 1839 to the Present*. New
York: Museum of Modern Art, 1982.

O'Brien, Susie. "Serving a New World Order: Postcolonial Politics in
Kazuo Ishiguro's *The Remains of the Day*." *Modern Fiction Studies* 42, no. 4
(Winter 1996): 787–806.

O'Reilly, Nathaniel. "The Voice of the Teller: A Conversation with Peter
Carey." *Antipodes: A North American Journal of Australian Literature* 16, no. 2
(December 2002): 164–67.

Orwell, George. *Coming Up for Air*. San Diego: Harcourt, 1950.

"Our Own Dickens." *The Advocate*, 5 March 2002, 62–63.

Perkin, Harold. *The Rise of Professional Society: England since 1880*. London:
Routledge, 1989.

Renk, Kathleen J. "Rewriting the Empire of the Imagination: The Post-
Imperial Gothic Fiction of Peter Carey and A. S. Byatt." *Journal of Com-
monwealth Literature* 39, no. 2 (June 2004): 61–71.

202 Robinson, Marilynne. "Modern Victorians: Dressing Politics in the Costume of History." *Harper's Magazine* 291 (July 1995): 72–77.

Rose, Michael E. *The English Poor Law, 1780–1930.* New York: Barnes and Noble, 1971.

Rosenbaum, S. P. *Victorian Bloomsbury: The Early History of the Bloomsbury Group.* New York: St. Martin's Press, 1987.

Rothstein, David. "*Brideshead Revisited* and the Modern Historicization of Memory." *Studies in the Novel* 25, no. 3 (Fall 1993): 318–32.

Rowbotham, Sheila. *Hidden from History: 300 Years of Women's Oppression and the Fight Against It.* London: Pluto, 1974.

Rushdie, Salman. *Midnight's Children.* New York: Penguin, 1991.

Said, Edward. *Culture and Imperialism.* New York: Alfred A. Knopf, 1993.

Samuel, Raphael. "Mrs. Thatcher's Return to Victorian Values." In *Victorian Values: A Joint Symposium of Edinburgh and the British Academy,* edited by T. C. Smout, 9–29. Oxford: Oxford University Press and the British Academy, 1992.

——. *Theatres of Memory.* Vol. 1, *Past and Present in Contemporary Culture.* London: Verso, 1994.

Schaaf, Larry J. "Notes on the Photographs in *The Pencil of Nature.*" Reprinted in *Henry Fox Talbot: Selected Texts and Bibliography,* edited by Mike Weaver, 107. Boston: G. K. Hall and Co., 1993.

Seabrook, Jeremy. "It's Not Natural: The Developing World's Homophobia Is a Legacy of Colonial Rule." *Guardian,* 3 July 2004.

Sontag, Susan. "Notes on 'Camp.'" In *Against Interpretation,* 275–92. New York: Farrar, Straus and Giroux, 1966.

Spurr, Barry. "Camp Mandarin: The Prose Style of Lytton Strachey." *ELT* 33, no. 1 (1990): 31–45.

Stallybrass, Peter, and Allon White. *The Politics and Poetics of Transgression.* Ithaca: Cornell University Press, 1986.

Stedman Jones, Gareth. "Why Is the Labour Party in a Mess?" In *Languages of Class: Studies in English Working Class History, 1832–1982,* 239–56. Cambridge: Cambridge University Press, 1983.

Stewart, Garrett. "Film's Victorian Retrofit." *Victorian Studies* 38, no. 2 (Winter 1995): 55–99.

Stoker, Bram. *Dracula.* Harmondsworth, UK: Penguin, 1979.

Strachey, Lytton. *Eminent Victorians.* San Diego: Harcourt, Brace and Co., n.d.

——. *Queen Victoria.* London: Penguin, 1971.

Sweet, Matthew. *Inventing the Victorians: What We Think We Know about Them and Why We're Wrong.* New York: St. Martin's Press, 2001.

Tagg, John. *The Burden of Representation: Essays on Photographies and Histories.* 203
Minneapolis: University of Minnesota Press, 1988.

Thatcher, Margaret. *The Downing Street Years.* New York: HarperCollins, 1993.

Thomas, Ronald R. "The Home of Time: The Prime Meridian, the Dome of the Millennium, and Postnational Space." In *Nineteenth-Century Geographies: The Transformations of Space from the Victorian Age to the American Century,* edited by Helena Michie and Ronald R. Thomas, 23–39. Princeton, NJ: Princeton University Press, 2003.

———. "Specters of the Novel: *Dracula* and the Cinematic Afterlife of the Victorian Novel." In Kucich and Sadoff, *Victorian Afterlife,* 288–310.

Trilling, Lionel. *E. M. Forster.* Norfolk, CT: New Directions, 1943.

Turner, Graeme. "'It Works for Me': British Cultural Studies, Australian Cultural Studies, Australian Film." In *Cultural Studies,* edited by Lawrence Grossberg, Cary Nelson, and Paula Treichler, 640–50. New York: Routledge, 1992.

Walvin, James. *Victorian Values.* Athens: University of Georgia Press, 1987.

Waters, Sarah. *Affinity.* London: Virago, 1999.

———. *Fingersmith.* London: Virago, 2002.

———. "Wolfskins and Togas: Maude Meagher's *The Green Scamander* and the Lesbian Historical Novel." *Women: A Cultural Review* 7, no. 2 (1996): 176–88.

Waugh, Evelyn. *Brideshead Revisited.* 1945. Boston: Little, Brown, n.d.

———. *Decline and Fall.* 1928. Boston: Little, Brown, n.d.

———. *A Handful of Dust.* 1934. Boston: Little, Brown, 1999.

———. *A Little Order: A Selection from His Journalism,* edited by Donat Gallagher. London: Eyre Methuen, 1977.

Wilde, Oscar. "Phrases and Philosophies for the Use of the Young." In *The Complete Works of Oscar Wilde,* 1205–6. London: Collins, 1966.

Williams, Raymond. "The Bloomsbury Fraction." In *Problems in Materialism and Culture,* 148–69. New York: Schocken Books, 1991.

———. *The Country and the City.* Oxford: Oxford University Press, 1973.

———. *Marxism and Literature.* Oxford: Oxford University Press, 1977.

Wolff, Janet. *AngloModern: Painting and Modernity in Britain and the United States.* Ithaca, NY: Cornell University Press, 2003.

Wolff, Larry. "'The Boys Are Pickpockets, and the Girl Is a Prostitute': Gender and Juvenile Criminality in Early Victorian England from *Oliver Twist* to *London Labour.*" *New Literary History* 27, no. 2 (Spring 1996): 227–49.

Wood, James. "Human, All Too Human." *New Republic,* 24 July 2000, 41–45.

204   Woolf, Leonard. *Beginning Again: An Autobiography of the Years 1911 to 1918.*
      New York: Harcourt, Brace and World, 1964.
      ———. *Downhill All the Way: An Autobiography of the Years 1919–1939.* New
      York: Harcourt, Brace and World, 1967.
      ———. *Growing: An Autobiography of the Years 1904–1911.* New York: Har-
      court, Brace and World, 1961.
      ———. *Sowing: An Autobiography of the Years 1880–1904.* London: Hogarth
      Press, 1961.
      Woolf, Virginia. *Mr Bennett and Mrs Brown.* London: Hogarth Press, 1928.
      ———. "A Sketch of the Past." In *Moments of Being,* edited by Jeanne
      Schulkind, 127–31. London: Sussex University Press, 1976.
      Wright, Patrick. *On Living in an Old Country: The National Past in Contemporary
      Britain.* London: Verso, 1985.

Index